# ROADSIDE HISTORY OF

ALABAMA  GEORGIA  Atlantic Ocean

10
98
Tallahassee  FLORIDA  Jacksonville
10
Pensacola  Lake City  St. Augustine
Panama City  98  75  Gaines-  95
Apalachicola  ville

Ocala  Daytona Beach
4
Gulf  Orlando
of  75
Mexico
4
Tampa  Ft. Pierce
St. Petersburg  Lake Wales  FLORIDA'S TURNPIKE
Sarasota  27
Lake Okeechobee
Punta Gorda  Palm Beach  95
Fort Myers  Ft. Lauderdale
Naples  75
Miami

N

FLORIDA

Key West  FLORIDA KEYS

**Florida**
A DYNAMIC LAND

0        50        100 miles
0    50    100 km

ROADSIDE HISTORY OF

*Florida*

Douglas Waitley

1997
MOUNTAIN PRESS PUBLISHING COMPANY

**Library of Congress Cataloging-in-Publication Data**
Waitley, Douglas.
     Roadside history of Florida / Douglas Waitley.
          p.     cm.
     Includes bibliographical references (p.    ) and index.
     ISBN 0-87842-366-4 (alk. paper). — ISBN 0-87842-367-2 (alk.
     paper)
          1. Florida—History, Local.   2. Historic sites—Florida—
     Guidebooks.   3. Florida—Guidebooks.   4. Automobile
     travel—Florida—Guidebooks.   I. Title.
     F311.W32    1997
     917.590463–dc21                                    97-39849
                                                            CIP

Mountain Press Publishing Company
P. O. Box 2399 • Missoula, MT 59806
(406) 728-1900

*To Jeff*
*beginning a new life in Florida . . .*

# Contents

# *Acknowledgments*

I have had the help of many persons in the compilation of this book. So thanks to the historical societies and private historians from Pensacola to Key West that furnished me with memoirs and personal recollections not available elsewhere. I have received excellent photos from the Historical Association of South Florida in Miami, the Orange County Historical Society in Orlando, and the Yonge Library of Florida History in Gainesville. But most of all, I found the Florida State Archives in Tallahassee to have an amazingly complete collection of vintage pictures.

Some highly skilled historians have read the manuscript and given me valuable suggestions. Among them are Niles Schuh and William Marina.

I would also like to mention my grandfather, Elbert G. Drew. Although it has been many years since he tramped Florida's sandy soil, he knew and loved the state and it was he who, in the 1930s, painted the beautiful scene of the Big Cypress Swamp that is both the centerpiece of my living room and the cover of this book.

Most of all I would like to thank Mary, my wife, for her companionship on the innumerable trips I made around this wondrous state.

# About the Cover Artist
## ELBERT G. DREW, 1867–1934

Elbert G. Drew was my grandfather. I was hardly higher than his knee as I watched him daub paints onto canvasses that seemed as large as bass drums. The colors did not make sense—a slash of crimson here, a splash of turquoise there. But when I backed up, it all came together as a lake or a mountain or a forest. What magic!

Grandfather was an elderly man when I got to know him. He was tall and had a white mustache and a little goatee that made him about the most distinguished person I could imagine. But he was a down-to-earth sort of man. Many times I sat with him on the second-story porch where he did his painting and listened to him do birdcalls for me—whippoorwills and bobwhites—I can still hear their plaintive calls.

From a family history that my mother wrote, I later learned that Elbert had been a top executive with Illinois Bell Telephone back in the early days when live operators handled all the calls and Elbert's phone number was simply five. But he always had a love of and a talent for art. In 1920 he formed the Business Men's Art Clubs of Chicago, with a membership of 170. This group eventually became affiliated with the Amateur Art Clubs of America, and Elbert soon became president of this organization.

Grandfather was sixty years old when he retired, and during the last seven years of his life he devoted his time to painting. With his wife, Harriet, he traveled extensively in Europe, and I remember well the painting of the Roman Forum that hung in the home where I grew up.

Elbert also spent a great deal of time in Florida. His paintings of Lake Eola in Orlando and the Bok Tower have become family treasures. The original of this book's cover painting is the center-piece of my living room. It represents a scene from the Big Cypress Swamp down by the Everglades.

So, Granddaddy, now a lot of folks are going to enjoy your painting as I have. Do I hear the song of a whippoorwill from on high?

—Douglas Waitley

# About the Author

Douglas Waitley is the author of twelve books on Americana. After receiving his master's degree in history from Northwestern University in Evanston, Illinois, it is not surprising that his first book, published in 1960, was entitled *Portrait of the Midwest*. Other books followed, and he appeared on NBC's "Today Show" for *Roads of Destiny*, a description of Indian trails, pioneer paths, and military routes between the Atlantic and the Mississippi River.

Waitley and his wife, Mary, moved to Florida in 1990. Intrigued with the state's colorful history, Waitley started doing research. His interest grew, as did his effort, and the result is *Roadside History of Florida*.

# Chronology

## OF FLORIDA HISTORY

500 M (million years ago)
: Florida is part of Africa.

400 M
: Africa and North America collide to form a supercontinent. Florida welds onto Georgia.

200 M
: Supercontinent breaks apart. Florida remains part of North America as an underwater limestone platform.

24 M
: Huge numbers of animals begin leaving their remains at Bone Valley, just east of Tampa.

2 M–10,000 B.C.
: Glacial era: ocean repeatedly rises and falls. Florida's Central Ridge forms.

13,000 B.C.
: Paleo-Indians reach Florida. They hunt mastodons and other Ice Age creatures.

A.D. 1000
: Native Americans build mounds at Tallahassee, Tampa, and many other sites throughout Florida.

1400s–1700s
: Apalachee and Timucua tribes live in northern Florida and the Calusas live in the south.

1513
: Juan Ponce de León discovers and names Florida.

1539
: Hernando de Soto lands near Tampa. Celebrates Florida's first Christmas at Tallahassee.

1564
: French build Fort Caroline near Jacksonville.

1565
: Spanish establish St. Augustine, the oldest continuously occupied town in the United States.

1565
: Spanish wipe out their French competitors.

1680s
: Franciscan mission system reaches its height, with thirty-one missions and twenty-six thousand Christian Indian followers.

1696
: Jonathan and Mary Dickinson, with twenty-four companions, are shipwrecked near Jupiter. Jonathan's account of their grueling struggle up the coast becomes a Florida classic.

1698
: Pensacola permanently founded.

| | |
|---|---|
| 1702–6 | British and Creek Indian slave-hunting forays devastate the Spanish mission system. |
| 1702–63 | Spanish Empire in decline. |
| 1763–83 | British gain control of Florida as the Spanish trade it for the city of Havana. |
| 1783–1821 | Spanish regain Florida. |
| 1818 | First Seminole War. Andrew Jackson invades Florida. |
| 1821 | United States purchases Florida from Spain. Andrew Jackson accepts transfer of province at Pensacola. |
| 1824 | Tallahassee becomes the territorial capital. |
| 1832 | Audubon paints birds in the Keys. |
| 1835 | Second Seminole War begins when Osceola murders the Indian agent at Ocala. |
| 1842 | Second Seminole War ends with the expulsion of almost all Seminoles from Florida. |
| 1845 | Statehood follows much debate over whether Florida should be one state or two, divided at the Suwannee River. |
| 1855–58 | Third Seminole War. |
| 1861 | Florida's first cross-state railroad runs between Fernandina and Cedar Key. |
| 1861–65 | Civil War. |
| 1881 | Hamilton Disston saves Florida from near bankruptcy when he purchases an enormous parcel of 4 million acres in southern Florida. |
| 1884 | Henry Plant's railroad reaches Tampa. |
| 1888 | Henry Flagler completes the Ponce de Leon Hotel at St. Augustine. |
| 1894–95 | The Great Freeze sets back Florida's development. |
| 1896 | Flagler extends the Florida East Coast Railway to Miami. |
| 1905 | Governor Napoleon Bonaparte Broward builds canals to begin draining the Everglades. |
| 1905–12 | Flagler builds the Overseas Railroad to Key West. |
| 1921–25 | Real estate boom: Carl Fisher builds Miami Beach; George Merrick builds Coral Gables; Addison Mizner revamps Palm Beach and starts building at Boca Raton. |
| 1926 | Real estate bust. The Depression begins in Florida. |
| 1928 | Tamiami Trail across the Everglades completed. |
| 1929 | Bok Singing Tower Gardens opens. |

| | |
|---|---|
| 1930s | Miami Beach art deco era. |
| 1930s | CCC preservation activities help save Highlands Hammock, near Sebring, and Ocala National Forest. |
| 1934 | Ernest Hemingway writes *To Have and Have Not,* describing Key West during the Depression. |
| 1935 | Malcolm Campbell sets a world speed record of 277 mph on the beach at Daytona. |
| 1935 | Hurricane wrecks the Keys's Overseas Railroad in early September. |
| 1936 | Cypress Gardens, Florida's oldest theme park, opens. |
| 1938 | Frank Lloyd Wright designs first of many buildings at Florida Southern College at Lakeland. |
| 1941–45 | World War II travel restrictions almost destroy Florida's tourist industry. |
| 1942 | Zora Neale Hurston, native of Eatonville, writes her autobiography, *Dust Tracks on a Road.* |
| 1946 | Harry Truman begins using Key West navy base as his little White House. |
| 1949 | Truman approves testing rockets at Cape Canaveral. |
| 1950s | Federal highway program begins. Florida tourism benefits greatly as interstates are built. |
| 1958 | Daytona Beach Speedway constructed. |
| 1959 | Fidel Castro takes over Cuba. Massive influx of immigrants to Miami begins. |
| 1959 | Busch Gardens opens. |
| 1961 | Moon race with Russia begins. Great expansion of Cape Canaveral. |
| 1968–74 | Richard Nixon uses his home in Key Biscayne. |
| 1969 | *Apollo 11* lands on the moon. |
| 1971 | Walt Disney World opens. |
| 1973 | Sea World opens. |
| 1980s | Revival of downtowns. |
| 1980 | Mariel boat lift sends 125,000 more Cubans mainly to Miami. |
| 1990 | Universal Studios Florida opens. |
| 1992 | Hurricane Andrew devastates Homestead in August. |
| 1995 | Hurricane Opal pounds the panhandle in early October. |
| 1995 | Seagram Co. buys MCA/Universal. |

| | |
|---|---|
| 1996 | ValuJet aircraft crashes in the Everglades. One hundred ten persons vanish into the muck and saw grass. |
| 1996 | A record 41 million visitors come to Florida. |
| 1997 | Kennedy Space Center opens the huge Apollo/Saturn V Center. |
| 1997 | Miami suffers severe financial problems. |
| 1997 | Universal Studios Florida pursues a $2.6 billion expansion program. |
| 1998 | Disney scheduled to open its fourth theme park, Animal Kingdom. |

# Introduction

## FLORIDA—A DYNAMIC LAND

Florida was not always a geographical part of North America. It began as an extension of Africa, and only after tectonic forces caused Africa and North America to collide some 400 million years ago did Florida become welded to southern Georgia.

After Africa moved away, Florida existed as a shallow ocean basin. Shellfish thrived here, and over the millennia their remains formed a layer of limestone bedrock up to four miles thick. When the Kennedy Space Center was being built, drillers found this bedrock 160 feet beneath the surface and anchored the huge Vehicle Assembly Building to it.

Over eons, rivers from the eroding Blue Ridge and Appalachian Mountains deposited huge quantities of sand on the submerged Florida platform. When the ocean level dropped during the Ice Age, this sand formed the low hills of the north and the long, narrow ridge that runs down the peninsula. The southern portion of this ridge supports the orange groves that grow along it in great profusion.

During the Glacial Age, beginning around 2 million years ago, a great deal of water became locked up in northern ice. The result was a drop in the ocean levels, which subsequently exposed the land. Then, when the glaciers melted and the oceans rose, Florida was again submerged. This cycle happened many times, and each rise and fall marked Florida with new seafloors. One example is I-95, which utilizes the bottom of the ancient Pamlico Sea for its route from Jacksonville to Miami.

## Florida's Regions

The state can be separated into three general geographic regions. North Florida, including Tallahassee and most of the panhandle, has gently rolling landscapes. The central portion of the state is largely flat (except for the long spinal ridge), with poor drainage and many lakes, such as the land around Disney World. And southern Florida is predominantly wetlands, exemplified by the exotic Everglades and the Lower Keys.

A member of the former Confederacy, Florida is surprisingly un-Dixielike. But you can still see reminders of the Old South along the byways off I-10 and around Tallahassee, Pensacola, and at Stephen Foster's Suwannee River memorial, west of Jacksonville. This area was the heart of antebellum Florida, with cotton plantations and slave quarters. The inhabitants are mostly native born, and their speech has a proud Cracker twang. Ocala, too, has retained its distinctive southern character, with horse farms and echoes of Marjorie Kinnan Rawlings's rustic novel *The Yearling.*

Things change around I-4, called by some the Great Wall of Orlando. Disney completely transformed this region, not only physically but demographically. Old-time natives are rare, for most of the current inhabitants are from the North. Politically, the area has large numbers of Republicans, distinguishing it from the northern portion of the state, which traditionally has been Democratic.

There is another demographic change evident in southeast Florida. Whereas northern Florida has almost no immigrants and central Florida's immigrant population is only 7 percent, in Miami's Dade County a full 45 percent of the inhabitants were born outside the United States, most in Cuba.

## The Aborigines

In prehistoric days, Florida was also divided into northern, central, and southern portions. The populous and prosperous Apalachee peoples ruled the panhandle, with their principal town near Tallahassee. Timucuan warriors controlled the area from Jacksonville to Daytona Beach and on into the central part of the state. They were a strong people, who built log homes and raised crops.

Several minor tribes lived along the Atlantic Coast. The Ais claimed the area from Cape Canaveral to Fort Pierce, barely surviving on creatures they managed to take from the waters around them. Even smaller and more destitute was the Hobe tribe, around Jupiter

*When the Europeans arrived, they found the Timucuan peoples living in substantial lodges along northern Florida lakes and rivers. This drawing was made by Jacques Le Moyne from Fort Caroline around 1564.* —P. H. Yonge Library of Florida History, University of Florida

Inlet. Both tribes figured prominently in the almost incredible saga of Jonathan Dickinson and his companions, who were shipwrecked among them in 1696.

To the south, the Tequesta peoples lived around the Miami–Fort Lauderdale area, and the Calusas lived on the southwest coast. Both groups were primitive and warlike.

### The Spanish Era, 1513–1763

Florida first entered Western consciousness in 1513, when Juan Ponce de León made landfall somewhere around Cape Canaveral. Because his arrival occurred during the season the Spanish called Pascua Florida, or the "festival of the flowers," Ponce de León named Spain's new possession La Florida.

The Spanish were certain that Florida held golden cities to match those they had so methodically looted in Mexico and Peru. In 1539 Hernando de Soto, who had participated in the Inca pillage, landed at or near Bradenton, on the southern shore of Tampa Bay. With over six hundred soldiers, he fought through the Calusa and Timucua tribes along what is now I-75 and I-10 until he reached the site of Tallahassee, where he went into winter quarters and celebrated the

*Much Florida architecture reflects the Spanish influence, which itself had a Moorish flavor. This structure is on Snell Island, Saint Petersburg.*

New World's first Christmas. From there he marched northward, ever deeper into the continent on his futile gold search, until he died and his body was dumped surreptitiously into the muddy Mississippi.

The first permanent Spanish settlement was made at St. Augustine in 1565. From here missionaries tramped the road that eventually ran westward for four hundred miles past the sites of Gainesville and Tallahassee to Pensacola. Over the years more than thirty Spanish cattle ranches sprung up in the hinterlands, particularly along the St. Johns River and the grassy belt from Gainesville to the Suwannee River.

Eventually the Apalachees and the Timucuans became part of the Spanish mission network, incorporating up to twenty-six thousand Native Americans—a number far larger than a similar mission system established in California many years later. The largest mission was San Luis, on the outskirts of Tallahassee, where its remains can be visited today.

Despite St. Augustine's success, the mission existed as a stepchild of the Spanish Empire. Its main purpose had been to protect the treasure fleets carrying Inca and Aztec gold to Spain. In this it was ineffective, and ultimately about its only reason for existence was to keep the aggressive British—who were in the Carolinas—out of Florida. Despite the erection of a frowning fortress called the Castillo de San Marcos (now a major tourist attraction), in this, too, St. Augustine failed. Between 1702 and 1706 British-led Creek warriors decimated Spain's Christianized Indians in a series of slave-hunting raids that utterly destroyed the missions and left Florida virtually unpopulated except for the outposts at St. Augustine and Pensacola.

The Spanish Empire decayed during the 1700s, with its demise coming in 1763 when, allied with France, Spain lost a war with Great Britain. In order to regain Havana, which the British had captured, Spain traded away the entire troublesome territory of Florida.

### The British Interlude, 1763–1783

If modern historians have minimized the first 250 years of Spanish rule, they have virtually ignored the years of British occupation. Yet when the British took possession of the Floridas, they went to great lengths to attract colonists, seeing a significant place in their empire for Florida sugar and indigo. Soon large, slave-based plantations sprung into existence, connected by the still-used Kings Road between Jacksonville and New Smyrna. Most of the plantations used the Halifax River to transport their goods to ocean vessels waiting at Ponce Inlet near Daytona Beach.

Meanwhile British traders fanned far out into the western wilderness, some of their exploits around Gainesville being told by the indefatigable explorer-botanist William Bartram.

The colonies of East and West Florida did not join their thirteen brethren in the Revolutionary War. Thus, with the conclusion of the conflict—which France and Spain had joined against Britain—the loser was forced to return the Floridas to Spain.

### The Spanish Again, 1783–1821

The Spanish apparently wanted Florida more as a means to thwart the British than as a valued province. Because Spain begrudged the few soldiers it had dispatched to Florida, the garrisons were inadequate to control the unruly Seminoles, who came down from the north to fill the vacancy left by the vanished Apalachees and Timucuans.

In 1818, after Seminole raiding parties hit American frontier settlements in Georgia, Andrew Jackson, spitting fire and steel, swept into Florida with an army of frontier ruffians. Offering a cursory apology to the Spanish authorities trembling in Pensacola, he conducted a successful campaign against the Indians, subsequently called the First Seminole War.

It was clear that American annexation of Florida was inevitable. Thus in 1821 the Spanish ceded the province to the United States, receiving in return a mere U.S. assumption of debts that American citizens claimed were owed them.

### Tallahassee, the New Capital

General Jackson accepted the transfer of the province at Pensacola, where he took over as military governor. But because Pensacola was too remote to be the permanent capital and because most people believed that Florida's main settlements would be in the upland strip between Pensacola and St. Augustine, the new capital was chosen midway between the two towns near some deserted fields the Indians called Tallahassee.

### The Second and Third Seminole Wars

The Seminoles were unhappy with the rough treatment they received from Jackson, and when Seminole leader Osceola murdered an Indian agent at Ocala in 1835 the Second Seminole War began. The Indians achieved several successes, most notably the annihilation of an army detachment near Bushnell and the destruction of the sugar plantations along the old Kings Road, leaving evocative ruins near Flagler Beach and New Smyrna. But the U.S. Army, with Tampa and Palatka as its principal supply ports, began a relentless war of eradication that resulted in Osceola's capture near St. Augustine and his subsequent death in prison. Most of the surviving Indians were herded together and shipped off to western lands. Those who were not captured tried to stay clear of the Americans, but in 1855 the Third Seminole War brought their removal—except for a few hundred who retreated into the then-boundless Everglades, where their colorfully garbed descendants greet tourists today.

### Statehood

By 1838 Floridians decided it was time to apply for statehood. Although the Second Seminole War was raging down south, the upper part of the territory, where a vast majority of the forty-eight thousand inhabitants lived, was largely peaceful. Thus that December delegates gathered in St. Joseph, an influential community on the Gulf of Mexico, to write the constitution that would be submitted to the voters one month later—the voters being white adult males. (Women were not expected to have thoughtful opinions on such complicated matters as politics; slaves had no rights whatsoever).

The constitution generated a great deal of controversy, for most people in St. Augustine and Jacksonville wanted the territory divided into two states, with the boundary being the Suwannee River. Citizens around Pensacola desired union with Alabama, but people in the densely populated area around Tallahassee overwhelmingly supported a single state, with their own town continuing as capital of course.

When the votes were in, a single state was approved by a thin margin of just 119 votes. Congress waited to grant statehood until 1845, when Florida, a slave territory, could be neatly balanced with the admission of Iowa, a free territory.

### Florida in the Civil War

The antebellum South flowered in northern Florida, where beautiful plantation mansions were found among the soft hills around Tallahassee and along the Suwannee River, made famous by Stephen Foster's melody in 1851. Travelers reported cotton fields as far as the eye could see. The Apalachicola River was alive with barges floating the large, heavy bales to the gulf port of the same name, where oceangoing vessels carried them to England and other distant countries.

Slavery thrived in Florida, and the remains of slave cabins can still be seen at such locations as the Bulow Plantation, near Flagler Beach, and the Kingsley Plantation, just east of Jacksonville. The fact that Florida's black population was nearly half of the state's total in 1860 shows the pervasiveness of the institution.

At first the Civil War had little effect on Florida, which was far from the battlefields. The state, with its small population, could contribute little to Southern manpower. But soon it became evident that Florida ports were ideal for smugglers of Union contraband. In addition, Florida became an important source of beef for Confederate armies. Much-used cattle trails led up the peninsula from the main ranges east of Sarasota and Fort Myers. Furthermore, along the gulf shores around Panama City, several thousand men actively gathered salt and transported it to distribution points in Alabama.

Eventually Northern strategists decided Florida must be taken out of the war. For this purpose, Union ships not only blockaded the coast but effectively patrolled the St. Johns River from their base at Palatka. Federals occupied every major port—Key West, Pensacola, and Tampa—and they wrecked Jacksonville.

Floridians fought back, defeating Union forces at the minor Battle of Olustee, forty miles west of Jacksonville. Then, during the last days of the war, a grab bag of Floridians beat another Union detachment attempting to take Tallahassee. Despite these victories, Florida had no choice except to surrender with the rest of the Confederacy in 1865.

## The Difficult Reconstruction Period, 1865–1876

Florida was in chaos with the defeat of the Confederacy. Not only was the economic system completely disrupted with the abolition of slavery, but capital for rebuilding the economy was wiped out when a new state constitution repudiated all debts incurred in support of the Southern cause. The Florida executive branch was nonfunctional with the suicide of Governor John Milton, and only the presence of federal troops prevented complete anarchy.

For the former slaves, freedom was a mixed blessing, for they had no way of earning a living. With the fields abandoned, there was great concern of famine. This prompted the federal commander to call on plantation owners to meet with their former slaves and ask them to remain on the land, working either for wages or a share of the harvest. The blacks had little choice but to agree, and thus was born the systems of tenant farming and sharecropping, which were to become almost as oppressive as the slavery they replaced.

Reconstruction was more successful in the political sphere, where black people used their newly gained voting rights to elect African Americans to the state legislature, under the aegis of the newly dominant Republican Party. But even in this, blacks were threatened by the Ku Klux Klan, and eventually poll taxes diminished the number of black voters to insignificance. Nonetheless, during the ten years of Reconstruction, the political power of black Floridians backed up by federal occupation troops caused many whites to flee the once-prosperous area around Tallahassee known as Middle Florida for the virgin lands of the peninsula. Jacksonville became the gateway to the south, and the St. Johns River began to hum with the sound of steamboats taking immigrants to such interior towns as Sanford, Enterprise, and Orlando.

*An 1880s excursion train pauses for picture-taking. Henry Flagler soon incorporated this and other lines into a system that ultimately reached Key West.* —P. H. Yonge Library of Florida History, University of Florida

## The Railroad Era, 1877–1900

By 1877 Florida was again on the move as Northern money began to flow into the state. The first major financier was Hamilton Disston. When he purchased 4 million acres from the state in 1881, he saved Florida from serious economic difficulties. Disston had an ambitious scheme to drain and develop the wetland area from Kissimmee to Lake Okeechobee. But bad planning and inclement weather brought his ruin and alleged suicide in 1896.

Other Northerners took over where Disston failed. Foremost was Henry Flagler, tough cohort of John D. Rockefeller as they forged the Standard Oil monopoly. Flagler, loaded with Standard Oil booty, built a magnificent resort hotel in St. Augustine. Then, almost as an afterthought, he formed a railroad line to provide land transportation for his patrons. Bad weather in St. Augustine caused him to extend his line to Palm Beach, where he not only constructed several more luxury hotels but an ostentatious mansion (which still stands) for himself and his new young bride. A cold spell in Palm Beach was all Flagler needed to continue building to Miami. From there he hurled his rails over the water to distant Key West, reached in 1912. His goal achieved, he died the following year.

Meanwhile, Henry Plant was erecting a rail web throughout western Florida, whose mileage more than matched Flagler's. Plant likewise built a string of fine hotels, chief among them the bizarre Turkish palace still standing in Tampa.

## The Incredible 1920s

During the first half of the 1920s, Florida indulged in perhaps the wildest real estate orgy ever to embarrass an American state. Plans were laid out for fancy subdivisions and fabulous towns—and many were actually built. Carl Fisher's Miami Beach and George Merrick's Coral Gables helped make Miami a wonder of the age. Up the coast, Addison Mizner, having re-created Palm Beach, began work on an even more glamorous development at Boca Raton. Meanwhile, on the gulf coast, circus magnate John Ringling worked on a watery paradise on the islands off Sarasota.

Millionaire hopefuls streamed toward the state along the Dixie Highway, much of which eventually became Florida's US 1. Most of them simply camped out in the tin-can tourist areas outside of the towns, for the hotels were always full. But for the upper crust, construction began on luxury palaces like the Vinoy Hotel in St. Petersburg, the Don CeSar in St. Petersburg Beach, the Biltmore in Coral Gables, and the Casa Marina on Key West—all of which stand today as representatives of an age of dreams and splendor.

The real estate bust hit Florida in 1926, as a horrendous fall in prices left the state in economic shambles. As a result, Florida was left with abandoned developments and a reputation for overblown promises liberally salted with actual deceit. A second staggering blow came just three years later, when the stock market crash helped create the Great Depression.

The bust meant little to the predominantly farming black population, for the prosperity of the 1920s had largely bypassed them. The imposition of sharecropping had long since created its own economic woes. Race relations were generally tense, with the climax coming in 1923 when a mob of whites, enraged at a report that a white woman had been raped by a black man, attacked the village of Rosewood, forty-five miles southwest of Gainesville. In the ensuing melee, six blacks and two whites were killed and Rosewood was completely destroyed.

## The Depression and World War II, 1929–1945

The 1930s was a decade of hard times, described by Ernest Hemingway, writing in Key West, and Zora Neale Hurston, writing in Eatonville. Even the elements were hostile, as in 1935, when one of the fiercest hurricanes ever to hit North America wrecked Florida's vaunted Overseas Railroad, knocking a relief train completely off the tracks and killing hundreds of people. Of course, Florida was not completely prostrate. Cypress Gardens, near Winter Haven, opened in the 1930s, becoming Florida's first theme park. Miami Beach indulged in an amazing construction spree, resulting in the beautiful Art Deco structures whose recent renovation has again brought them into the public eye. And Frank Lloyd Wright began designing the buildings that were to make Florida Southern College in Lakeland famous.

Despite scattered construction, the state's economic situation remained grim. About the only concerted activity in Florida during this period involved Franklin Roosevelt's Depression-relief agencies, such as the Civilian Conservation Corps (CCC), among whose suc-

*Newsreel crews like this helped keep Florida in the limelight in the 1930s. The coats would come off and the shivers vanish when cameras started rolling.* —Florida Cypress Gardens, Inc.

cesses were the Highlands Hammock Park, outside of Sebring, and the preservation of the Ocala National Forest. Another agency, the Works Progress Administration (WPA), also completed many improvements, one of them Daytona's oceanfront band shell and clock tower.

The 1940s did not treat Florida much more kindly. World War II brought restrictions on travel that almost destroyed what remained of the tourist industry. The armed forces took over most of the former luxury hotels, including the fabulous Breakers at Palm Beach, which served as a hospital. During the early part of the war, Florida's beaches were often unavailable due to oil pollution from ships sunk by German submarines. Horrified tourists at Cocoa Beach and Jacksonville Beach even watched as torpedoes exploded tankers only a few miles away!

## The Modern Era

The turnaround in Florida's fortunes began in the late 1950s, when the federal highway program began routing a pair of major expressways through the state. And Florida contributed its own turnpike that eventually linked I-75 with I-95. The expressways helped bring a surge of tourists that revitalized the state's economy. The booming economy attracted businesses, and businesses attracted workers. Soon Florida was one of the fastest-growing states in the country. Among the newcomers were masses of retirees, who eventually made up a quarter of Florida's population—the largest elderly population in the United States.

The stupendous demographic change brought a corresponding alteration of Florida's political makeup. Traditionally the state was controlled by the northern rural counties, whose representation in the legislature was far out of proportion to the growing central and southern counties. Old-time Democratic politicians, known as Tallahassee's Pork Chop Gang, ruled the state and were unsympathetic to tourism and opposed to desegregation. It took a federal court ordering reapportionment in 1967 to break the power of the Pork Choppers.

Reapportionment brought a major political adjustment. So great had been the influx of newcomers, most from affluent Northern Republican families, that although the Democrats remained effective in the state legislature, Florida began appearing regularly in the Republican column during presidential elections.

The Civil Rights Act of 1964 helped African Americans regain the political privileges that had supposedly been granted them a century earlier. Over that period, they had grown to view Florida as an essentially hostile place and had migrated north in such large numbers that, whereas in 1900 they were 44 percent of the population, by 1970 they made up only 18 percent.

One of the most significant developments in Florida's economy in general, and of central Florida in particular, was the coming of Walt Disney. The interstate highways were vital in Disney's decision to start a theme park here. When he flew over I-4 and saw it cutting across the center of the state, linking I-75 in the west and I-95 in the east, as well as Florida's Turnpike in the center, his decision was made.

Disney World opened in 1971, and the rush was on. By the late 1970s Florida's cities were reflecting the new prosperity. Orlando's Church Street Station and International Drive brought fun-loving tourists in numbers never dreamed of a few years earlier. Tampa's Busch Gardens, at the western end of I-4, and the Kennedy Space Center, near the eastern end, added to the state's lure.

During the 1980s, Miami, Jacksonville, and downtown Tampa were also on the move. Miami became the home port for a host of cruise ships, and the Bayside Marketplace revitalized the waterfront. Jacksonville called the 1980s the Billion Dollar Decade, as glass skyscrapers formed a glittering backdrop for its attractive Jacksonville Landing. Tampa, too, had its new skyscrapers, and by the 1990s Ybor City was fast becoming a popular entertainment center.

In many ways the 1970s and 1980s were more difficult for towns than for the large cities. As shopping malls began mushrooming outside the cities and in the suburbs, the smaller business districts that once were regional market centers slowly withered. A feeling of hopelessness took hold of civic leaders as the tax base dwindled, and run-down, deserted storefronts became more common than prosperous enterprises.

But in the late 1980s and early 1990s a renaissance occurred, at least in some towns. Perhaps Delray Beach provided the spark; it certainly was one of the earliest towns to understand that the revitalization of a downtown depended on the grassroots efforts of its own citizens—not on government handouts and advice from outside "experts."

*A spacious pontoon boat takes passengers on scenic excursions along
the St. Johns River above Sanford.*

In 1985 a statewide Main Street program was inaugurated to aid
towns with populations between thirty-five hundred and seventy
thousand—with DeLand in central Florida as one of its first selections. The state acted as an advisor only, and each town had to come
up with its own plan to bring back its downtown. Community involvement was stressed. The qualifications were strict, and ten years later
only thirty-five towns had been able to meet them. Among the
business districts that have been spruced up and revitalized are
Chipley and Marianna in the panhandle; Venice, Dunedin, and Tarpon Springs on the gulf coast; Sebring, Sanford, and Ocala in central
Florida; Key West in the south; and New Smyrna and Titusville along
the Atlantic.

The achievements of the men and women of the past are part
of modern Florida. We travel the pathways they blazed, and later
paved with bricks, and still later turned into expressways. We linger
on the land where they had their campfires or where they constructed
their log cabins or their hotels and skyscrapers.

The people of the past knew they were building for the future. They knew we would come—just as we know others will follow us. They must have stood on the seashores, on the hilltops, or on the riverbanks and sometimes mused about the future, as Walt Whitman did so many years ago:

> *I am with you, you men and women of a generation,*
> *or ever so many generations hence,*
> *Just as you feel when you look on the river and sky,*
> *so I felt,*
> *Just as any of you is one of a living crowd,*
> *I was one of a crowd . . .*

*Beautiful Lake Eola, with parks and walking paths, graces Orlando's downtown.*

# ⊰ 1 ⊱

# *Orlando and the Theme Parks*

## FUN AND FANTASY

## Orlando

*Boomtown*

Orlando has been many towns. In 1835 it consisted only of Fort Gatlin, a minor army post during the Second Seminole War. At this time, a U.S. soldier named Orlando Reeves was killed by the Indians somewhere near the shores of Lake Eola, and most historians believe it was he who became the town's namesake. The locale first had the simple designation "Orlando's grave."

Orlando was little more than a weathering grave marker until 1880, when the railroad arrived. Within four years the population shot up from barely two hundred to almost seventeen hundred.

By World War I a new Orlando was emerging. In 1917 Newton Yowell and Eugene Duckworth completed the handsome, five-story brick building that still stands at 1 South Orange Avenue. It became such a popular department store that a few years later they installed a Japanese tearoom on the mezzanine, which was a tremendous attraction to women shoppers. The profits from the store were such that Duckworth sold out to Benjamin Drew, and then Duckworth entered politics. In 1920 this dynamic and feisty little man of barely five feet four inches became mayor.

Soon Stanley Ives and H. H. Dickson put up an equally handsome brick building directly across the street at 2 South Orange. They, too, had a department store, and the competition between theirs and Drew's was legendary.

During the Roaring Twenties the growing city, with a population of twenty-seven thousand, became a shopping center for much of

*Orlando's Orange Avenue in the 1920s. The Yowell-Duckworth Building is in the right foreground. Down the street is the Angebilt Hotel.* —Orange County Historical Museum

central Florida. The downtown could now support a theater, so the Beacham was built at 46 North Orange. Braxton Beacham, who had made a fortune in Florida real estate, was tremendously proud of his theater. The Beacham hosted many premier shows, one of the most successful being that put on by John Philip Sousa and his entire marching band. The Ziegfeld Follies also drew record crowds. But the theater's main staple was silent films until management installed equipment so the actors could actually talk!

In 1924 the Orlando Bank and Trust built a tower at 102 South Orange that scraped the sky at ten stories. Not to be outdone, its chief competitor, the State Bank, erected an even grander ten-story monolith at 1 North Orange.

With all the activity, Joe Ange, builder and real estate promoter, decided that Orlando needed a first-rate hotel. So up it went, eleven stories of brick with limestone trim. What should he call it? Why, the Angebilt Hotel, of course. And here, in 1926, one of the earliest radio broadcasts was made, on WDBO.

In 1927 county officials entered the building binge as they erected an impressive four-story, classical-style courthouse at 50 North

Magnolia. This building underwent extensive retrofitting in 1997 to become the home of the Orange County Historical Society.

Orlando in the 1920s was a smug little world. Locals could only marvel at the wonders that had been wrought. Lucy Lawrence took the elevator to the top of the Angebilt Hotel, where she stood in awe at the vista and later wrote down her impressions. She recalled that when she first came to Orlando the roads were of sand. Now, "extending as far as the eye can reach are the bricked highways that knit this city to its sister cities." She remembered the old gaslights that used to sputter along the streets until they were turned off at midnight. Now she saw "electric lights that are like the jewels in some gorgeous necklace." She exclaimed how "today we have department stores that rival those of a big city managed by men of vision and enterprise."

Yet, although Lucy did not know it, an era of disillusionment was approaching, of which her men of vision and enterprise had not the slightest inkling.

It began with the stock market crash of 1929. The next year, the full effect of the Great Depression was on, and the impossible happened: the State Bank, housed in that great skyscraper at Orange and Central, closed its doors. So, too, did its fierce competitor, the Orlando Bank, housed in its own skyscraper just down the street. Next, in panic, crowds descended on the First National Bank at Orange and Church, demanding the return of their deposits, which, of course, the bank had put out in the form of loans. This bank, too, went under. When it reopened in 1934 as the new First National (now the SunTrust), it was able to pay depositors just 30 percent of their accounts.

The Orlando of the next four decades was a far different city from the cocky place of the twenties. Although improvements came, they did not involve the downtown, which remained in a state of shock.

Many of these improvements involved Lake Eola, which became a showplace when the exclusive, nine-story Eola Plaza (now the Park Plaza) apartment complex was built on the southern shore in 1950. It was the costliest structure ever erected in Orlando, and it was from here that Walt Disney announced his exciting theme-park plans a decade and a half later.

To enhance Lake Eola, a fountain was installed in 1957. Then, in 1961, the Robert Meyer Group from Jacksonville bought the old high school on the western shore. There they constructed the motor hotel that eventually evolved into the Harley when it was purchased by Leona Helmsley, whose saga as hotel queen and prison inmate make an incredible story, summarized by her most famous boast: "Only the little people pay taxes."

Although the downtown had been largely bypassed by the improvements, this was to change in a strange manner.

### The Whiz-Bang Kid and Church Street Station

In 1972 twenty-eight-year-old Bob Snow stood before the deserted railroad depot on Church Street, near the heart of downtown Orlando. The station was dilapidated, with paint peeling and the roof leaking. Yet it was no worse than the rest of the neighborhood. Drunks loitered around the Strand Hotel flophouse. Ne'er-do-wells came and went from the Goodwill store that was operating from the closed Bumby Hardware. Farther down Church Street was a grimy pawn shop. And Sam's Bar and Grill in the Teele Building made the air bitter with the odor of stale beer and greasy burgers. While Snow contemplated the scene, a patrol car pulled up. The officer urged him to get moving. "You don't want to be here after dark," he warned.

But Snow did not see a decrepit neighborhood. Instead he saw a row of vintage buildings crying to be rehabilitated. He saw nightclubs, restaurants, shops, and arcades. Inside the old train depot he pictured an antique gift shop, and outside, a real steam locomotive with a string of period coaches.

It would be a tremendous challenge. But he believed he could do it, for hadn't he recently turned a run-down warehouse and hotel in Pensacola into the highly successful Seville Quarter? This experience had led him to seek a location for a larger development, and he had just finished scouting fifteen cities. He was in Orlando for that purpose but had about given up. Indeed, his taxi had almost reached the airport when the driver happened to tell him about the decaying railroad depot. Almost as soon as he viewed it, he knew this was what he had been looking for.

Of course, there was the matter of financing. Few bankers had confidence in Snow's Church Street Station project. Even fewer believed that this very young man with the outlandish handlebar mustache and a tendency toward braggadocio had the moxie to turn a down-and-out area into a family entertainment center.

Somehow Snow managed to wheedle a loan from the First National Bank of Orlando. Then he set up temporary offices in the Victorian depot, which had been built back in 1887 by railroad tycoon Henry Plant. Next he began turning the old Slemons Department Store, at the corner of Church Street and Garland Avenue, into a nightclub.

It was a labor of love, not only for Snow but for his whole crew, who began calling themselves the Good Time Gang. They tried to keep the building's original fixtures—thus the pressed-tin ceilings remained. And as the interior neared completion, Snow brought in valuable antiques that he had collected on personal trips all over the world.

By the summer of 1974, Slemons had become Rosie O'Grady's Good Time Emporium. A Dixieland band, singing waiters, and even a red-hot mama belting out raucous ditties—they were all there. Snow loved it, for he had helped pay his way through college by playing trumpet in such a band. He was there to personally greet the guests and work the beer tap.

Rosie's was an instant success. So with money coming in, Snow marched down Church Street to the First National Bank and paid off his loan with two hundred thousand dollars in cash while his Dixieland band blasted "Happy Days Are Here Again" through the staid bank lobby.

Snow quickly got a new loan under more favorable terms. Then he began working his way along the north side of Church Street. Next to Rosie's was a 1919 building that once had housed Leon's Jewelry and Second Hand Shop. After two years of intensive labor, Leon's became Apple Annie's Courtyard. A year later, the run-down Strand Hotel emerged as Lili Marlene's Aviators Pub and Restaurant. And by 1978 the Teele Building, once home to the venerable Sam's Bar and Grill, had been transformed into Phineas Phogg's Dance Club.

Now Snow turned his attention to the south side of Church Street. The Purcell Corral, a western-wear store, was in a decaying 1920 building across from Rosie O'Grady's. It was a natural to become a country-western nightclub. So the interior was almost gutted and decked out with what the *Orlando Sentinel* called "the usual Church Street array of colored glass and antiques." In 1982 it reopened as the Cheyenne Saloon & Social Club, a family-oriented entertainment palace seating up to a thousand people.

Amid all the frolic and fervor, Snow had a 141-ton, authentic Orange Blossom Special steam locomotive chug to its permanent home in front of the refurbished depot. The fact that it had been used in the 1957 John Wayne movie *Wings of Eagles* gave it added

*Church Street in 1886 (facing west) just after the first railroad station was built. The Bumby hardware store on the left is brand new.* —Florida State Archives

*Church Street today (facing east). Bumby Emporium is in the foreground. Turret of the 1889 railroad station and the massive SunTrust tower are in the background.*

luster. Snow hoped to have the train make excursions along the historic route through Winter Park to Sanford.

One of the pioneers along that route had been Joseph Bumby, who, freshly arrived from England in the 1870s, opened the Bumby Express, a stagecoach and freight line between Orlando and Sanford. The express made the fifty-mile round-trip in just twelve hours! However, hardware, not speed, was Bumby's main interest. Since Church Street was then a prime commercial area, Bumby constructed one of the town's first brick buildings there in 1886. From this building Bumby and his descendants sold farm goods and other essentials for eighty years. But the store was defunct by the time Bob Snow appeared.

In 1984 Snow constructed a gaudy walkway over Church Street connecting Lili Marlene's with Bumby Hardware. Then work began on the old building, which Snow, with a friendly nod to the ghost of the dead Englishman, turned into the Bumby Emporium and Arcade. Ever ready with novel ideas, when he repaved the Bumby sidewalk with bricks he let visitors inscribe messages on them—at a cost of $13.95 per brick. On opening day, Snow was there stomping through the sawdust in his flashy cowboy boots and western shirt with gold-tipped collar.

Around this time, Snow talked the city into closing Church Street in the evenings and using police on horseback to patrol the area. Snow helped with the initial expense by ostentatiously depositing a saddlebag jammed with $6,500 in front of Orlando's startled mayor.

In 1988 Snow opened his largest addition to the Church Street complex. This was the seventy-thousand-square-foot Exchange, giving Church Street an imposing facade on I-4. The building looked like something resurrected from the Columbian Exposition of 1893, but it was all new. Snow believed its attractive shops would double the number of Church Street visitors, which already stood at a yearly 2 million. This made Church Street Florida's fifth-largest tourist attraction!

Snow's operations caused independent operators to open attractions along Church Street east of his development. Most impressive was a bilevel, Middle Ages–style market occupying both sides of the street and enclosing a much-needed public park with benches and fountains. But the proprietors did not have Snow's magic, and the building ended up in the hands of Barnett Bank, which in turn sold it to Dutch investors in 1994.

As for Bob Snow, in a surprise move he suddenly sold out, giving as his reason a desire to seek new enterprises. With an estimated profit of $48 million, he was apparently ready to meet the challenge offered by the city of Las Vegas, where he built Main Street Station in a past-its-prime part of town. Snow sunk nearly all he had into the venture, but within four months he had filed for bankruptcy. To satisfy his creditors, he even put his treasured collection of antiques on the block.

Does Snow ever reminisce about his dazzling successes in Orlando? "Those were exciting days," he recalled to a reporter. "Every morning was a new day, and every day was Dixieland bands and cancan girls and Red Hot Mamas. But you can't look back."

Though Bob Snow is not there, Church Street Station rollicks on. Mamas still bellow at Rosie O'Grady's. The Cheyenne Saloon still stomps to country music. Musical combos have begun livening other joints along the street, and the activity has spilled out onto Orange Avenue, which has become so jammed with cars at night that signs now warn sight-seers not to cruise the block more than three consecutive times.

### The Great Orange Avenue Revival

With Church Street Station providing the spark, nearby Orange Avenue, Orlando's main thoroughfare, started to revive. It began in 1984, when the city formed an organization called Streetscape, whose objective was to bring businesses back to the area. Through Streetscape the six main blocks of Orange Avenue from Jefferson to South Street were closed to traffic while bulldozers and backhoes dug out and replaced the antiquated wooden sewers put in during the Duckworth administration. Then, after more powerful utility lines were buried beside the new sewers, the street was repaved. Before the project was completed, sidewalks were turned into curved brick walkways, and trees were planted every thirty feet. At the same time, off-street parking was nearly doubled.

The result was dramatic. Orange Avenue regained much of its old sparkle. Businesses began opening. Old buildings that had once been eyesores were renovated. Furthermore, with proper sewers and electric power, large modern buildings could now be accommodated. So at the end of 1984 work began on a magnificent bronze-colored glass tower, soon nicknamed "the Copper Whopper," at 111 North Orange, on the corner of Washington.

*Orange Avenue today with the Yowell-Duckworth Building on the right. The Streetscape project of the 1980s brought in the trees and widened the sidewalks.*

As the activity increased, SunTrust concluded the time was right to construct its own office tower on Orange Avenue. It was thirty-five stories, the maximum height allowed by the Federal Aviation Administration, and the architectural style was art deco, reminiscent of the 1930s. Particularly "playful" (to use one art critic's description) were the four green pyramids at the top. Made of fiberglass, they hid the radio antennas that were to be placed there.

### The Rise and Fall of William du Pont III

At almost the same time that the SunTrust was revitalizing the south end of downtown, a newcomer named William du Pont III was planning a development more than three times larger for the north end. Although du Pont was barely out of college and had almost no business experience, the fact that he was worth $125 million could more than make up for these deficiencies.

Bill, as he liked to be called, had married an Orlando girl and, having attended universities in North Carolina and Kentucky, spoke with a slight southern drawl. That is, when he spoke at all, for he was a quiet, somewhat withdrawn young man who felt the du Pont name was as much a handicap as an asset. More than anything, Bill wanted to prove that he could be a big-time businessman by his own efforts.

In the summer of 1984, du Pont announced plans for the largest development Orlando had ever seen. Along Orange Avenue and west to I-4 he was going to construct three huge office towers, plus an upscale hotel of 650 rooms, retail space totaling 125,000 square feet, a major trade mart, a bevy of restaurants, and garages for nearly four thousand cars. The development would cover the better part of six square blocks. When the director of the regional planning office heard about it, he was "stunned," to use his own word.

Du Pont Center took off with a roar. By 1988 the first building was ready for occupancy, and the prestigious First Federal Association Savings and Loan moved in and emblazoned its name on the twenty-eight-story building's highest pinnacle. William du Pont had arrived.

Optimism ran high. The exclusive Westin Hotel chain was enthusiastic about leasing the projected seventeen-story hotel. Thus encouraged, preliminary work began.

Bill du Pont became Orlando's most celebrated citizen. Perhaps his greatest feat was snagging a professional basketball franchise

*The former Du Pont Center was designed to be the first of three huge towers before young William du Pont suffered financial reverses.*

for the city after the National Basketball Association had rejected a local group. Young William seemed to have a sorcerer's touch, for by 1990 the Magic basketball franchise's value had shot up to $70 million, more than double his original purchase price.

But at the same time, the high-flying millionaire was having financial problems. Work on the proposed hotel was stopped so abruptly that piles of earth were left where they had last been deposited during soil testing. Then it came out that du Pont had lost $10 million when a local savings and loan he had invested in collapsed. In addition, income from the du Pont Center was way off, for not only was the building far from full, but the First Federal itself had run afoul of government regulators. Within a year the institution would cease to exist—leaving the vast space it had rented vacant.

By August 1990, du Pont's company was unable to make payments on a series of loans, and by October the lawsuits began. Du Pont, forced to return his flagship building to his creditors, lost all he had invested in it. His lofty plans for the other towers, the hotel, and the rest of the buildings were scrapped.

The events staggered Orlando's financial community. But not for long. The Barnett Bank, one of the creditors, became the new anchor tenant. Barnett, for its part, was delighted to put its name where it could reach the clouds. The joy was short-lived, however, for Barnett was soon gobbled up by megagiant Nations Bank.

In 1997 Barnett's corner of downtown was greatly enhanced by the addition of the Orange County Court House, a skyscraper with a cylinder-shaped top. Although the courthouse is an admirable addition to Orlando's skyline, its erection played out almost as a comedy of errors. Due to changes in federal regulations, misinterpretations of work specifications, and general goof-ups, expenses ran far over budget. By the time the building was completed, the project manager was suing Orange County, and the subcontractors were suing the project manager. The result was seven full volumes of claims. Perhaps the greatest incentive to getting the behind-schedule building completed was the desire of all parties to get into the new courtrooms with their lawsuits.

## International Drive

The planners of I-4 never dreamed that a great complex of theme parks, hotels, restaurants, and amusements of innumerable and strange varieties would sprout from the wetlands west of Orlando.

I-4 was designed simply to connect I-95 along the east coast with I-75 along the west coast. It was not even designed originally to go through Orlando!

Disney insisted that several interchanges be put in so visitors could get to the Magic Kingdom, EPCOT, and Lake Buena Vista. Even so, it was thought that the Disney on-site hotels would provide lodging for all the overnight tourists visiting the park. However, this was not the case, and in 1972, less than a year after Walt Disney World opened, a Sheraton went up at Sand Lake and International Drive. "There was nothing there before we came," recalled James Russell, one of the owners. "I mean nothing except a ma-and-pa motel or two. I-Drive only ran north. To the south it was all just deserted orange groves. One of our partners took a look at the site, groaned, and wanted to abandon the whole thing."

But Russell had correctly judged the demand. With two hundred units constructed around swimming pools and lagoons, the Sheraton was filled from the day it opened.

The construction of the Sheraton set the stage for wild expansion along International Drive. Soon the road was extended far southward until it linked up with US 192, the main entrance to Disney World. Along the way it passed the massive Orange County Convention Center, Sea World, and a series of large hotels including the Peabody, Omni Rosen, and the Marriott World Center.

A trip along I-Drive affords a ramble past luxury and honky-tonk unrivaled this side of Las Vegas. Coming from Orlando on I-4, get off at Kirkman Road and go one street south to International Drive. Half a mile to your left is the large Belz Factory Outlet, with many good buys. Turning right, I-Drive passes Wet'n Wild, a multistory maze of water slides ideal for a warm day. At the southeast corner of Sand Lake Road is the Marriott, formerly the Sheraton, the original major motel on the strip.

A newer, wider portion of I-Drive begins just south of the Marriott. The Mercado is a large shopping center with many good shops and some excellent restaurants. At the next bend in the road is the Orange County Convention Center, opened in 1983. Huge to start with, it was constantly expanded until by 1998 it became one of America's six largest centers. Beside it is the Omni Rosen, and opposite is the twenty-seven-story Peabody Hotel.

The Peabody is a southern tradition dating back to 1869. The original hotel in Memphis catered to such Civil War celebrities as

Bedford Forrest, who, when asked how he won so many battles knowing so little about military tactics, grunted that he simply got there "fustest with the mostest." The Florida building opened in 1986. You might want to visit the lobby, with its $1.5 million worth of paintings, pottery, and statuary. There are, in addition, the Peabody's famous ducks.

The ducks started as a delightful joke—and have remained so. The duck caper began in Memphis in the 1930s, when some hunters deposited a few of their live duck decoys in the hotel fountain. The incongruity of the situation tickled the patrons, and by the 1940s the ducks' entrance and exit was heralded by rolling out a red carpet and playing a Sousa march.

Each day at 11 A.M. and 5 P.M., descendants of the ancestral ducks re-create the decades-old pageantry in the Orlando Peabody lobby, which is open to the public. You can also have something to eat at Mallards or take afternoon tea in the foyer of Dux Restaurant.

From the Peabody, continue south on International Drive. You will pass State Route 528, which, as the Bee Line Expressway, runs directly to Cape Canaveral. At 10100 I-Drive you will find the Sheraton World Resort.

The Sheraton chain had an interesting beginning. The founders were a pair of Harvard classmates who during the 1910s tried their hands at many ventures, including the assembly of Model T Fords and the importation of paper-fiber suits! After the stock market crash of 1929, they began investing in run-down hotels, which they fixed up and operated at a profit. They called themselves the Standard Equities Corporation until they purchased a building in Boston with a large electric sign. Rather than go to the expense of tearing down the sign, they renamed their company after it: the Sheraton.

The Sheraton lobby is three stories high, with wood panels and a skylight. The twenty-eight–acre grounds contain mainly two- and three-story buildings. Visible immediately south is the blue glass edifice of Harcourt Brace, whose unusual story is told under the Sea World section later in this chapter.

Farther down I-Drive is Sea Harbor Drive, leading to the Renaissance Hotel, across from the entry to Sea World. It is famous for having the world's largest atrium. The ceiling is ten stories high. Glass elevators go up to the surrounding floors, from which private interior balconies look out over the wide expanse. On the main floor, there is a waterfall that cascades from beneath a raised platform supporting a restaurant. The lobby floor is of shimmering marble squares, and near the center is a two-story ornamental cage with tropical birds.

Continuing down I-Drive, you will soon see the spire of the Marriott World Center. The hotel is worth a visit—and don't forget to ride the glass elevator. You will enjoy its awesome vistas. Unfortunately, the hotel has provided no rooftop viewing area, but if you get off at the twenty-seventh floor you can enjoy a good perspective through the picture windows. The view to the west is particularly rewarding, for you can see Disney World's Contemporary Hotel and Space Mountain, as well as the golf ball of EPCOT and the peaked green roof of Disney's Dolphin Hotel. In the distance to the middle is Pleasure Island, with the paddle-wheel steamer *Empress Lilly*, named after Disney's wife.

The hotel itself is like some great Medieval castle with a distinctive modern touch—a far cry from Willard Marriott's original root beer stand. The hotel, built in 1986, has nine restaurants, snack bars, and lounges; an eighteen-hole golf course; and one of the most fabulous swimming pools you'll find anywhere. The Marriott does not own the hotel; it acts as the management company.

From the Marriott, go a short distance west to get back on I-4.

# Walt Disney World

### Walt Disney's Triumphs and Tragedies

The legend about Walt Disney and the creation of Mickey Mouse is one of those so good that if it isn't true it should be.

Picture a young, struggling artist in a room so threadbare that his only solace is a mouse who lives in his wastebasket. The little critter becomes so tame that he climbs onto the artist's drawing board and partakes of the crumbs from the man's miserable meals. In return for this companionship, the artist immortalizes the mouse in his cartoons.

Although Disney never confirmed this story, the part about him being poor is true. The Disney family goes back to humble peasants in Isigny, France. They migrated to England with William the Conqueror, at which time they added a *d* to the name Isigny, feeling it gave them class (for it suggested aristocratic roots). So the family was known as D'Isigny until they ultimately merged into the English community as Disney.

Walt's parents were married in Florida, where his father tried his hand as a cattleman in Kissimmee and as a hotel manager in Daytona

Beach. He was not a success at either place, and the family soon moved north. In 1901, Walt was born in Chicago, although he was to spend most of his formative years in rural Missouri. It was here that young Walt first displayed his artistic bent by painting a tar pig on the side of the family's whitewashed farmhouse, an unappreciated project for which he paid dearly.

At age twenty-one Walt became interested in animated cartoons. So he went to Hollywood with only a cardboard suitcase and forty dollars in his pocket. Once there, he set up a tiny studio with his older brother, Roy, who operated the secondhand camera. Besides the brothers, there were a pair of pen-and-ink girls to fill in Walt's cartoons. Walt married the one known as Lilly, who became his steadfast companion for the rest of his life.

In 1928 Walt's first Mickey Mouse film appeared. Walt intended to call the character Mortimer Mouse, but, as the story goes, Lilly insisted on the more friendly Mickey. Walt had a warm feeling for Mickey and, when talkies came in, Walt's falsetto was Mickey's voice.

Walt had a genuine love of youngsters. "If all the world thought and acted like children," he said, "we'd never have any trouble." Thus it was one of the bitterest events in his life when the doctor told him that, though he and Lilly had one daughter, they could never have another child. The problem was with him. And though they later adopted a second daughter, that did not alleviate the fact that Walt could never have the son he so ardently desired. Many people close to Walt, including Lilly, believed that his affection for Mickey Mouse was a substitute for the son he never had.

Disney's cartoons were an instant success. By 1930 it was estimated that more than 400 million people had seen a Mickey Mouse film—including England's sedate Queen Mary and Italy's strutting dictator Benito Mussolini. When *Snow White and the Seven Dwarfs* came out in 1937, it assured Disney's preeminence in the field.

But by the early 1950s Walt was growing bored with cartoons. *Alice in Wonderland* had been a box-office failure and *Peter Pan* had not done as well as expected. When Walt discussed a Disney amusement park, the idea was ridiculed. "Almost everyone warned us," he later said, "that Disneyland would be a Hollywood spectacular—a spectacular failure." But Walt went ahead, optimistic as ever, and from the day the California park opened in 1955 it was a roaring success.

There had never been anything like it. Whereas amusement parks had traditionally been conglomerations of Ferris wheels, roller coasters, and fun houses, Disney's was mostly built around the theme of his cartoon characters, so he called it a "theme park." Disneyland also had a nineteenth-century-style downsized train, modeled on the one he ran around his own yard. Yet Disneyland had a futuristic aspect, as America's first monorails carried visitors on elevated tours of the park.

Disneyland was different in many other ways. The sleazy hawkers that were so frequent at carnivals and circuses were replaced by scrubbed young men and women. Furthermore, the park itself was clean, and restaurants on the premises served food that was actually good.

Disneyland's tremendous success took Walt and Roy, who handled the finances, by surprise. The company's gross income more than doubled in 1956. By 1957 profits had doubled again!

But Walt was always looking for new worlds to conquer. As early as 1958 he was considering a second park. Florida was the ideal location, due to its year-round favorable weather. Soon the site was narrowed to either near Ocala or Orlando. Disney's agents reported that Ocala was better, but Walt wanted to look for himself. So he flew over Florida in his private Beechcraft. Beyond Ocala, he began following Florida's Turnpike. When he approached Orlando, he saw construction being done on I-4, which crossed the Pike just west of town. Beyond lay mile upon mile of almost uninhabited wilderness.

The location was perfect: it had good transportation and was inland, away from hurricanes. Furthermore, acreage could be purchased for a song if he was careful to keep his identity quiet. So Orlando it was.

When Disney's agents had secretly bought all the land they needed, Walt revealed his plans. Orlando was agog. Nothing this momentous had ever happened to the sleepy place of only 30,000. Hardly any tourists stopped here, for Miami to the south was the chief destination. But it was clear that this was about to change. And did it. Within a decade the town had jumped to 250,000, and Miamians were speaking ruefully of the Great Wall of Orlando that kept tourists from venturing beyond central Florida.

Construction of Disney World was not easy. When Walt's engineers flew over the area they were appalled, for the site was mostly mosquito-infested wetlands. From out of this had to emerge elevated land and fresh blue lagoons!

*Walt and Roy Disney announce plans in 1965 for a future theme park to be built in the swampy land west of Orlando.* —Florida State Archives

Work on the Magic Kingdom came first. Here, many of the rides were to be repeats of the tried-and-true attractions so popular in California. New, however, would be the hotels right on the premises. The Polynesian would represent a lodging in the South Pacific, while the Contemporary would be an ultramodern structure where monorail trains would actually coast right through the lobby!

Yet, strangely, Walt had little interest in the Magic Kingdom or in the hotels. He concentrated on what he referred to as his City of Tomorrow. It would be a model community. Thirty thousand people would live there—mostly employees of Disney World. Disney would own the homes, so the company would have control over how the town developed. There would be no slums and no crime. In Walt's words, it would become "a showcase for American industry and research, [for] schools, [and for] cultural and educational opportunities."

This town would be constantly changing as the inhabitants solved various problems of community living. It would be an experiment that would furnish the nation and the world with a prototype for living in future harmony. With this in mind, Walt named his project the Experimental Prototype Community of Tomorrow: EPCOT for short.

EPCOT quickly took on a special urgency, for Walt's health was deteriorating. He had a constant and growing pain in his neck that made it difficult to move his head. In 1966, when he went to a doctor, Walt learned that the pain was from a growth of calcium. But, far worse, the exam also revealed a malignancy on one of his lungs. Although he had the lung removed, the prognosis was still pessimistic.

Now it became a race against time. Aware that his days were numbered, he wanted to establish the guidelines of EPCOT, since it was with this project he believed his place in history would lie.

Oddly, he was more worried about the future of EPCOT than his own. Why was it going so slowly? What did it matter that the city would not bring in profits the way the Magic Kingdom would? Couldn't his associates see that it would provide a blueprint for uncountable benefits to humankind? Wasn't that more important? The very day before his death, he made Roy promise to see EPCOT through.

On December 15, 1966, Walt passed away. The band at Disneyland played "When You Wish Upon a Star." There was a moment of silence throughout the park. Then the rides resumed. Walt wanted it that way.

Roy attempted to continue for his brother. Walt Disney World opened in October 1971 to tremendous accolades. Roy shared in the elation. But he had given his all, and one month later he died of a cerebral hemorrhage.

Now the scepter was passed to others who did not understand Walt's passion for EPCOT. Believing his dream was impractical, they completely revised the sketchy plan Walt had left. Gradually most of EPCOT became mere showcase buildings for trade goods from specific countries. Rides were thrown in as additional attractions. This is not to say that the company stinted on EPCOT. Far from it. Some financial advisors even thought it had spent so much on the attraction that it was in danger of bankruptcy.

EPCOT had its grand opening on October 24, 1982. Walt's wife, Lilly, was there for the dedication. "May EPCOT Center entertain, inform, and inspire," she said.

"Entertain"—it certainly did; from the beginning it was exceedingly popular. "Inform"—yes, there was a good deal of information, if one could find it amid the rides, trinkets, and fireworks. "Inspire"—

*Walt Disney World several months before opening in 1971. Upper right, the Contemporary Hotel; center, Cinderella's Castle.* —Florida State Archives

that's another question. Walt wanted EPCOT to provide an experimental prototype community that would enable its inhabitants to reach a new plane of coexistence.

Have Walt Disney's successors succeeded in this goal? You be the judge.

### Disney's Town of Celebration

Some Disney officials like to point out the new town of Celebration as a fulfillment of Walt's "experimental prototype of the city of the future." At I-4 and US 192, Celebration was opened to the public in 1996. It is truly an exciting place to visit. Designed to eventually accommodate a population of twenty thousand, it has a central business district with restaurants, shops, a movie theater, and other amenities, all built around a pretty little lake. In planning the town, Disney's experts visited modern towns in many different locations, including Florida's unique village of Seaside, on the upper gulf coast.

Humans, not autos, are featured in Celebration. There are alleys for cars and out-of-sight parking lots downtown. The streets are mainly for the inhabitants to walk, bike, or skate. There are few, if any, cul de sacs, and all the streets lead somewhere—thus promoting visitation among neighborhoods. Most of the homes have front porches to promote neighborliness.

Modern architecture has little place at Celebration. The homes and commercial buildings show styles from the 1920s and earlier, although the movie theater has an Art Deco motif reminiscent of the 1930s. The *Orlando Sentinel* used the word *whimsy* to help describe Celebration, "where theme-park fantasy meets Norman Rockwell America."

Celebration is well worth the visit. Here you will see Mickey's version of yesterday. You may even want to buy a home there and live in a fantasy forever and ever—if you can.

### An Inexpensive Tour of Disney World

One can have a very enjoyable tour of Disney World without spending much money. Disney World is divided into three major segments: the theme parks, the hotels, and Downtown Disney (formerly Disney Village). An admission fee is charged to enter the theme parks, which include the Magic Kingdom, Animal Kingdom, EPCOT, and MGM Studios. However, if you are short on time or just want to get the flavor of Disney World without the expense, you can get off I-4 at exit 27, Lake Buena Vista (Apopka-Vineland Road), then go one block north to Hotel Plaza Boulevard, where you turn left past large hotels to the parking lot at Downtown Disney.

Entry to Downtown is free. There you can browse through shops of many kinds and enjoy a snack or full dinner at one of the many restaurants, including some that are quite spectacular.

Then catch a free bus to the main transportation center. Here, at no extra charge, you can board the monorail for a tour around the Seven Seas Lagoon.

Your first stop will be the Polynesian Hotel, which, with the Contemporary Hotel, was the only on-premises lodging during the park's early years. You will certainly be impressed by the lobby, which is centered around a tropical jungle, with palms and banana trees reaching up two and a half stories, and brilliantly colored birds hopping about with no cages to restrict them. Then walk to the waterfront, where you can sit on the beach while watching sailboats and water sprites cut through the blue. You can rent one of these boats, if you wish.

Your next monorail stop will be the Grand Floridian Beach Hotel, a plush Victorian structure with a five-story lobby done in white and beige. Again, you can stroll to the waterfront, where there is a snack bar along with beach chairs.

Back on the monorail, you will pass the Magic Kingdom before cruising directly into the lobby of the Contemporary Hotel. There, on the main floor you can enjoy sandwiches or a full meal, while gazing at a mosaic reaching up to the ceiling many stories above and watching the monorails rumble gently overhead. For a spectacular view of the Seven Seas Lagoon and the Magic Kingdom, take the elevator to the spacious lounge at the top of the Contemporary. If you are there at the right time, you will be treated to fireworks shooting up over Cinderella's Palace.

The Contemporary has a fine beach on Bay Lake, where you can get refreshments. From here, for a fee, you can take an excursion boat around the lake.

The next stop is back at the transportation center, where you can transfer to another monorail system at no charge for a ten-minute ride to EPCOT. Here, while the train makes a slow turn around Spaceship Earth, commonly called Walt's golf ball, the monorail's intercom describes what you're seeing. Beyond the pavilions on your left is the World Showcase Lagoon, bordered by exhibition buildings from France, Mexico, China, and many other nations.

Once back at the transportation center, the bus will take you back to Downtown Disney. The total trip with no stops takes around two and a half hours.

## Universal Studios

Universal is the oldest continuously operating movie studio in the United States, tracing its existence to a tiny storefront nickelodeon that Carl Laemmle opened in Chicago in 1906. According to legend, Laemmle called his fledgling company Universal after seeing the name on a plumbing truck.

Universal's independence ended in 1952, when it was bought by Decca Records. Ten years later Decca Records, in turn, was purchased by MCA, which was to eventually build the theme park.

MCA began its colorful life in 1924 as the Music Corporation of America. Its founder, Jules Stein, was putting himself through school tooting his saxophone with a band when he found his group got more jobs than it could handle. So Stein began booking other bands.

Eventually nearly all the nation's top big bands of the 1930s became his clients.

Stein then branched into other booking fields. Over the years he corralled an impressive stable of movie stars that included Kirk Douglas, Clark Gable, Jimmy Stewart, Bette Davis, and Marilyn Monroe. In 1949 MCA became a producer of television shows, two of its best-known series being *Wagon Train* and *Alfred Hitchcock Presents*. By this time MCA had its appendages in so many places that show people referred to it as "The Octopus."

In 1959 MCA bought Universal's Hollywood 420-acre back lot, complete with studios and equipment, and began turning it into a public attraction. Then, three years later, it bought Decca Records, including Universal itself. By the mid-1970s the back lot had been transformed into one of the nation's largest theme parks.

The guiding genius at MCA was now Lew Wasserman, Stein's hand-picked successor. He dearly wanted to own a park in Orlando, for he savored competition with Disney. As early as 1976 he attempted to acquire Sea World, but he was stymied as the result of a coup engineered by William Jovanovich (see Sea World section later in this chapter), the aggressive head of Harcourt Brace Publishing. So in 1981 Wasserman bought 423 acres near Disney World and began building his own theme park.

The Disney people were greatly agitated that MCA was elbowing into their territory, especially since they themselves were planning a theme park oriented around their own subsidiary, MGM Studios. MCA needed Florida's help in enlarging the roads and ramps around I-4, and when the state was slow coming through, MCA sensed the unseen hand of Disney. MCA president Sid Sheinberg complained to the state through the *Orlando Sentinel* that "Disney's ability to decimate you by acting in a predatory way is chilling. Do you really want a little mouse to become one large, ravenous rat?" State funds were forthcoming.

Now it became a race to determine which movie theme park would open before the other. Most experts assumed there was not enough demand for two such parks, and the first to establish itself would take all.

MCA worked furiously. It was at a distinct disadvantage because the company wanted its rides to be more thrilling than Disney's, which would require more complicated engineering. MCA's flagship ride was designed around its tremendously successful movie *Jaws*. The plot involved a mechanical shark attacking a boat filled with people. To be realistic, the shark had to be propelled through water, mouth opened, with the equivalent force of a five-hundred-horsepower truck. At the same time, the electrical mechanisms driving the equipment had to be resistant to violently rushing water.

The race with Disney was neck and neck. Though MGM was completed first, MCA felt Disney had not had time to woo a hard-core audience. Omitting some vital testing, MCA hurried Jaws into operation and opened its park with a star-studded ceremony in June 1990—just six months after Disney.

Universal's Florida debut was horrible. When the shark was supposed to attack, it lay indolently on the bottom—except for the times it almost exploded against the boats, jabbing its teeth into the pontoons and giving the terrified patrons more realism than they expected. Another thrill ride, Earthquake, often produced so feeble a tremor that it would not even disturb a sleeping mouse. Hundreds of angry guests demanded refunds. Universal sued the manufacturer, then began to work feverishly reconstructing the rides.

It was three anxious years before Jaws was officially reopened. This time, rigorous testing had been done—and redone. Additions were also made, like the enormous fireball that erupted when the guide fired

*Universal Studios' Jaws ride became operational in 1993.* —Universal Studios

a grenade at the shark, and the clouds of steam and funky smells that engulfed the boats as the beast was conquered in the grand finale.

On opening day, a teenager was asked how she liked the ride. "I *love* it!" she exclaimed. "And it actually works!"

A great many other people loved Jaws, as well as Earthquake, Back to the Future, and the other big-name rides. By the mid-1990s more than 7 million people were thronging to the park each year, bringing it into a virtual dead heat with Disney's MGM.

Universal has been on a successful thrill ride of its own in its competition with Disney. When Disney went on a fury of expansion in the mid- and late 1990s, Universal earmarked up to $2.6 billion for its own new attractions. Included is an "entertainment zone" featuring nightclubs, restaurants, and various other types of entertainment for which there will be no admission charge. In addition, due to open before the year 2000 is its second theme park, called Islands of Adventure. Islands is a huge project that will give Universal an even more major presence in Orlando.

## Sea World

Sea World had a rather unusual beginning. The original idea that germinated in the minds of four fraternity boys from UCLA was to build an underwater restaurant in Mission Bay near San Diego, California. However, they found there was more enthusiasm for a hands-on aquarium than a human eatery. So in 1964, Mission Bay, California, became the site of the first Sea World. The popularity of the attraction enabled the company to go public, and six years later it built another park near Cleveland.

When Walt Disney made headlines with his planned development just outside of Orlando, Sea World decided it was time to get its feet wet in Florida. Thus, in 1971, management announced it would buy 125 acres off I-4. Two years later the park opened. It was an immediate success, attracting 1.7 million visitors the first year—a figure that doubled within a decade.

The company's prosperity roused the interest of predators that Sea World's management regarded as more dangerous than their sharks. One of these was MCA, owner of Universal Studios, which had just produced the box-office hit *Jaws.* Many Sea World execs feared that MCA intended to convert their park into rides and gimmicks, like Universal's park in California.

The savior came in a strange form: that of William Jovanovich.

Jovanovich was an unusual person. Born to Yugoslav parents in a Colorado coal camp, he did not learn English until he went to school. Beginning his career as a humble textbook salesman, by the time he was thirty-four he had fought his way to the presidency of Harcourt Brace, the nation's number one textbook publisher. Under Jovanovich's firm, almost tyrannical regime, the company's sales shot up from $8 million in 1954, when he assumed power, to over $300 million by 1976, when he acquired Sea World. Along the way, Jovanovich added his name to the company, which became Harcourt Brace Jovanovich, or HBJ for short.

Jovanovich took an active and decisive role in shaping Sea World. Indeed, he became so interested that he actually moved his company headquarters from New York to a site within viewing distance of Sea World. Here the impressive HBJ building, with its distinctive blue glass walls, became a landmark along International Drive.

Under HBJ, Sea World continued to grow. A particularly innovative attraction called Shark Encounter came on line in 1979. It involved a long acrylic tube that was encased in six hundred thousand gallons of seawater. Visitors were carried slowly through the tube on a moving belt while vicious sharks lurked around and above them.

In 1984 Jovanovich opened an even larger attraction. This was Shamu Stadium, home to the Shamu family of killer whales. When Baby Shamu was born the following year, Sea World was ecstatic. The small whale instantly became the park's largest attraction. Newspapers kept the eager public informed of Baby Shamu's progress, such as when her baby teeth broke the gum line and when her mother began teaching her to eat fish.

But there was another side of the Shamu experience. Environmentalists argued that whales were too sensitive to live within the confines of a man-made ocean, and that at certain times of the year, killer whales were used to migrating up to one hundred miles in a single day. They said that because of this, a whale in captivity would live only ten years, whereas in the wild the life span was well over thirty. Sea World, priding itself on the humane treatment it offered all its creatures, disputed the environmentalists' conclusions.

William Jovanovich loved the park and would visit it often from his nearby office. But beginning in 1987, most of his attention had to be centered on a takeover attempt by British corporate raider Robert Maxwell. Maxwell tried to win over Harcourt's stockholders

*Sea World in 1984 was constructing Shamu Stadium.* —Sea World of Florida

with a purchase offer of more than $2 billion. To prevent defections, HBJ borrowed heavily in order to pay each stockholder a more-than-generous dividend of forty dollars per share. This, some said, was merely a bribe to keep Jovanovich in power. Although such a bonus insured stockholder loyalty, it left HBJ foundering in an ocean of debt.

In the midst of the uproar about this action, the sixty-eight-year-old Jovanovich resigned. But the urgent need for funds to meet the debt payments continued, and in 1989 HBJ sold Sea World as well as Cypress Gardens, which HBJ also owned, to Anheuser-Busch, operator of the huge Busch Gardens in nearby Tampa.

Despite the sale, Harcourt Brace Jovanovich was unable to emerge from the financial whirlpool, and in 1991 an event similar to the very one Jovanovich tried to avoid came to pass: HBJ became a subsidiary of General Cinema. Although its main office remained at 6277 Sea Harbor Drive, close to Sea World and the Renaissance Hotel, "Jovanovich" disappeared from the company's name. Today Sea World, saved for the future by the controversial Jovanovich, thrives under Busch.

*Sidewalk cafes abound along Ocean Drive in Miami Beach's art deco district.*

# ≈ 2 ≈
# Miami and Vicinity
## WHERE THE FANTASY BEGAN

## Miami

Miami had a slow beginning. In 1567 the Spanish planted a mission on Miami Beach, but the Indians were not receptive so it was quickly abandoned. Although the U.S. Army built Fort Dallas at the mouth of the Miami River in 1836, it saw no major action during the Seminole Wars, and by the time trader William Brickell arrived in 1870, about all that remained of the fort were the walls of two buildings. Brickell opened a general store on the south bank of the Miami River, almost opposite the old fort, but about his only customers were destitute Seminoles, who often camped close by.

A young widow named Julia Tuttle arrived in 1887, fixing up the old fort's officers' quarters for herself and her two children. Then she put up a tall flagpole so visitors could find her home amid the dense jungle that surrounded it. She also bought a great deal of land along the bay front and the Miami River.

Realizing that she needed a railroad to make her land valuable, Julia hassled Henry Flagler about extending his line down from its terminus at Palm Beach. In return she offered him much of her prime land, an offer made much more enticing when she sent him a fresh-cut bouquet to show that, although the Great Freeze of 1894–95 had wiped out crops as far south as Palm Beach, Miami remained warm and sheltered.

After visiting Miami, Flagler took Julia Tuttle's offer, and on a great day in 1896 a high-stacked, wood-burning locomotive pulled into the little town. Less than a year later Flagler's Royal Palm Hotel opened—

a true showplace with electric elevators, a swimming pool, and six grassy knolls upon which visitors could play a strange new game called golf.

## Miami and the Boom to End Booms

Although Julia died of what was probably a brain tumor the following year, the town took off without her. During the early 1900s Miami's population doubled, then doubled again. Many wealthy and well-known people began building winter homes here. One was James Deering, cofounder of industrial giant International Harvester, who moved into the mansion he called Vizcaya in 1916.

By 1920 Miami boasted nearly thirty thousand citizens. Three years later the figure was forty-seven thousand. But that was slow. Beginning in 1924, things *really* began to happen.

As land prices soared, the roads to Florida became clogged with people wanting to partake in the boom. Soon northern newspapers were fueling the speculative flames: "Something is taking place in Florida," wrote the usually staid *New York Times,* "to which the history of developments, booms, inrushes, speculation, [and] investment yields no parallel."

Flagler Street became a bustling, open-air emporium where realtors worked newcomers to the blare of brass bands and liberal draughts of bootleg liquor. Stories of incredible fortunes were told and retold—and many were actually true. For just 5 or 10 percent down, you could take a "binder" on a parcel of land, with no further payments for a month. By then you could expect to have sold it for thousands more than you paid.

Everyone knew the prices were absurd. One speculator calculated that in order to collect rents sufficient to justify the price of a parcel on which he had just taken a binder, he would have to construct a two-hundred-story office building. But what did it matter? Somebody else would pay more within a week or two. "Impossible things were happening under my very eyes," wrote a T. H. Weigall, fresh from England, "and with everyone else, I was living now in a wild dream."

Soon huge buildings were rising along Biscayne Boulevard, including the *Miami Daily News's* eighteen-story tower, which was the tallest, most showy structure in the city. And on Flagler Street, plans were being made for the monumental Dade County Court House. The atmosphere was heady, and sometimes buyers actually rioted in their

*Flagler Street at the corner of Southwest First Avenue in 1925. Bus caravans wait to take speculators to Coral Gables or Miami Beach. The Dade County Court House is at the extreme left.*

*Flagler Street at Southwest First Avenue today. The now-venerable Dade County Court House is at the extreme left.*

frenzy to purchase already overpriced property before a rival snatched it.

For those wary of Miami's inflated prices, long bus caravans formed on Flagler Street to carry them out to new elysian fields called Coral Gables or Miami Beach.

The Miami boom was such that the railroads could not handle the tremendous influx of passengers, supplies, and building materials. In the summer of 1925, more than eight hundred freight cars were stalled on Miami's sidetracks. A hundred and fifty more were backed up for five miles to the north! The railroad had no choice except to declare an embargo on all inbound freight except foodstuffs.

The embargo put a severe burden on harbor facilities. By December, thirty-one ships hovered offshore waiting for docking space. Then, in January 1926, a vessel sank at the harbor entrance, completely cutting off all water traffic.

Now, with the lack of imported materials, construction activity plummeted, and speculators began to question the suddenly shaky real estate market. In September, a hurricane caused more than a hundred deaths and the destruction of thousands of buildings. People realized that Miami was not the paradise the promoters had promised.

The bust came with devastating rapidity. Paper fortunes were lost. Weeds began growing along the avenues of dozens of unfinished communities. On Flagler Street the bands were silent and the flimflam artists had departed. It was a predictable end to one of the greatest boom-and-bust cycles in American history.

## Miami and the Cubans

There is no question that the central event in Miami's recent history is what has been called "the Cuban Invasion." It had its roots in 1959, when Fidel Castro's Communist forces took over Cuba and began expropriating property. Soon, not only business owners but doctors, bankers, and other professionals were ordered to give up virtually all they owned to work as servants of the Communist bureaucracy. That or flee the island.

Flee they did—and in staggering numbers—to Miami, only a short plane hop to the north. Upon their arrival, most were almost destitute. So in 1960 the Eisenhower administration—engaged in the cold war with the Soviet Union, who supported Castro—gave the immigrants aid through the Cuban Refugee Program. This provided the newcomers with food, clothing, and housing assistance. Most of the Cubans were registered in the old Miami Daily News Building at 600 Biscayne Boulevard, which, with its spectacular pink and white Spanish-style shaft, they called Freedom Tower.

The Cubans intended only a short stay—just long enough to organize an expedition to their homeland and depose the hated Castro. Equipped and trained by the CIA, fifteen hundred men made a successful landing at the Bay of Pigs in 1961. But from there everything went wrong. The Cubans thought American military aid had been promised, but just-elected President Kennedy had not been fully briefed and refused to allow U.S. involvement in the actual fighting. The expected uprising among native Cubans did not materialize, and Castro's response was far quicker and more decisive than anticipated. Confronted by twenty thousand troops with tanks and jets, the invaders were forced to surrender within three days. Castro took the freedom fighters prisoner, but after twenty months of severe American pressure he returned them to the United States. Kennedy honored them with a ceremony in Miami's old Orange Bowl.

The episode had been traumatic for the expatriate community, who now realized that they would be remaining in the United States far longer than anticipated. As a result, many of the displaced Cubans sought help from the Small Business Administration in establishing enterprises similar to those they had operated in Cuba before Castro. Although the total cost to U.S. taxpayers was one billion dollars, the SBA and other programs worked, and by 1979 the eight hundred thousand Cubans had established themselves comfortably in Miami.

Much of the black population of the city, with whom the Cuban refugees often competed for jobs, housing, and government assistance, did not welcome the Cuban influx and from the late sixties began to protest what they considered negligence by social agencies. Then, in 1980 the racial tensions became worse as Castro emptied his jails and sent 125,000 more Cubans to Miami in the notorious Mariel Boatlift. This, at least indirectly, resulted in the devastating Liberty City riot of that year.

As time passed, the Cuban immigrants gradually broke into the upper political and economic levels of Miami society, and in 1985 elected one of their own as mayor. When the Summit of the Americas Conference was held in Miami in 1994, it became apparent that the city was well on its way to becoming the financial and business center for Latin America. This reorientation of Miami to the countries to the south was due largely to the Cuban influence.

Some observers are concerned that the Cuban influence is too strong, and that eventually Miami will become a semidetached part of the United States, so aligned with Latin America as to become almost part of it. But these concerns are probably not realistic, for the great American melting pot is bubbling actively in Miami, where the younger generation prefers to speak English over Spanish. Ironically, there's a worry now that the young people will lose their ability to relate to Latin Americans, diminishing the economic ties to South and Central America that have proved so beneficial to Miami's economy.

### Downtown Miami Today

Today Flagler Street is once more full of hustle, although of a quite different sort from the Roaring Twenties. The six blocks between Biscayne Boulevard (US 1) on the east and the Metro-Dade Cultural Center on the west throb with the activities of Cuban Americans and other Hispanics. Strolling the street is like taking a trip to Latin America. Yet the Miami of the twenties still breaks through, particularly in the form of the still-imposing Dade County Court House, at Flagler and Northwest First Avenue. Planned during the boom, its lofty tower was intended to symbolize the stunning future, but by the time it was completed in 1928, the boom had disintegrated into vanished dreams and empty wallets.

Other vintage buildings remain. There is the ten-story former Olympia Vaudeville Theater at 174 East Flagler, constructed in 1925. Maurice Gusman refurbished its ornate auditorium and presented it to the city in 1975.

At 19 West Flagler is the thirteen-story Biscayne Building, also a product of the dizzy mid-twenties. Founded in 1896 as the Bank of Biscayne with the help of Henry Flagler, it was one of the many projects that failed during the bust.

On Flagler across Northwest First Avenue is the handsome group of buildings known as the Cultural Center. Created as part of the Decade of Progress 1970 bond issue, the complex contains the public library, the Center for the Fine Arts, and one of the nation's finest historical museums.

At its eastern end, Flagler Street leads to Bayfront Park, which was part of Biscayne Bay until it was created from dredgings in 1925.

William Jennings Bryan, perennial Democratic presidential hopeful, conducted Bible lectures here. It was here, too, that an assassin shot at President Franklin Roosevelt in 1933, killing instead Anton Cermak, mayor of Chicago.

Bordering Bayfront Park on the south is the thirty-four-story Inter-Continental Hotel, which has wonderful views of Biscayne Bay as well as of the Miami River. William Brickell's two-story trading post once stood across the river. Flagler's great Royal Palm Hotel was immediately west of the Inter-Continental. Its location is now a parking lot, for the proud building fell prey to lowly termites and was demolished in 1930. Fort Dallas originally stood near here, but in 1929 the Daughters of the American Revolution had the officers' quarters—where Julia Tuttle made her home—moved stone by stone to Lummus Park at North River Drive and Northwest Third Street, and here it remains today, fenced off from the public and largely forgotten.

On the north end of the Bayfront Park is the Bayside Marketplace, an exciting potpourri of thirty restaurants and miscellaneous snack bars, as well as more than a hundred shops, many boasting arts and crafts from local artisans. Until recently this was Pier Five, a run-down area frequented by Miami's charter fishing fleet.

### The World of Calle Ocho

The hub of Cuban life is along that portion of the Tamiami Trail (US 41), once known as Southwest Eighth Street, but now usually

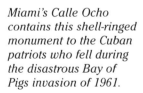

*Miami's Calle Ocho contains this shell-ringed monument to the Cuban patriots who fell during the disastrous Bay of Pigs invasion of 1961.*

called by its Spanish name: Calle Ocho. The heart of the district is between Southwest Twelfth and Seventeenth Avenues, where Miami has offered zoning breaks to business owners who decorate their buildings with Spanish embellishments. But the Hispanic section has long since expanded beyond there—for more than half of Miami's citizens are Hispanic.

Calle Ocho exudes the flavor of Latin America. At Sixteenth Avenue is Maximo Gomez Park, where Latinos play fierce games of dominoes. At Fourteenth Avenue, the sidewalk in front of the McDonald's has embedded stars honoring Latin celebrities. And at the corner of Thirteenth Avenue is a small park where an eternal flame burns for the men who died in the Bay of Pigs invasion. It is the most revered site in Little Havana.

### South Miami Is a Special Place

When James Deering built his Vizcaya mansion south of the main part of Miami, he was only acknowledging the uniqueness of the exclusive little area known as Coconut Grove. Today Vizcaya, at 3251 South Miami Avenue, is a delight to tour. There are thirty-four luxurious rooms filled with priceless paintings, tapestries, and furniture. President Ronald Reagan entertained Pope John Paul II at Vizcaya in 1987. Seven years later, President Bill Clinton hosted the Summit of the Americas here.

Coconut Grove has always been known for its upscale ambiance. It was founded in the late 1800s not as a commercial center, but as a winter resort for the wealthy. Under the leadership of Commodore Ralph Middleton Munroe, the Grove, with its sheltered harbor, became popular with yachting families and northern intellectuals. In 1891 Munroe built his home, called the Barnacle, at 3485 Main Highway, and today it is open for tours. Munroe started a trend that resulted in the area boasting Miami's first Millionaires Row. Coconut Grove is still an enclave of the well-to-do. But it is not stuffy. Instead, there are many blocks of beckoning shops, well sprinkled with appealing eating establishments. Particularly active are the CocoWalk and the Streets of Mayfair entertainment centers on Grand Avenue.

The picturesque Dinner Key Marina is slightly north on Bay Shore Drive from downtown Coconut Grove. The key was once just a secluded alcove where locals enjoyed picnics, hence its name. But at the dawn of the air age, the U.S. government dredged the bay so that seaplanes could use it, and in 1930 Pan American Airways

*The Miami City Hall was originally the Pan American Airways seaplane base when it opened in 1930. Pan Am's "flying boats" attracted large crowds to watch their takeoffs and landings.*

inaugurated service on what they called "flying boats" to Latin America. So great was the popular interest in aviation that the following year Miami began work on what was to become the world's largest seaplane base.

During its heyday in the 1930s, large crowds gathered here to gape at the thundering craft as they cut through the water and finally lumbered into the sky. Many people had never seen an "aeroplane" before. But by 1946, land planes had largely replaced the colorful Pan Am Clippers, so the terminal was converted into Miami's city hall—and so it remains today.

### Miami's Financial Woes

Modern Miami is in a difficult situation. The tremendous influx of Cubans, Haitians, and other Third World peoples has been accompanied by an exodus of so many wealthier longtime residents that the city has been left with a diminished tax base. As a result, city expenses have exceeded revenue—a matter not helped by corruption, which was so gross that the FBI was called in. By 1996, when city officials revealed a $68 million budgetary shortfall, the city's credit rating pummeled to junk-bond level. Bankruptcy was considered, and a headline in Orlando's largest newspaper chortled, "Miami Lies at Death's Door."

Though city finances face a difficult future, Miami itself has a firm economic underpinning. In particular, there are the admirable harbor facilities that have made the city the world's leading cruise port. Furthermore, no other Florida city enjoys Miami's ability to tap the vast, burgeoning Latin American market. Three-fourths of Florida's exports head south, most of them passing though Miami. Business leaders recognize the value of locating in downtown Miami. Indeed, in 1997 a northern investors' group shelled out the highest price per square foot ever paid in Florida to purchase the First Union Tower.

## Key Biscayne

Key Biscayne is a narrow barrier island off the coast of southern Miami. It can be reached via the Rickenbacker Causeway, which has a convenient entrance off I-95 and US 1. The causeway, named in honor of World War I flying ace Eddie Rickenbacker, is an experience in itself with its magnificent views of Miami. The road also leads to the Miami Seaquarium, established in 1955 as one of the world's first major oceanariums. Dolphin shows and innumerable exhibits of living sea creatures make the Seaquarium a popular attraction. So, too, is the nearby is Planet Ocean, with its wraparound theater where twenty-three projectors take visitors on thrilling excursions beneath the depths.

Key Biscayne is also the location of Crandon Park, with two and a half miles of white sand. Here are excellent picnic facilities shaded by coconut palms. This was formerly the site of Miami's zoo. At the

*Key Biscayne presents a magnificent panorama of Miami from the Rickenbacker Causeway.*

*The large, rectangular object protruding into the bay is a helicopter pad built beside President Nixon's Key Biscayne home. The five houses along the water made up the Nixon compound.* —Historical Museum of South Florida

southern end of the island, in the four-hundred-acre Bill Baggs State Park, is the historic Cape Florida Lighthouse. The ninety-five-foot lighthouse was unsuccessfully besieged by Indians during the Second Seminole War.

### Key Biscayne and the Demise of Richard Nixon

Once, Key Biscayne's fame rested solely on its being the location of Richard Nixon's home at 516 Bay Lane, reached by way of Crandon Boulevard and Harbor Drive. During the hectic years of Watergate, Nixon relished Key Biscayne as a retreat from his mounting problems. He loved the island because it was scenic, it was subtropical, and, most of all, it was isolated. Nixon was by nature a reclusive sort of person who craved time away from others. He was awkward socially—a strange characteristic for someone who placed himself so vigorously in the public spotlight.

From earliest manhood Richard Nixon had his eye on a political career. He was hardly out of the navy when he won a seat in the U.S. House of Representatives; later he was elected to the Senate. His strong, almost virulent anticommunist stance made him a natu-

*President Richard Nixon (far right) and vice president Spiro Agnew relax at Key Biscayne in 1969 after winning the election. With them are their wives, Pat Nixon (far left) and Judy Agnew. Reelected in 1972, both men were forced to resign before the term was up.* —Florida State Archives

ral running mate for General Dwight Eisenhower in 1952. Thus at the age of just thirty-nine he became vice president of the United States.

Ike and Nixon won second terms, then Nixon ran as the Republican presidential candidate against John F. Kennedy. However, it was a Democratic year, though Nixon's margin of loss was razor thin. In 1968 he gave it another try and beat Hubert Humphrey.

Although Nixon and his wife, Pat, had been vacationing on Key Biscayne for seventeen years, they began using the home on Bay Lane more extensively after the election. When they came here in 1968 to celebrate the victory, their mood was joyous, especially at Christmas with the arrival of daughters Tricia and Julie, the latter accompanied by her new husband, David Eisenhower, grandson of the former president. At this time, aides and advisors also converged at Key Biscayne, for the need was urgent to fill posts for the cabinet and agency heads.

To handle the influx of officials, a large helicopter platform was built into the bay beside the Nixon compound. And to control the throngs of sight-seers wanting to pester the reclusive president, Bay Lane was closed to the public, with guardhouses at each end.

There were five buildings in the compound, with the family residing in the one on the corner. Nixon used another as an office— in which he often slept. He and Pat often relaxed beside the compound's swimming pool.

Nixon's first term was a resounding success. He began the dialogue with Communist China that would realign world politics. And he was the first president to visit Moscow—capping it with the world's first nuclear-arms-limitation agreement.

The Republican Convention of 1972 was held at Miami Beach, where Nixon was renominated to the ecstatic roar, "Four more years!" After giving his acceptance speech, he took a helicopter to Key Biscayne to share the experience with Pat. In November the nation awarded him a second term by one of the largest landslides in presidential history.

Although Nixon started his second administration by ending U.S. involvement in the distasteful Vietnam War, clouds gathered concerning a mysterious break-in at the Democratic National Headquarters in the Watergate complex. Questions were asked regarding the president's role, and soon the word *cover-up* began to circulate. During this time, Nixon took increasing refuge at Key Biscayne. It was here that he stored some of the devastating tapes of the conversations that would confirm his activities in the Watergate affair.

During 1973, investigators relentlessly followed leads that got ever closer to the White House. In November, when Nixon was visiting Disney World, he went on national TV to proclaim weakly, "I am not a crook." But by now nearly everyone was convinced that he was deeply involved in the obstruction of justice that had already tainted many of his inner circle. By the end of the year, the House Judiciary Committee was talking about impeachment. At this time, Nixon's lawyers came to Key Biscayne and advised him to leave the presidency.

One can imagine Nixon pacing the bay shore as he pondered his action. No president had ever resigned. How could he do it? The utter humiliation of it all! He refused.

But there was no escaping the noose that drew ever tighter. Nixon became despondent, secretive, distrustful of almost everyone except his old friend and neighbor Charles "Bebe" Rebozo. He could not sleep, and the nights on Key Biscayne became interminable. Perhaps in his bitter brooding he mused on the supreme ironies that led him to this sorry state. The recordings that were his undoing had been taped by himself. And he had not even installed the recording machines—that had been the handiwork of his predecessor, Democrat Lyndon Johnson.

At last there was no alternative. On August 9, 1974, Richard Nixon resigned the presidency and left the White House in disgrace.

# Coral Gables

Coral Gables is immediately west of southern Florida's Coconut Grove and runs on both sides of US 1 from Southwest Thirty-Seventh Avenue to Southwest Fifty-seventh Avenue.

During the early 1900s the Merrick family raised vegetables on a farm here, living in a small home made of a local limestone that resembled coral to these Massachusetts pioneers. The young son, George, would take a mule wagon five miles down the shell road to peddle their produce at Miami's Royal Palm Hotel. But George Merrick had no intention of remaining a farmer, for he aspired to be a writer of romantic fiction. Even when his father sent him to law school, George continued to write. He was good at it, too—one of his stories captured first prize in a contest and was published in a New York newspaper.

George's stay in college ended abruptly in 1911 when his father died, and he became master of Coral Gables. Although the farm prospered, George, still a dreamer, envisioned the area around his farmhouse as a well-planned city, complete with schools, parks, churches, hotels, and even a university. With this in mind he began purchasing large parcels of surrounding land, and by 1921 he had quietly increased his acreage from the original 160 to 1,600. Now the glory days began!

With a handpicked group of architects planning what he called the "city beautiful," Merrick started promoting Coral Gables as the perfect community. Eventually more than three thousand salesmen were handling his properties, and a fleet of thirty-passenger buses hurried prospective buyers from Miami to Coral Gables. He even cajoled the famous William Jennings Bryan, three-time Democratic candidate for president, into giving peppy sales briefings beside the lovely Venetian pool he had fashioned from an old quarry.

Merrick was riding high. He signed a $75 million agreement with a home builder—at the time the largest such contract ever awarded

An unsuspecting George Merrick (right) and hotel magnate John Bowman pause for a photo on the steps of the Biltmore Hotel just before Florida's great real estate bust began in 1926. —Historical Museum of South Florida

in Florida. At about the same time, he donated 160 acres plus $5 million to start the University of Miami. Finally, to cap it all, Merrick constructed the gorgeous Biltmore Hotel, which opened with a glittering formal banquet on January 14, 1926.

To help handle reporters Merrick hired a talented young Englishman named T. H. Weigall, who later wrote his reminiscences in one of the most entertaining books of the era. "I suppose I was slightly mad; we all were," Weigall recalled in *Boom in Paradise*. Yet he himself was actively fanning the flames that drove the fire.

Weigall was in awe of his boss. Merrick was a broad-shouldered man who conveyed the impression of massive power, although he was only five feet, nine inches tall. Yet he was difficult to know, for there was still the essence of the withdrawn poet about him. He tended to avoid people, but though he was seldom seen his presence was always felt, and Weigall called his rule "dictatorial." He had an office in the Biltmore tower, where he made his plans and dreamed his dreams. When the great man emerged, he cruised around town in a long two-seat auto that Weigall found "rakish."

However, by 1926 the boom was suddenly over. Weigall, more perceptive than most, sensed the coming crash. "The whole feeling of the place was different," he remembered. "Something that was

*The Biltmore Hotel at Coral Gables was a showplace when it was built in 1926. It still is.* —Historical Museum of South Florida

very faintly sinister seemed on that morning to have mingled with the air."

Merrick's downfall came swiftly. Within three years he was bankrupt, and his holdings, including the fabulous Biltmore Hotel, passed into other hands. After losing Coral Gables, Merrick and his wife, Eunice, ran a small fishing camp in the Keys—until 1935, when the same hurricane that obliterated Flagler's railroad also blew Merrick's camp into oblivion. In 1940 Merrick took a job as Miami's postmaster, and though the position was a good one, the excitement of $75 million deals was gone. Two years later he died of a heart attack, at the age of fifty-six.

As for the Biltmore Hotel, it went through a series of vicissitudes. During the Second World War the army—then the Veterans Administration—took it over, using it as a hospital until 1968. The building remained vacant for ten years, then it was renovated at last and reopened with all its former splendor in 1987. Today the Biltmore, at 1200 Anastasia Avenue, is a showplace. Its lobby is worthy of a Romanesque church. Its outdoor swimming pool, the largest in America when it was built (fast-living Johnny Weissmuller, star of the Tarzan movies, churned the water here during the 1930s), is a pleasure to behold—and food is served poolside.

The University of Miami campus is a short distance south of the Biltmore, beside Granada Boulevard. The center of town is on Coral Way. Here you will find the impressive Colonnade Hotel, a Merrick

*During Florida's wild real estate boom of the 1920s, William Jennings Bryan, three times Democratic presidential hopeful, gave sales talks beside Coral Gables' Venetian pool.*

masterpiece in which he had his main office. Be sure to visit the rotunda, with its Roman columns, fountain, and marble floor. The hotel has many historic photos on display, including one autographed by baseball legend Babe Ruth. There is a beautiful outdoor swimming pool on an upper floor with an expansive view of the city.

The Venetian pool, at 2701 De Soto, is well kept up and open for public swimming. Bryan gave his sales pitches from a platform floating in the pool's center. The golden-voiced orator's activities at Coral Gables abruptly ended when he was called to Dayton, Tennessee, to help defend divine creation against the teaching of evolution in the famed Scopes "Monkey Trial." The endeavor undermined his health, already precarious from years of diabetes, and Bryan died in May 1925, just weeks after the case ended with John Scopes's conviction and the assessment of a nominal hundred-dollar fine, which was later overruled.

The Merrick homestead (the original Coral Gables) at 907 Coral Way is open to the public. George Merrick began humbly and ended quietly, but there was a lot of sparkle in between. "It all happened so quickly," his wife, Eunice, reminisced years later. "I have no regrets. It wasn't easy—but it certainly was interesting."

# Miami Beach

*A Bittersweet Love Story*

When the dream spinners write ads for Miami Beach, they usually picture palm trees, moonlit sand, and a romantic couple beside the lapping waves. The romance is not a fiction. It is here today. And it was here yesterday when Carl Fisher created the island. The tale of Carl and his wife, Jane, is one of Florida's most tender and sad love stories.

Jane was just fifteen when she first saw Carl. He was a dashing swashbuckler, twenty-two years her senior, who was making a fortune with the manufacture of auto headlights. Jane was enamored with him from the moment he donated funds for her team's baseball uniforms. As for Carl, he was entranced with the perky blond girl, and his love-name for her was "wench." They were wed in 1909 at Jane's Indianapolis home.

In 1911 Carl sold his auto-light company, emerging with a profit of $5.6 million. He was uncomfortable with such a sum lying idle in the bank, so when he and Jane were wintering in Miami and he discovered that an old duffer named John Collins was trying to develop a mangrove island out in Biscayne Bay, he became interested. Learning that Collins had run out of funds, Fisher gave him the money he needed in exchange for land in the southern portion of Collins's five-mile oceanfront spread.

Seventeen-year-old Jane accompanied Carl on an inspection of the purchase. Later she wrote about this experience, as well as of her life with Carl in general, in a poignant book entitled *Fabulous Hoosier*. As they tramped through the dank jungle that would one day be the exclusive Lincoln Road shopping strip, "mosquitoes blackened our white clothing. . . . Other creatures that made me shudder were lying in wait in the slimy paths or on the branches of the overhanging trees." She wondered what her husband could see in this awful place.

But when they reached the beach, Carl pulled out a stick and drew his dreams in the sand. "Look, Honey," he said. "I'm going to build a city here! A city like magic." And, as he talked, Jane melted. He showed her where they would construct their own home, almost where they were standing on the wild, deserted beach. "As I always did," Jane recalled, "I fell under the mesmeric spell of his voice."

In 1913 Carl began creating Miami Beach. First, he imported hundreds of laborers with machetes to hack away the palmettos and

*In 1915 dynamic Carl Fisher helped trailblaze the Dixie Highway from the Midwest to Miami. During the 1920s his artful ballyhoo brought Miami Beach national attention.* —Historical Museum of South Florida

mangroves. Then he brought in teams of mules to wrench the tenacious roots from the marshy earth. When the land was laid bare, Fisher hired a fleet of dredges to suck sand and muck from Biscayne Bay and flush it through large pipes over the island. The men inland who worked on the dredgings had to wear thick hip boots to protect them from snakes. Smudge pots burned constantly to smoke away the voracious mosquitoes.

During the summer, crews often worked by torchlight to escape the torrid heat of day. "Late at night," Jane reminisced, "Carl and I would cross the bay . . . to the Beach and walk out on the pipe lines with big baskets of sandwiches and pots of coffee for the men."

It was an almost impossible task, but slowly the land emerged. Once there was something to build on, Carl began Lincoln Road, named after his presidential idol and composed initially of crushed coral taken from a reef offshore. Then he constructed the seven-story Lincoln Building. He had his sales offices there, and prospective land buyers were usually whisked onto an elevator to the top for an impressive view of Miami Beach as it was being developed.

Soon Carl erected the magnificent Flamingo Hotel at the foot of Lincoln Road, facing Biscayne Bay. It rose eleven stories and, with floodlights illuminating its tower, could be seen at such a distance that it became a navigational landmark for ships far out in the Atlantic.

While all this was going on, Carl built a dream home for Jane. Called the Shadows, it was so close to the ocean that on stormy nights the waves seemed almost to come through the huge glass windows and merge with their thick, sea-green living-room carpeting.

Jane was happy in these early years. Often she would curl up in her small red chair at Carl's feet, with their beloved dog, Rowdy, beside them. She was entranced by the changes Carl had wrought. "Overnight our man-made paradise was discovered by choruses of singing birds and brilliant clouds of butterflies. I called everyone into the garden the morning the butterflies came. . . . I can still see Carl's smile."

Jane was not just a passive observer. One day, when she and Carl were strolling down Lincoln Road, she commented that the town needed a house of worship. Carl grunted that no one had time for preachers. But she persisted, and at last he roared, "Where in hell do you want your gee-dee church?" The building went up on some of the most valuable land along Lincoln Road, and for years it was known as the Gee-Dee Church.

Jane also played a role as Carl began to promote the island. He remodeled Collins's casino just up the beach from their house and installed a pavilion for partying and Roman pools for swimming. Jane loved the pool and was an excellent swimmer. But more than that, she wore the first form-fitted bathing suit in Florida. It had a shockingly short skirt that actually showed her knees. When Carl saw what a sensation her outfit caused, he began a massive advertising campaign that soon resulted in *bathing beauty* and *Miami Beach* being almost synonymous.

Carl was a master of ballyhoo. To show the public that Florida could actually be reached by car, in 1915 he led a conspicuous cavalcade of fifteen autos from Indianapolis to Miami. He called his expedition the Dixie Highway Pathfinding Tour. The route they took soon became a major thoroughfare to Florida.

To attract the wealthy set, Carl installed a polo field. Then he would ride all around the island on his polo pony followed by the press as he inspected the building sites. When golf began to attract sportsmen in the early 1920s, he put in a course, then invited President Harding to be his guest, giving him as a caddie Rosie the elephant. That kept Miami Beach in the headlines for a long time.

Jane gloried in the flapper era. She claimed she became "the queen of Miami Beach." She wore the first lipstick south of the Mason-Dixon line. She bobbed her hair in the daring style of Irene Castle. And she actually wore her skirts way up above her ankles!

Carl, for his part, was amused by his young wife. But he had no personal use for fancy clothes and never wore formal attire. His favorite dress always included his battered wide-brimmed hat, once white but now gray.

Jane was in her mid-twenties and loved the fast life. But Carl's attention was on his Miami Beach project. "Many mornings I woke . . . to find Carl had not come upstairs," Jane wrote. "I would go down and find him lying on the rug beside Rowdy, staring into the dead ashes of the fire . . . he had been planning . . . the night through. I understand that now. I didn't then."

They both yearned for a child, and after Jane became pregnant the bond between them was renewed. When the baby boy was born, Carl doted over him and Jane loved him as nothing else. But one day the baby grew quiet and cold in Jane's arms. She screamed for the nurse. But nothing could be done. Their son was dead.

More than a tiny life was snuffed out at that moment. Unspeakable sorrow clouded the gaiety that had once been theirs. Carl took to drinking and cursing and sometimes flew into inexplicable rages. Jane immersed herself in parties and teas. Now they rarely caressed, and Jane realized, "We had entered separate worlds . . . [yet] neither would hold for us anything we really wanted."

In 1925 Jane took a trip to Paris by herself. There, she was back in the dazzle of youth: the theaters, the galleries, and "the entertaining men . . . ready to kiss the hand, dance and sympathize with the neglected wife of an American millionaire."

Carl wrote her a letter that she kept for the rest of her life. He said that he understood her desire to be with people her own age. "If you have some real man and want to marry, then perhaps you may be happier." Soon they divorced.

Jane was thirty when she returned to America. Not only she, but Florida itself, was quite different. The bust of 1926 had struck. Carl had sold the Shadows, and the new owners had torn it down. Another door to their past had slammed shut.

Jane went to see Carl, "not with any idea of again being Carl's wife. That was over; but there was between us as great a friendship, I believe, as ever existed between a man and a woman."

*Jane Fisher, former wife of the city's developer Carl Fisher, and J. N. Lummus, former mayor, attend an anniversary celebration in 1950.*
—Florida State Archives

Carl was having many problems. Added to the real estate bust was the devastating hurricane that caused untold damage at Miami Beach. Furthermore, he was overextended with another major development in New York. His nerves were frayed, and incessant drinking was ruining his constitution. As he realized that his health as well as his once-enormous wealth was draining away, he began deeding property to Jane, just in case he would not be around.

When Jane was with Carl, "I would look at him misty-eyed," she recalled. "I couldn't remember a time in my life when Carl had not been protecting me, sharing my life, building around me new, more wonderful, undreamed-of worlds." Nonetheless, in 1927 Jane remarried.

Carl, too, found a new spouse, but he was not happy. The 1930s were hard on him. He lost almost everything and ended up living in a small house in Miami Beach. When he shuffled down the streets, scarcely anyone recognized the overweight, alcoholic old man. For himself, Carl felt no affinity with the strange art deco buildings rising on the land he had created.

Despite it all, Carl and Jane remained in close contact. In 1939, when Carl became ill, Jane came to his bedside. He was just a shell of his former self, and it was difficult for her to see through the misshapen body to the man who had once been her young and powerful husband. She left in tears. A few weeks later Carl died. Among his last words were: "Where's Jane? It's getting dark."

"He had always hated having me out after sunset," Jane recalled. "In this last darkness he remembered."

## Miami Beach Today

The Shadows, Carl and Jane Fisher's mansion, was by the ocean a short distance south of Collins Park, which itself is at Collins Avenue and Twenty-Second Street. On the north side of the park, the Holiday Inn occupies the site of Fisher's Roman Baths, where Jane displayed her shocking bathing suit.

Lincoln Road, five blocks south, is open only to pedestrian traffic. Fisher designed the thoroughfare to be an exclusive shopping area, but it went through some difficult times until it was recently rehabilitated. Now it is artfully landscaped, and fresh coats of paint are everywhere.

*Carl Fisher designed Lincoln Road to be Miami Beach's upscale shopping boulevard. It has gone through hard times but is on the way to its former glory.*

The church that Jane Fisher talked Carl into building is in active use and stands at 500 Lincoln Road. Carl Fisher's seven-story office building is at the corner of Jefferson. It, too, has been thoroughly rehabilitated and now supports a cafe with a sidewalk extension.

But the main historical attraction of Miami Beach lies in its amazing art deco revival. The 1930s brought a flowering of art deco architecture that has made Miami Beach's historic district one of the largest on the National Register. Today most of the buildings have been renovated, and block after block sparkles, perhaps even more brightly than they did in the days of Franklin Roosevelt.

The Miami Design Preservation League has an art deco guide that describes in detail six walking tours through this city of nearly one hundred thousand people. But for many visitors, a stroll down Ocean Drive will probably suffice.

Nearly all the pastel-colored buildings along the drive are art deco, with streamlined corners and sleek, horizontal window "brows." Many buildings have stylized images of the sun, representing the sunbathing craze that took hold of the nation in the 1930s. Others have zigzag patterns symbolic of radio waves—reflecting the radio's popularity in the 1930s. Geometric patterns were profusely utilized, often in the form of circular windows. Glass bricks made their earliest large-scale appearance here.

Many hotels have sidewalk cafes, ideal for coffee sipping and people watching. Across Ocean Drive is Lummus Park, named for an original landowner and the town's first mayor, elected when there were only thirty-three registered voters.

*This Carl Cowden mural on Tampa's Franklin Street Mall shows the former thoroughfare as it was in its 1920s heyday.*

# ☞ 3 ☜
# Tampa and St. Petersburg
## BAGHDADS ON THE BAY

## Tampa

Tampa owes much to its marvelous bay. But it was not always there, for during the Ice Age, when vast quantities of water were stored in northern glaciers, the gulf dropped by three hundred feet and the bay area became a wide valley. Here streams from the interior converged to run across a sandy plain to the Gulf of Mexico, which then lay 125 miles to the west.

### Fort Brooke and the "Wild Men"

Prehistoric tribes found Tampa Bay to their liking, and nearly two dozen ceremonial mounds, some up to fifty feet high, were erected around the shore. By the time the Spanish arrived, the Mound Builders had vanished and their place had been taken by the Timucua tribe, estimated to have numbered up to seven thousand in the vicinity. The Timucuans were fierce fighters, as Hernando de Soto found when he pushed through them in 1539. The tribe left us with their name for the bay, *tanpa,* meaning "sticks of fire," but that is about all they left. The Timucuans eventually fell prey to British-led Creek warriors from the north, and when American Colonel George Brooke built a fort here in 1824 the Timucuans had been displaced by Creek rebels called *seminoles,* or "wild men."

The fort, which ran along the Hillsborough River between modern Kennedy and Whiting Streets, had a beautiful setting, with the river on one side and a grove of wide-branching live oaks and fragrant wild oranges on the other.

*In the 1890s Henry Plant erected a railroad empire in western Florida even larger than that of his arch rival, Henry Flagler, on the east coast.* —Florida State Archives

When the Seminoles, under the leadership of Osceola, became a threat to the military in 1835, Major Francis Dade set out from Fort Brooke with 107 troopers to reinforce Fort King in modern Ocala. But the Indians ambushed and massacred almost the entire force near Bushnell. Thus began the Second Seminole War.

Although Fort Brooke feared an attack after the horrifying Dade disaster, the fortress there was far too strong for the Seminoles to attempt such an action. It was protected by a wall of upright sharpened logs and a pair of blockhouses. Furthermore, outside the wall were a series of eight-foot-deep pits concealed by straw with pointed stakes along the bottom.

After the war, Fort Brooke continued as a quiet government base. "Tampa, or more properly the Military Reserve, is a charming spot," wrote naval officer Edward Anderson in 1844. "It is overgrown with huge old oaks spreading their arms abroad in every direction & giving a shade which is at all seasons delightful." The post became even less active through the next two decades, until it was given the coup de grâce by Union troops in 1864. By that time a sleepy fishing village had established itself around it, though there was little growth until Henry Plant completed his South Florida Railroad in 1884.

## *Henry Plant and the Exotic Tampa Bay Hotel*

Henry Plant started his career as a lowly mail clerk on a New York steamboat. But he soon got a job with the Adams Express Company, where his rise was aided by his considerable business abilities and abetted by his marriage to the daughter of an influential U.S. senator. After the Civil War, Plant, who had moved to Augusta, Georgia, as Adams's regional agent, began buying bankrupt southern railroads. Soon he expanded into Florida.

Plant was determined to do for Florida's west coast what Henry Flagler was doing for the east coast. Therefore, in 1888, Plant began erecting the great Tampa Bay Hotel. While the hotel was going up, Plant and his second wife, Margaret (his first having died of tuberculosis), spent the better part of three years rummaging through the world's antiques for items with which to grace the hotel. Eventually the lobby and other public rooms contained everything from a Marie Antoinette sofa to inlaid cabinets from ancient Japan.

Nothing like this had ever been seen hereabouts. This is how an enthralled writer for the *Tampa Daily Journal* found it on opening day, 1891:

> The Tampa Bay Hotel is a beautiful building with its turrets, domes and minarets towering heavenward and glistening in the sun, its long verandas with graceful cornices of light horseshoe arches and fancy scroll work.

The reporter went on to describe the grand ball, attended by an array of women of "kaleidoscopic beauty." As they paraded past him, he rhapsodized in embarrassingly dated prose: "There was a most dazzling display of lovely toilettes, which enhanced the queenly grace and beauty of the fair ladies."

Of course Plant invited his rival, Henry Flagler, to come to Tampa and see what a true luxury hotel should be. Flagler wired back the perfect squelch: "Where's Tampa?" Yet he did show up.

The hotel offered a great many things to do. Guests could boat on the river, race horses on the hotel track, or hunt in the wild countryside. And there were parties and balls enough to make anyone giddy with excitement. Plant also built an adjoining casino, where actors and actresses, some world famous, put on spectaculars during the season, which lasted from December through April. When not used for theatrical productions, the casino floor could be removed to reveal a large heated pool, ideal for swimming and general cavorting.

*An 1896 Plant System ad showing the Tampa hotel and adjoining casino/theater. The theater floor could be removed to uncover a swimming pool where bathing beauties could display their stylish swimsuits.* —Florida State Archives

The height of the hotel's activities came in 1898, during the Spanish-American War, when it became headquarters of the thirty thousand troops gathering for the invasion of Cuba. At this time it was filled with strutting, gold-braided officers, including the boisterous young Colonel Teddy Roosevelt, who drilled his rowdy Rough Riders on the hotel grounds. Journalists, too, swarmed about the hotel. Among them were Stephen Crane, who had just married a Jacksonville madam, and artist Frederic Remington, told by his boss, William Randolph Hearst, "You furnish the pictures and I'll furnish the war."

When Henry Plant died in 1899, his holdings included 1,200 miles of main track. By comparison, Flagler's system had only 466 miles (although this did not include the glamorous extension to Key West he completed thirteen years later).

Plant had accomplished all his life's ambitions except one: he wanted his grandson to carry on as head of his railroad empire. The only problem was the fact that young Plant was a mere seedling, less than four years old. So Henry had arranged to have his holdings put into a trust until little Plant was twenty-one. But wife Margaret, enraged that she had not inherited everything, brought suit. After

*Today Henry Plant's Tampa Bay Hotel, bizarre by modern standards, belongs to the University of Tampa, which has turned part of it into a fascinating museum.*

three years of vicious litigation, she successfully had the trust dissolved; thereupon she promptly sold the entire system to the Atlantic Coast Line.

The Tampa Bay Hotel was not included in this liquidation. The odd fact was that no one wanted the hotel because the tourist boom that Plant envisioned had not materialized, and the five-hundred-room building was seldom more than half full. In 1905 Plant's heirs, eager to be rid of the white elephant, virtually gave it to the city of Tampa.

In the ensuing years, Henry Plant's once-proud building deteriorated, until in the early 1930s it was converted by the Works Progress Administration into college use and turned over to the University of Tampa, which continues to use it today.

## *Tampa in the Early Twentieth Century*

By 1900 Tampa's population had risen to sixteen thousand—and it doubled within the next ten years. The main source of wealth came from the export of phosphate, recently discovered in such stupendous quantities around Mulberry, just thirty miles east of town, that Tampa became (and still is) the exporting source of a large portion of the world's supply of this essential fertilizer ingredient.

As the waterfront became a mass of tracks and wharves, more space was needed. So in 1905 Harbor Island was dredged out of the muck and soon bristled with facilities for the all-important phosphate trade. With the population shooting up, citizens demanded a new city hall to reflect Tampa's strength and growth. Thus in 1915 a magnificent building with a soaring clock tower rose above the city's skyline.

Now Tampa began reaching out. St. Petersburg lay just nineteen miles on the other side of Old Tampa Bay, but to get there one had to cross nearly fifty miles of swamps and wetlands. So in 1922 work was begun on the Gandy Bridge—which was to include three miles of causeway and two and a half miles of actual bridging. When it was completed two years later, it was the longest auto toll bridge in the world. Hundreds of tourists came to Tampa just for the thrilling over-the-bay drive.

Tampa, with the rest of Florida, suffered greatly during the Depression. But World War II brought the city back to life when the army built MacDill Field. The government then constructed a broad highway from MacDill to Drew Field, the city's little airport that would one day become Tampa International. The highway, named after Dale Mabry, an army pilot who had been killed in a dirigible accident, became a major factor in opening the sparsely populated western lands, which were annexed in 1953.

### Gussie Busch and His Gardens

The greatest event for Tampa after World War II was the arrival of the Anheuser-Busch brewery in the late 1950s. Originally the Busch family never intended to have anything like the huge theme park that has become one of Florida's major attractions. Selling beer—that was the consuming passion of four generations of Busches, reaching all the way back to the grand patriarch, Adolphus.

Adolphus Busch was an ambitious lad of just eighteen when he arrived in St. Louis from Germany. St. Louis in 1857 had a large Teutonic population that made Adolphus feel right at home. He felt so at home that he married Lilly Anheuser, daughter of a wealthy soap manufacturer who also dabbled in beer making. Adolphus called Anheuser's brew "dot schlop," and proceeded to make Budweiser into something of which he, Lilly, and their thirteen children could be proud. Soon the massive Anheuser-Busch brewery, with battlements worthy of a Rhine fortress, became one of St. Louis's most impressive structures.

Now a rich man, Adolphus bought a winter mansion on Millionaires Row in Pasadena, California. There, in 1892 he began a garden that eventually turned into a showplace with sunken gardens and fountains. Then, to please his grandchildren, he brought in exotic birds. But with his mind still on business, Adolphus formed the largest segment of the garden into a circular bed where the flowers formed Budweiser's trademark eagle.

In 1911 Adolphus and Lilly decided to open a portion of the Pasadena grounds to the public. Busch Gardens, as the estate was named, became quite popular, which made old Adolphus happy, for he needed barrels of goodwill to combat the forces of Prohibition. When Adolphus died two years later, Lilly remained at Busch Gardens until she passed away in 1928. At this time the estate was broken up and the gardens destroyed.

Adolphus's son, August, was a quiet man, very different from his bon vivant father. During the 1920s, when Prohibition was law, August had to struggle to keep the brewery afloat. He tried many things, even producing livestock feed. Most humiliating of all, he made a nonalcoholic Budweiser.

This was an agonizing period for August, and at times it seemed as if he preferred the company of the menagerie of animals he kept at Grant's Farm, the Busch estate outside of St. Louis, to that of his business associates. Adding to his misery was an illness that brought excruciating pain. In 1934 August took a pistol and shot himself.

August Jr. took over. Nicknamed Gussie, he was a throwback to his grandfather. He enjoyed boxing as a pastime and transferred his aggression into business. He was a ruthless and fearsome competitor who took on a personal vendetta against the Schlitz Company, then the nation's number-one brewery. As Schlitz expanded, Gussie matched them brewery for brewery. Thus, after Schlitz built a plant in Tampa, Gussie did likewise.

When the Tampa plant opened in 1959, Gussie put in a hospitality center with a modest garden, where visitors could enjoy free beer and pretzels while they watched a trained-bird show. The center became ever more popular, so in 1964 Gussie built the Old Swiss House Restaurant, named after a similar establishment in Lucerne, Switzerland, where he had met Trudy, the lovely blond waitress who became his third wife.

In 1966, impressed by the success of the Old Swiss House, Gussie installed a monorail that took visitors on a mile and a half excursion

*A boisterous extrovert, August Busch Jr., known as Gussie, built Budweiser's Tampa brewery in 1959, at which time he began installing Busch Gardens around it.* —Busch Entertainment Corp.

through what was called the Serengeti Plain—eighty acres stocked with live animals. But Busch Gardens was still mostly a place to promote Budweiser, as tours of the brewery were the main attraction. The Old Swiss House also had another use. "Before we cleaned it up," one Busch executive complained, "it was sort of a playground for Gussie and his entourage. It was notorious for all the beautiful women on the staff who entertained the gentlemen who came down there on their vacations."

The success of Disney World, just down the pike, changed things. In June of 1972, Anheuser-Busch formed a separate division for Busch Gardens. The result was a programmed expansion plan. Almost every year, something new was added. The first big event was the opening of the Moroccan Village, in 1975. This was followed by the completion of the Congo area, with the African Queen Boat Ride, two years later. Soon there were roller coasters, a whitewater adventure ride, and a special park for kiddies. Then, in 1990, the Old Swiss House was renovated into the Crown Colony House, thereby removing an incongruous Alpine restaurant from the heart of "Africa."

But the main thrust of Busch Gardens became its animals. The park was stocked with everything from giraffes running wild to South

*Busch Gardens has just opened in this 1960 photo. The former brewery is left center. The Hospitality House glows with four triangles. In 1975 the Moroccan Village will be built in the far upper right vacant lot.* —Florida State Archives

American llamas and Australian koalas. In 1992 Busch added the Myombe Reserve, a three-acre habitat for gorillas and chimpanzees.

Although at age seventy-six Gussie was replaced as company president by his son, August III, he had many more years of vigor in him. So he devoted himself to the St. Louis Cardinals baseball team, which he had bought many years earlier.

The fans at Busch Stadium loved it as the gate in right field swung open and Gussie drove out in a bright red beer wagon pulled by a team of his beloved Clydesdale horses. He always wore a cowboy hat, which he waved as the Budweiser theme song, "Here Comes the King," rocked out over the cheering stands.

Even into his eighties, Gussie maintained his boisterous lifestyle. He loved gin more than beer, and he could hold a bellyful of martinis. He still enjoyed his beachfront vacation home at Pass-a-Grille, Florida, where the company had long maintained a luxurious yacht. It was from here that he announced he had remarried, this time to his secretary, who was almost twenty years his junior.

In the autumn of 1989 Gussie sensed his time had come at last. He retired to his St. Louis mansion. About him were the numerous trophies he had won as a horseman. One of his colleagues found him. He was "sitting there with tears in his eyes" as he recalled the past. Gussie knew he was dying. He had phoned Trudy, his third wife, for consolation; he had always loved her despite their divorce.

So Trudy comforted him as his long and colorful life ebbed away.

### A Rapid Survey of Busch Gardens

Busch Gardens is Tampa's most popular tourist mecca, drawing well over 3 million visitors yearly. For those who would like a peek at the park without purchasing entry tickets, management has complimentary shopping passes. These passes permit the holders thirty minutes in the park, during which time it's assumed they will browse the Moroccan Village shops, where hundreds of unusual items are for sale at good prices. In addition, a snake charmer, a Moroccan brass band, and several quick-serve restaurants help make even the briefest stay interesting.

For nonshoppers, the thirty minutes allows a hurry-up walk through the Moroccan Village in one of two directions. The first direction leads past the alligator pond to the Crown Colony House, which, as the Old Swiss House, was once Gussie Busch's stomping ground. From the wide veranda you get a panoramic view of the Serengeti Plain, with perhaps a giraffe or two ambling past your line of vision. On the way back, if you have been judicious with your time, you can detour through the Myombe Reserve for a glance at the fascinating world of the great apes. The other direction through the village takes you to the Bird Gardens, which was the first display when the brewery was built in 1959. The Hospitality House was the original Busch Gardens building. Food is served on a spacious patio that permits a fine view of some fountains and a small pond. The pond flows into a larger pond that's brightened by huge numbers of colorful flamingos.

Both excursions are designed for people with only a little time to spare. They are just enough to whet your appetite and make you want to purchase a full admission and return for a full day.

### Tampa's Decline and Renaissance

Despite the success of Busch Gardens, Tampa could not escape the serious decay so typical of central shopping areas across the nation in the 1960s and 1970s. Downtown Tampa's share of the city's retail sales plunged from 15 percent in 1962 to under 5 percent in 1977. Businesses shuttered their doors, and many buildings became derelict.

In a frantic effort to lure customers back, the city turned Franklin Street into a pedestrian mall. Since Franklin was one of Tampa's main retail thoroughfares, anchored by the venerable Maas Brothers Department Store, it was expected that shoppers would return. But they did not, and by 1979 the downtown was virtually moribund.

But seldom has a city had such a dramatic turnaround as Tampa in the 1980s. It began with an act of faith by the city's leaders. The key was the creation of the Tampa City Center Esplanade. This involved the conversion of two entire blocks of Franklin Street into multilevel, landscaped brick terraces. The esplanade was bordered on one side by the spectacular thirty-eight-story Tampa City Center and on the other by the 540-room Hyatt Regency Hotel. Both buildings were glass-sheathed eye-catchers.

The bold action inspired confidence in private builders. During the next decade more skyscrapers followed—and with them a resurgence in the downtown. This resurgence spilled over to the waterfront, where portions of Harbor Island were cleared of indus-

*The 1915 city hall, once Tampa's most impressive structure, is humbled by the glass-sheathed skyscrapers of the city's 1980s renaissance.*

trial eyesores and the handsome Wyndham Hotel was constructed. The building spree continued into the following decade, when the exciting Florida Aquarium became an instant major attraction upon its opening in 1995.

## Touring Downtown Tampa

To see downtown Tampa, park at the city garage at Franklin and Whiting, which is next to the City Center Esplanade. From the garage, the elevated People Mover makes regular trips to Harbor Island and the world-class Wyndham Hotel.

The esplanade is a marvelous creation. There are sunken gardens, fountains, water cascades, palm trees of many varieties, and ample restaurants, surrounded by beautiful glass buildings that give it all a futuristic feel. Balancing tomorrow is the 1915 city hall at the north end of the esplanade. The tower displays a clock called Hortense, named for the lady who promoted its purchase.

Interestingly, the esplanade was the site of the old Fort Brooke cemetery, obliterated by the debris of decades until construction of the city garage in 1980 unearthed the bones of 144 individuals, including 42 Seminoles.

Walking north from the esplanade, you enter the Franklin Street Mall, which begins at Kennedy. Now you are back in the 1920s. Although considerable renovation work still needs to be done, the mall itself, with its potted trees and benches, has done much to make strolling up Franklin Street pleasant.

Be sure to note the story-and-a-half mural on the storefront just beyond Madison. Done by Carl Cowden III, it shows this portion of Franklin as it was in 1925, when it was jammed with shoppers and streetcars and lined with thriving businesses.

Farther up Franklin is the 1923 Exchange National Bank, with the classical architecture of the era. The old Maas Brothers Department Store is at the corner of Zack Street. Built in 1905, it was the finest such store in this part of Florida until it closed in the late 1980s. Half a block farther north is the Tampa Theater, housed in an ornate, ten-story building that became one of the city's most impressive landmarks when it was completed in 1926.

Five blocks from the esplanade is Polk Street, with railroad tracks running along Plant's original route. Two streets west on Polk is Ashley Drive, where there is a city parking garage. Ashley, home to some of the city's tallest skyscrapers, is perhaps Tampa's premier thoroughfare.

Turning south on Ashley, you will pass the Tampa Museum of Art, built on land once occupied by the Atlantic Coast Line's ugly train shed. A block farther south, at Ashley and Madison, is the visitor center, with maps and other information.

At Kennedy Street, a block south of Madison, the Hillsborough Bridge leads to Plant's Tampa Bay Hotel, now home of the University of Tampa. There is a fine public museum in the building, and many of the display rooms are much as they were when they housed the opening-day guests in 1891.

## Seeing Ybor City

A trip to Tampa would not be complete without a visit to Ybor City, reached from downtown by going north on Thirteenth Street, or from I-4 via a marked exit. Ybor City has had quite a roller-coaster ride from the days when Don Vicente Martinez Ybor's cigar factory was the world's largest.

Other cigar makers joined him, until eventually there were more than two hundred factories employing ten thousand workers. Most of the workers were from Cuba, Spain, and Italy. Seventh Avenue became the center of their lives. Here they formed their social clubs, and a society distinct and separate from the rest of Tampa evolved.

During Prohibition, rumor had Ybor involved in a local bootleg brewery. A raid by federal agents in 1927 resulted in Ybor's arrest and a six-month jail sentence—a decision later reversed.

As cigar factories in other parts of the world began to industrialize, Ybor's workers were unable to compete with machines, and a decades-long depression settled in on the community. Businesses left and homes were abandoned. But the district, with its quaint buildings and unusual history, reemerged in the early 1990s as one of Tampa's main entertainment centers.

To see Ybor, drive first along Seventh Avenue, the heart of the city, to the popular Columbia Restaurant at Twenty-second Street. The Columbia has been a Ybor focal point from its founding in 1905. Ferdie Pacheco, in his lively memoirs entitled *Ybor City Chronicles,* recalls how the conductors of the streetcars that used to run down Seventh would dash into the Columbia each morning for a cup of coffee, leaving their vehicles and impatient riders sitting in the middle of the street. Pacheco also remembers how the restaurant expanded by building El Patio, the beautiful addition formed like the courtyard of a mansion in Seville. Columbia's owners intended to make an upstairs room available for gambling during World War II, but bullets from a local gang and pressure from the law made them decide on a more prudent course.

West on Seventh Avenue at Eighteenth Street is the impressive Italian Club, and two blocks farther the Spanish Club, a pair of vivid reminders of the importance of these meeting places in the life of Ybor's inward-oriented society during the first half of the twentieth century. It was in the Spanish Club that Ferdie Pacheco as a teenager attended crowded bashes in the second-floor recreation room. The older men would enjoy dominoes in the cool confines of the basement, where smoky cigars created their own friendly contentment.

Also be sure to visit Ybor Square, at Thirteenth Street and Ninth Avenue, across from a large parking lot. Here, shops and more restaurants occupy portions of Vicente Ybor's 1886 cigar factory. You should also go through the excellent state museum a few blocks east down Ninth. It is housed in the old Ferlita Bakery, which once produced thirty-five thousand loaves of Cuban bread each week.

### The Gandy Bridge

Travelers leaving Tampa for St. Petersburg have their choice of crossing Old Tampa Bay by I-275 or by the Gandy Bridge, reached via the Crosstown Expressway (Florida 618). History buffs will want to drive the Crosstown, which closely parallels the old Plant railroad. Tampa Bay Hotel guests would often take excursion trains down these tracks to Port Tampa, where they dined in another Plant hotel that was built over the water. During the Spanish-American War, soldiers bound for Cuba took this line to transports at Port Tampa.

Moderns see nothing spectacular about the Gandy Bridge. But it was once considered a wonder as it leaped over the water for five and a half breathtaking miles.

## St. Petersburg

Although St. Petersburg, with a population of 240,000, is usually linked with its slightly larger neighbor, Tampa (285,000), the two cities are as different as if they were a hundred miles apart—not just across a bay.

It is true that St. Petersburg was originally part of Tampa's Hillsborough County. But the town chafed under Tampa's domination, and in 1911, after a bitter fight, Pinellas County was created— the strange name being a contraction of the ancient Spanish des-

Peter Demens, cofounder of
St. Petersburg, with his
daughter. He named the city
after his hometown in Russia.
—Saint Petersburg Museum of History

ignation: Pinal de Ximenes's point. However, it was not the Spaniards but an unusual gentleman named Peter Demens who gave St. Petersburg its start.

### The Czar's Guard

Demens entered adult life as Piotr Dementief, captain in the Imperial Russian Guard. After the czar was assassinated in 1881, Dementief, who held overly liberal views, fled to America. He settled near Sanford, where he built a lumber mill and became Peter Demens. His main business was selling cross ties to the Orange Belt Railroad, a rickety little line running from the St. Johns River to nowhere. When the directors could not pay their bills, they simply unloaded the struggling line on Demens.

The plucky Russian felt that if he could somehow extend the railroad to a port on the Gulf of Mexico, he could make it pay. With money from queasy backers and land grants from the doomed visionary Hamilton Disston, Demens began construction. But when his finances dried up, angry creditors chained his engines to the tracks until he scrounged the money to pay them. One of Demens's backers was so shocked by the incident that he died of a stroke. Later a violent mob of workers, unpaid for three weeks, threatened to lynch Demens if their wages were not met by nightfall. Once more he frantically scraped up the necessary money.

Given the obstacles, it was almost a miracle when the first Orange Belt train wheezed down the Pinellas peninsula on June 8, 1888. Demens, tremendously proud of his accomplishment, named the rail terminus St. Petersburg, after his hometown in Russia.

Demens should have saved his elation, because the line, which ran through an almost uninhabited wilderness, had little to haul. Thus, a year later he was forced to sell out. Thereupon he moved to California, where he found a less stressful career as a newspaper reporter.

### The Great Pier War

Demens's line soon fell into the hands of crafty Henry Plant. With it came the railroad pier that extended from the foot of First Avenue South three thousand feet into the bay. Such a distance was necessary to reach water deep enough for ocean ships to dock. Because Plant was a fierce competitor and refused to allow independent operators to use his docks, D. F. Brantley built his own pier just three blocks away at Second Avenue North. Soon another operator constructed a third pier at the foot of Central Avenue, barely a block north of Plant's. Thus began the great pier war.

The pier war continued for several decades and ended when the city decided to clear the downtown area of its freight facilities and move them south to Bayboro Harbor. The area once occupied by Plant's pier eventually became Demens Landing, now the site of the Municipal Marina.

But the Brantley Pier remained, to be used for recreation, not freight. In 1906 the original pier was rebuilt, with electric streetcars clanging down it to boat docks at the end. Although this structure met an untimely demise in the fierce hurricane of 1921, it had been so popular that the city began construction of what was proudly called the Million Dollar Pier in 1925. Its main feature was a two-story casino, built to accommodate the influx of pleasure seekers coming to St. Petersburg via the just-constructed Gandy Bridge, which linked the town to Tampa and points north.

### The Fabulous Twenties

During the first half of the 1920s, St. Petersburg, as well as much of Florida, spun on a whirligig of paper prosperity. It was the era of the promoter, personified in St. Petersburg by C. Perry Snell, a big, brash man whose fortune was established when he purchased prime real estate at give-away prices from the Orange Belt Railroad. Snell, the richest man in St. Petersburg, planned a daring subdivision on an island he planned to make in Tampa Bay. He brought in dredges and hucksters, and by the end of 1925 had sold $7 million worth of lots, even though most were still just muck and mangroves.

In 1926, while work was proceeding on Snell Island, the promoter began the Snell Arcade, which, with its highly ornamented tower, was the city's finest structure when it opened two years later.

Meanwhile other large buildings were going up. Chief among them was the Coliseum Ballroom, a gargantuan edifice with a Moorish motif that became the hot spot for St. Pete's flappers. When Paul Whiteman or Rudy Vallee played there, the floor was packed with up to two thousand boozy partygoers.

But the biggest event during the Roaring Twenties was the grand opening of the Vinoy Hotel on New Year's Eve 1925. The hotel was the largest construction project up to that time in Florida history. Located on the waterfront near the Million Dollar Pier, the Vinoy was a dazzling addition to the city's tourist attractions. Celebrities flocked to it, among them Calvin Coolidge, Babe Ruth, and F. Scott Fitzgerald.

*Saint Petersburg's Million Dollar Pier and Casino around 1930. The Vinoy Hotel stands proudly in the background.* —Saint Petersburg Museum of History

*This is the original Snell Island Bridge. Now rebuilt, the structure still carries autos to the upscale development Perry Snell created from bay dredgings during the 1920s.* —Saint Petersburg Museum of History

## Plunging to the Economic Depths

The bust of 1926 and the ensuing depression of the 1930s left St. Petersburg in shambles. Its economy had depended on tourism, which almost vanished during the hard times. One measure of the catastrophe was indicated by bank deposits, which stood at $46 million in 1925 and barely $4 million in 1931. Construction virtually ceased, and no new major buildings were put up for forty years. The Vinoy hobbled along, but the coliseum had to include boxing matches to stay solvent. As for Perry Snell, he lost the arcade to foreclosure and died a poor man.

St. Petersburg worked toward a comeback. Strangely, its greatest problem involved the city's very success in attracting retirees. For many years, old folks were so numerous that rows of green rest-benches as close together as bus seats lined Central Avenue. But the penny-squeezing oldsters were not much help to the city's faltering economy, so St. Petersburg worked hard to get rid of its stodgy image as "God's Waiting Room." The benches were removed and efforts were begun to lure younger spenders.

## The Saga of the Baseball Franchise

A prime goal in the city's new image involved obtaining a major-league baseball franchise. Never has a city gone through such frustrations. In 1984 St. Pete believed it would get the Minnesota Twins when a local businessman purchased 42 percent of the team. Although the deal did not go through, baseball commissioner Bowie Kuhn agreed that the city should receive top consideration in the future. The future came the next year, when the Oakland A's seemed in the bag. But St. Petersburg's overtures were enough to get Oakland to entice their team back with a favorable stadium lease it couldn't pass up.

Despite two failures, in 1986 the city council debated whether to build a stadium, assuming that would automatically lure a team to the area. Several days before the vote, baseball commissioner Peter Ueberroth sent an urgent telegram noting that St. Pete was "not a strong candidate" for a team and urged the city not to build the stadium. Ignoring the warning, the vote was six to three in favor, and four years later (and $36 million over budget) the stadium opened. It was perfect for Florida's torrid summers, featuring air-conditioning beneath a dome that was slanted to allow the coolness to reach most seats. The only problem was that St. Pete still had no team.

Oh, of course there had been more foul balls. The Chicago White Sox had told the Illinois legislature they were moving to St. Pete unless they were given a new stadium. In a stormy session that was broadcast live in the St. Petersburg area, the northern lawmakers finally agreed to the Sox's demand. St. Pete fumed, for it felt it had been used merely as a pawn. Then there was the incident with the Texas Rangers, ultimately snatched from St. Pete by a group led by George W. Bush, the president's son.

And the saga continued. In 1991 the right to a National League expansion team was about to go to St. Pete, but the city's ownership group fell apart at the last moment and it went to Miami instead. The next year, the Seattle Mariners had their eyes on St. Pete, but a Japanese consortium stole them in a move that left the entire nation stunned.

Incredibly, the worst was yet to come. In 1992 the San Francisco Giants' owner actually agreed to sell the team to St. Pete, but the deal was squelched by the league owners. St. Pete was so furious that it began a lawsuit that sought compensation for the $3 billion it figured would be lost over the next twenty-five years. When the Florida Supreme Court ruled in favor of the city, the National League made plans to take the case to the United States Supreme Court. But litigation ended in 1995 when St. Petersburg was at long last granted an expansion franchise.

### Touring St. Pete and Vicinity

Tours of St. Petersburg should start at the historic pier, the emotional heart of the city. The current structure, which replaced the Million Dollar Pier in 1973, is highlighted by a five-story building in the unusual form of an inverted pyramid. Here are restaurants, shops, an aquarium, and an observation deck with wonderful views of the harbor. A more intimate acquaintance with the harbor and the bay beyond can be gained aboard the cruise boats that leave from the pier.

In 1914 several thousand spectators lined the pier to watch Tony Jannus take off in a Benoist seaplane on the world's first commercial air flight. He soared over the bay at an elevation of all of fifty feet, along a route later taken by the Gandy Bridge. Twenty-three tense minutes later, he landed at Tampa before a cheering crowd. A replica of the plane, as well as other exhibits, are in the excellent Museum of History at the approach to the pier. Nearby is the impressive Museum of Fine Arts.

Downtown St. Petersburg has many interesting buildings, chief among them the former Snell Arcade, at 405 Central. The Coliseum, at 535 Fourth Avenue North, has been splendidly maintained and continues to host major events, including ballroom dancing. The new sports stadium is on First Avenue South between Tenth and Sixteenth Streets.

The Renaissance Vinoy Hotel still graces the waterfront at 501 Fifth Avenue North. A marvelous job was done restoring it while preserving the building's National Register status. Lunch or dinner looking out toward the harbor is a pleasurable experience—one similarly enjoyed by the hotel's ritzy guests of the Roaring Twenties.

A short ride north along the waterfront on North Shore and Coffee Pot (yes, that's a street) leads to Snell Island. The long entry-parkway, with its statues of lions and panthers, impresses moderns the way it impressed Perry Snell's prospective buyers in the 1920s. At the end of Snell Isle Boulevard is the 1920s Club House, an Ali Baba fantasy with its exotic minarets and highly decorated Arabian Tower.

W SPA BEACH AND VINOY PARK HOTEL, ST. PETERSBURG, FLORIDA

*Early photo of the Renaissance Vinoy Hotel. The beach is now part of a marina.* —Renaissance Vinoy Resort

It is now part of the Vinoy's golf course, which was built by Snell in the 1920s. Nearly two dozen of Snell's Mediterranean-style homes, distinctive with their red tile roofs, grace the island's winding streets. His own mansion still stands at 375 Brightwaters Boulevard Northeast.

As for Peter Demens's old Orange Belt Railroad, the tracks have long since made the scrap heap. But much of the right-of-way remains as the Pinellas Trail. The rails-to-trails begins at Thirty-fourth Street South (US 19) and Eighth Avenue South. Although this is a largely industrial area, the route ultimately leads through scenic country as it continues thirty-four miles west and north through Dunedin to Tarpon Springs, where it can also be picked up at US 19 and the Anclote River.

## St. Petersburg Beach

*A Hotel Born from Music and Dreams*

At St. Petersburg Beach, the Don CeSar Hotel rises ten bold-pink stories above the Gulf of Mexico. Built during the real estate boom of the 1920s, it was a dream come true for its creator, Thomas Rowe, a frail little man separated from his wife. He was a born romantic

*The Don CeSar Hotel under construction in the 1920s. Its owner, mild mannered Thomas Rowe, lived in the penthouse. Sally Rand did her fan dance in the ballroom.* —Don CeSar Beach Resort and Spa

and named his hotel for an opera character, perhaps because he had a crush on the female star. We know that the shy, dapper fellow had an eye for the ladies: none other than the famous exotic dancer Sally Rand did her seductive fan dance in his ballroom.

The Great Depression had a devastating effect on the hotel, but Rowe continued living there until his death in 1940. During World War II, the army converted the building into a hospital, with the penthouses serving as operating rooms and an area on the ground floor as a morgue. After the war, the hotel housed offices of the Veterans Administration, who allowed the building to deteriorate.

This deterioration accelerated after 1967, when the government moved out and the structure stood vacant. By 1971 it had become such an eyesore that a local newspaper called it a "pink elephant" and even suggested that "razing may be the only answer." But the building was saved in 1972, when new owners restored it to its past splendor. Since then, celebrities such as George Bush and Jimmy Carter have partaken of the Don's hospitality.

Although the rooms are expensive, casual visitors can still walk the halls, eat in the restaurants, and stroll the sands where F. Scott Fitzgerald and his beautiful yet quirky wife, Zelda, once capered in the carefree twenties.

# Clearwater

### *The Beautiful Belleview*

The town of Clearwater is thirteen miles north of St. Petersburg on Alternate US 19. Of prime interest historically is Henry Plant's Belleview Hotel. Plant had intended to build this luxury palace in St. Petersburg but pulled out in a pique when locals refused his demand for what they regarded as exorbitant concessions. St. Petersburg missed a lot, for the Belleview, completed in 1897, became a most popular hostelry. Sometimes as many as fifteen private railroad cars were parked on the east front siding.

Plant died in 1899 and, after many vicissitudes, the hotel was purchased by a Japanese interest in 1990, at which time it became the Belleview Mido. The Japanese refurbished it and added on, and now the hotel again occupies a premier place among America's grand resorts, as well as being on the National Register of Historic Places.

Across the narrow bay from the Belleview Mido is Sand Key, boasting one of the world's top twenty beaches. Easily accessible by bridge, Sand Key has a large public park with bathing facilities, as well as a magnificent view of the Gulf of Mexico.

*Railroad tycoon Henry Plant built the Belleview Hotel in 1897 at Clearwater. It was recently refurbished and expanded by a Japanese company, who renamed it the Belleview Mido.*

# Dunedin

Dunedin is one of the most appealing little gems on the Pinellas Trail. The historical museum is in the old railroad station, where the trail crosses Main Street. Immediately west is the former Bank of Dunedin. This 1913 building is currently occupied by the chamber of commerce, whose restoration set the stage for the revitalization of the rest of downtown. Now arty shops and eateries thrive amid bright-colored old-time storefronts and a pleasant streetscape. It is also possible to rent bicycles or skates for a quick glide along the Pinellas Trail.

To see more of Dunedin, a block-and-a-half stroll west on Main Street will lead to the marina. On this site in the early 1870s was a horse-powered cotton gin, and a few years later the general store of J. O. Douglas and James Somerville. It was these two men who named the village, in memory of their native Scotland. A long pier into the St. Joseph's Sound ensured the town a good connection with ships from most of the world.

The location was not only commercially profitable, but the water view was so enticing that wealthy families soon chose to live in Dunedin. They loftily called their most exclusive street Victoria Drive, after the Queen of England. Yet, though their homes were some of the area's finest, they chose to keep the six-block avenue unpaved.

Victoria Drive, which runs north from the marina, is still unpaved, giving it a delightful yesteryear flavor. Most of the original old homes continue to grace Victoria's leisurely way. James Somerville's, built in 1888, is at 1037. The 1893 residence of the Bouton family is at 937. The homes at 951, 1005, and 1015 went up in the 1910s, when autos were a novelty and big-wheeled bicycles the rage.

# Tarpon Springs

## *The Days of the Greek Sponge Divers*

Tarpon Springs is seven miles north of Dunedin. Although the town was incorporated in 1887 as a stop on the Orange Belt Railroad, its real beginning dated from the Spanish-American War, when the sponge industry fled Key West in fear of Spanish warships from Cuba. Sponging was done mainly by experienced men from Greece. Diving gear was introduced in 1905, and eventually some two hundred boats operated out of the channel along the street named for the Greek Dodecanese Islands.

*Sponge boats still operate out of Tarpon Springs's colorful harbor.*

The Tarpon Springs sponge fleet went out twice a year, remaining at sea for more than five months at a time. The diving boats were tended by mother ships, which brought food and fresh water. At night the fleet would tie up to the mother ships, and the men would sing or tell stories by lantern light.

A diving outfit was cumbersome and heavy, weighing nearly two hundred pounds, and was topped by a large helmet with a glass window. Men aboard the ships would hand-pump air to the divers, who would remain submerged for two hours at a time as they harvested sponges with long rakes and deposited them in net bags. Their only communication with the boat was by tugs on their life-line: need more hose, pump more air, emergency—pull me up quickly!

Tarpon Springs's peak years were during the 1930s. After that, disease in the form of "red tides" and, later, the invention of plastic sponges brought hard times. Yet sponge boats still use the harbor, and the sponge dock along Dodecanese Boulevard is now a National Historic Landmark.

The town is extremely popular with tourists, and Dodecanese has become jammed with souvenir shops, many with quaint gifts reminiscent of the sponge industry. A sponging museum is on the boulevard. So, too, is the Sponge Exchange, with origins dating back to 1908. The exchange includes a modern mini–shopping mall, appealing in its white paint and blue trim so characteristic of the Greek islands. Farther west along the boulevard is the Pappas Restaurant, having grown from a 1925 mom-and-pop operation to a huge establishment with Greek food, classical statuary, and a marvelous view of the harbor.

With the docking area's commercialism, it is refreshing to experience the vaulted tranquillity of the St. Nicholas Greek Orthodox Church, at 36 North Pinellas Avenue. The original structure dated from 1907. The current church was built from stones quarried in Greece and used for the Greek pavilion at the New York World's Fair in 1939. It is a small-scale replica of the beautiful Santa Sophia in ancient Constantinople.

The Pinellas Trail runs though downtown on a course that was once the Orange Belt Railroad, a pioneer line that linked St. Petersburg with Sanford, then an important port on the St. Johns River. The trail runs through Dunedin and Clearwater on its thirty-four-mile route to St. Pete. It is ranked among the top five "rails-to-trails" in the entire nation. Bikes and skates can be rented at various locations.

## The Bridge of the Golden Sails

Heading south from St. Petersburg on I-75, the way leads over Tampa Bay via the spectacular Sunshine Skyway Bridge. There are actually two separate, quite different bridges. And therein lies a dramatic story.

The ten-mile-wide bay entrance had long been crossed by a car ferry when in 1954 a highly touted bridge with an eight-hundred-foot span for ships' passage was completed. It carried such heavy traffic that seventeen years later a second span was added. But on May 9, 1980, during a blinding downpour accompanied by sixty-mile-an-hour winds, a large freighter crashed into the bridge. As a span collapsed, the cars on it tumbled into the bay, killing all thirty-five motorists who were on the bridge at the time, except the lucky one whose pickup truck happened to land directly on the freighter's deck.

The disaster resulted in a complete redesign of the replacement bridge. To guide wayward vessels away from the foundations, forty circular pilings, called "dolphins," were securely anchored to the bedrock. And the central span allowed ships a twelve-hundred-foot, not eight-hundred-foot, clearance. The bridge also had an aesthetic appeal, as the spans were supported by a web of golden-colored cables tied to twin masts that rose twenty-five stories above the roadway. This new Sunshine Skyway Bridge was completed in 1987.

What became of the old bridge? A creative use was found for it. The wrecked portions were dismantled and deposited in the western portion of the channel to form fish reefs. The still-standing portions were converted into drive-on piers from which anglers can not only haul in grouper, snapper, mackerel, and tarpon but at the same time savor a thrilling, windswept vista of blue and gold.

*The impressive Union Terminal, renovated in the 1980s,
is now Jacksonville's convention center.*

# ~ 4 ~

# *Jacksonville*

## CITY ON THE RIVER

Jacksonville was the natural site for a major city, since here was the narrowest crossing of the St. Johns River for many miles. The British called it Cow Ford, an ideal crossing for the Kings Road, which they built between 1771 and 1777 to connect with the plantations that reached as far south as New Smyrna. After the Spanish claimed Florida in 1783, they put up a small fortification beside the Kings Road on the south riverbank.

By the time Florida became a U.S. territory in 1821, a few Americans had already settled at Cow Ford. The following year, Isaiah Hart, Lewis Hogans, and John Brady donated land for a town, and the first streets were laid out in the place named Jacksonville, in honor of Andrew Jackson, the provisional governor.

Isaiah Hart built a rather spacious boardinghouse at the northwest corner of Bay and Market Streets and managed to attract a few wealthy northerners over the winter. But the frontier hamlet's permanent population was barely a hundred until the advent of the steamboat.

### The Steamboat Era

Although the first steamboat had thrilled New Yorkers in 1807, it took a number of years before inventors discovered how to overcome the boats' unfortunate tendency to explode. So it was not until 1829 that the first steamboat crossed the treacherous sandbar at the mouth of the St. Johns River and chugged up to the gaping townsfolk at the Jacksonville Landing.

At first the steamboat was more a curiosity than anything else, for there was little reason to travel upriver—not with the smoldering Seminole problems. But when the Second Seminole War erupted in 1835, the army found that steamboats were ideal for transporting troops and supplies deep into the interior. Thus Jacksonville took on some importance as the port of embarkation. Soon other military posts were strung along the river, with a major one being Fort Mellon, two hundred miles up from Jacksonville, where the St. Johns widened into Lake Monroe (now the site of Sanford).

When the war ended and most of the Seminoles had been herded off to the West, the lands along the St. Johns opened up for settlement. Again steamboats played a key role.

One of the first civilian captains was Jacob Brock, a native New Englander who had made enough money transporting cotton around Charleston to have his own steamboat constructed. Named *The Darlington,* it had two decks, the lower one for machinery and freight and the upper one for passengers. It could carry forty travelers in comfort, with staterooms for overnight accommodations and a private salon for the ladies.

Brock brought *The Darlington* to Jacksonville in 1851 and immediately had a thriving river trade. An ambitious man, Brock then built a hotel beside Lake Monroe at a little place called Enterprise. Next he began once-a-week steamboat service to his hotel. Leaving Jacksonville at dawn each Sunday, Brock's boat overnighted at Palatka, then reached Enterprise the next evening, covering the distance in just two comfortable days—a trip that would take a man on horseback five arduous ones.

Brock was a rough and boisterous ship captain, as if right out of Mark Twain's novels. Almost vainly proud of the ship's whistle, he got immense pleasure from blasting it when ladies walked by— just to see them jump. As for his language, even among steamboat captains he had "a notable reputation for the lavish and original nature of his profanity," wrote a contemporary. But at the bottom, "a kinder-hearted . . . or more congenial man never walked a deck."

During the Civil War, Brock became a Confederate blockade runner until he was captured at Fernandina and interned for the rest of the war. Then his boat was incorporated into the Union blockade fleet that dominated the St. Johns. After the war, Brock bought *The Darlington* back and resumed steamboating. However, as the competition became more intense, Brock did not fare well. Eventually financial woes forced him to sell his hotel, and just before he died in 1877 at the age of sixty-six, he was forced into bankruptcy.

*An 1880s steamboat outing. Notice the "grande dame" on the woodpile seat of honor.* —Jacksonville Historical Society

Steamboating reached its peak in the 1880s, when Jacksonville's waterfront bristled with wharves and warehouses. At this time, more than seventy vessels operated out of the port. Foremost among them was Count DeBary's line, with thirteen ships using the company piers at the foot of Laura Street.

The end of steamboating came abruptly. By 1881 a railroad linked Jacksonville with Savannah, and within three years a line reached south to connect Jacksonville with Palatka. Henry Flagler began putting together the Florida East Coast Lines, and in 1889 his rattling steel bridge spanned the St. Johns, formally sounding steamboating's death toll.

### The Cottage at Mandarin

In 1867 the Jacksonville area received a most unusual winter resident: Harriet Beecher Stowe, author of *Uncle Tom's Cabin,* the most inflammatory antislavery book ever written. When Abraham Lincoln met Mrs. Stowe, the president greeted her, "So this is the little lady who made this big war."

After the Civil War, Harriet came to Jacksonville to rent a plantation that she wanted her son, Frederick, to manage, seeing in it a means to divert him from his growing dependency on alcohol. While Harriet was in the vicinity she visited Mandarin, which then was an independent hamlet fifteen miles upstream from Jacksonville. Finding what she regarded as an ideal winter home for herself, her twin daughters, and her husband, who had just retired, she purchased it.

Harriet loved Mandarin, a tiny community of only twelve homes. Just down the road from her cottage was a combination church and school, and Harriet participated in both. So, too, did her husband, Calvin, who preached and conducted Bible lessons.

The Stowe cottage was small, with a story-and-a-half gable roof. They spent most of their time on the wide porch, which was shaded by a massive live oak. At one end of the porch was a dense jasmine vine with perfumed yellow flowers that bloomed from January until March.

Harriet enjoyed sitting on her porch looking out on the broad St. Johns. She was there so often that steamboats slowed down so passengers could see the famous lady. When they waved, she waved back.

*Harriet Beecher Stowe, her husband, twin daughters, son Frederick, and Mother Beecher (with the white hair) relax in front of their winter cottage at Mandarin, near Jacksonville, around 1873.*
—Jacksonville Historical Society

Harriet wrote a book about her experiences at Mandarin. Entitled *Palmetto Leaves* and published in 1873, its popularity attracted many tourists to the area; and no wonder, for her descriptions of life along the St. Johns were idyllic.

The river at this point was nearly five miles wide. "The great blue sheet of water," she wrote, "shimmers and glitters like so much liquid 'lapis lazuli.'" Some of her neighbors had sailboats and "on this great, beautiful river you go drifting like a feather or a cloud; while the green, fragrant shores form a constantly-varying picture as you pass."

Once she, her husband, and their daughters, vivacious young ladies, took Captain Brock's steamboat up as far as Enterprise, "where the river narrows so that the boat brushes under overhanging branches, and then widens into beautiful lakes dotted with wooded islands."

There was a long wharf between the Stowes' cottage and that of their neighbor to the south. It was here that Harriet met old Cudjo, a former slave sitting forlornly on a bale of cotton. During the past four years he had labored on a plot of land nearby, had built himself a log cabin and a barn, and had raised a fine cotton crop.

But through legal shenanigans, a foreigner took control of the land and ejected Cudjo, who now had a single cotton bale for all his work. Harriet's white neighbors, rallying behind Cudjo, contacted influential people in Washington and won the land back for him. When Harriet met Cudjo again, he told her that the foreigner had himself been evicted and that when the man begged Cudjo to sell his land, Cudjo had replied that he'd be glad to sell it to him for ten thousand million dollars. Thus the affair ended.

As the years passed, the Stowes' winters at Mandarin began to lose their appeal. It was essentially a "still and lonely" life, Harriet admitted. After Calvin became ill, he was not much of a companion. And Harriet's daughters increasingly tended to her household and business affairs, so she had a lot of empty time.

As for her son, Fred, the grove had not helped alleviate his drinking problem. Finally, at Harriet's suggestion, he took a vacation to San Francisco, where he vanished without a trace. Harriet was devastated, and it is said her hair turned white almost overnight.

Harriet was now in her seventies, and the annual trek from the north had become ever more difficult. Also, memories of Fred haunted the grounds. So in 1884 the Stowes decided to live year-round in

Hartford, Connecticut. After Calvin died, Harriet became a virtual recluse, dwelling in the golden days of childhood until she passed away in 1896.

## The Madam and the Famous Writer

By the beginning of the twentieth century, Jacksonville, with a population of fifty thousand, had become Florida's largest city. Much of its prosperity came from the pine-log rafts nearly a quarter-mile long that were floated down the St. Johns River. The logs were sawed into planks at a large mill that was beside McCoy's Creek, just west of the modern Acosta Bridge. The lumber was then carried to northern cities by the fleet of three-masted schooners crowding the wharves along the Jacksonville Landing.

The sailors and merchants who flooded into the city looked for good times, and sporting houses sprung up to accommodate them. The most famous was the Hotel de Dream, on Jefferson Street. It catered strictly to upper-class gents and was run by Cora Taylor, a lady out of legend. Cora came from a refined Boston family in which artists and musicians were common. But she was not of the traditional mold. She had a buoyant personality that craved new sensations, new experiences. "Unenthusiastic natures, how much they miss!" she was to write in her diary. "I have lived five years in one all my life."

In 1895, at age thirty, she bounced into Jacksonville, already having shucked off a lover and two husbands, one of whom had been a titled English captain. She bought the Hotel de Dream, a real classy place, with a piano man and a roulette wheel that almost always gave a fair whirl. She abhorred hard liquor, and if you got drunk in her pleasure parlor, you had to do it on her beer at an unheard-of dollar a bottle.

One day Stephen Crane rambled in. Although barely twenty-four, he was already famous as the author of *The Red Badge of Courage,* heralded as the best fictional account of the Civil War. To Crane's delight, Cora had read some of his writings, and from there they instantly hit it off—so much so that Cora soon sold the hotel, went off with Crane to cover war stories in the Balkans, and eventually married him in Greece. Here she showed a new talent as she wrote war impressions that appeared in ten American newspapers.

But the idyll was over when Crane died in 1900, possibly of an illness contracted in Florida. Cora returned to Jacksonville, where she was soon back at the old trade, continuing until she died suddenly of a heart attack ten years later.

### Boom—Bust—Boom

In 1901 a horrible fire caused much of wooden Jacksonville to vanish in a fearsome sheet of flames. The column of smoke rose so high that it could be seen five hundred miles away. More than two thousand buildings were destroyed, and nearly nine thousand people were made homeless.

But a booming new city of brick, stone, and ambition quickly rose. By 1912 the huge four-story St. James Building had filled the entire block along Duval Street across from Hemming Park. Simply called The Big Store, it became a magnet for shoppers throughout northern Florida. Seven years later the Union Terminal was completed. With its massive row of forty-two-foot classical columns, it was the largest railroad station in the South. Such a great structure was needed to handle the hordes of people coming into the city on the twenty-five daily passenger trains.

The 1920s were ushered in by the construction of the Acosta Bridge. Then downtown began to sprout an inspiring assortment of

*Cohen's popular Big Store drew eager shoppers from all over north Florida after it was built in 1912. The building still stands across from Hemming Park.* —Jacksonville Historical Society

*Jacksonville's riverfront some time before construction of the I-95 bridge (dashes) in 1954. The Jacksonville Landing complex has replaced the ugly docks above the twin-spired Main Street Bridge.* —Jacksonville Historical Society

large buildings. Chief among them was the Barnett National Bank, which at eighteen stories remained Jacksonville's tallest skyscraper for almost thirty years.

Prosperity ended for Florida with the great bust of 1926. Although the Main Street Bridge was built in 1941, not much other construction went on downtown until 1975, when the landmark Independent Life Tower went up. Then came the 1980s, the Billion Dollar Decade, marked by the opening of the Jacksonville Landing and construction of three more major skyscrapers, capped by the Barnett Center's forty-two-story tower that dominated the skyline.

### Touring Downtown

Most visitors head for Jacksonville Landing, on the north bank of the St. Johns River at the foot of the Main Street Bridge (US 1 and 90). Parking is available on the east side of the bridge. The landing replaced a dingy wharf area that once rang with the curses of rough longshoremen. Now it is a sparkling recreation area with outdoor entertainment and excellent restaurants and shops overlooking the river.

## A Historical Walk

Many tourists enjoy the four-block walk from Jacksonville Landing up Laura Street to Hemming Park, the heart of old Jacksonville. Some interesting sights lie on the route:

1.  Northeast corner of Laura and Bay: the Old Bisbee Building. Begun in 1901, just four months after the great fire left downtown a smoldering ruin, the two-story building is a marvel of terra-cotta ornamentation

2.  Northeast corner of Laura and Forsyth: the Jacksonville National Bank. This classical-style structure was also constructed just after the fire. With its solid stone exterior, it was called the Marble Bank by the enthralled patrons who parked their carriages in front.

3.  Northeast corner of Laura and Adams: the Elks Club. This building opened during the boom of the 1920s. The five Venetian arches on the second floor give it a Mediterranean look.

4.  Southwest corner of Laura and Adams: the Barnett National Bank. This skyscraper, which went up in 1926, was for many years Jacksonville's signature building. Notice the row of obelisks at the top and the lion heads between the third and fourth stories.

5.  Northwest corner of Laura and Adams: the Greenleaf and Crosby Building. Completed in 1927, this structure is lavishly decorated with everything from eagles to urns. It was originally to have been six stories, but at the last moment of planning, four stories were erased from the right wing. Two more stories were added to these four and placed on the left wing to make it twelve stories.

6.  Southwest corner of Laura and Monroe: the Snyder Memorial Methodist Church. This Gothic-style building was completed in 1903 to replace the original, which had become tinder in the 1901 fire. Constructed of granite trimmed with limestone, it was obviously designed to withstand anything except the Final Conflagration.

## Hemming Park: Heart of Old Jacksonville

Hemming Park, bordered by Laura, Monroe, Hogan, and Duval Streets, dates back to Isaiah Hart's survey of 1857. The Confederate

monument, donated by Charles Hemming, was unveiled during a
gathering of Southern war veterans in 1898. Three years later, the
statue atop its tall pedestal stood aloof and unharmed while flames
consumed everything around it.

The Cohen Brothers Big Store at Laura and Duval was easily
Jacksonville's largest and most impressive building when it was
completed in 1912. It was an early mall, with private shops around
Cohen's anchor department store. The upper two stories were offices.
The Big Store closed in 1987, when the Cohens submitted to the
inevitable and moved to the suburbs.

## The Riverwalk

Water taxis make regular and frequent runs between Jacksonville Landing and Riverwalk, across the St. Johns. It is well worth
the short trip, for the view of the Landing, with its backdrop of glass-
sheathed skyscrapers, is breathtaking. So, too, is the close-up of the
Main Street Bridge, built near the original cow ford, although the
depth of the water forced the cattle to swim, not ford, to the other
side. Later a ferry ran across the river, leaving from the Dixieland
Amusement Park, at the foot of what is now the Main Street Bridge.

Riverwalk is a broad boardwalk that was begun in 1986, a year
before the Jacksonville Landing. It meanders for about a mile along

*Friendship Fountain frames Jacksonville's skyscrapers.*

the St. Johns, from the Marina Hotel on the eastern end and past the just-renovated Hilton Hotel to the spectacular Friendship Fountain on the western end. The fountain is near the site of the old ferryman's house that stood beside the Kings Road. There are some nice restaurants along the way and a small but informative historical society museum.

Compared to the landing, Riverwalk is quiet and staid. Yet the scene is expansive. Downriver is the stadium of the Jaguars, the city's long-sought National Football League team that began playing in 1995. Jacob Brock's shipyard was just west of the stadium. Upriver is the new Acosta Bridge and beside it the 1890 railroad bridge built by Henry Flagler.

Eight blocks west of the Landing on Water Street is the former Union Terminal, renovated during the 1980s into the impressive Prime F. Osborn III Convention Center. Water Street began as a railroad spur, running across marshes from the Julia Street Wharf to the railroad freight yards, near what became the Union Terminal. The neighborhood around the old terminal is also being reborn. Once it housed ladies of the evening, with Cora Crane's Hotel de Dream at the southwest corner of Jefferson and Ashley.

### The Harriet Beecher Stowe Home

Mandarin, the location of Harriet Beecher Stowe's winter home, can be reached on Florida 13, south from downtown Jacksonville.

*Harriet Beecher Stowe worshiped at the original Episcopal Church in Mandarin. A hurricane destroyed this church as well as the Stowe-dedicated window. The current award-winning building was completed in 1966.*

The original road was completed in 1915 as part of the famous Dixie Highway that connected Florida with the Midwest. The road was only nine feet wide, and the surface was of bricks laid by convict labor. A mile after passing I-295, watch for Mandarin Road, draped with oaks and Spanish moss. The Stowe cottage was located on the river, immediately west of 12408 Mandarin Road. The site is now occupied by a house that would dwarf Harriet's modest cottage. The church/school that was so important to Harriet is about sixty yards away, at 12447 Mandarin. It was built in 1872, after the first building burned down. Stowe solicited northern friends to get funds for the new building.

Downriver is the Episcopal Church, attended by the Stowe family. It was organized the year Harriet came to Mandarin, and the current building was constructed in 1883. When Calvin Stowe died, Harriet asked that a window be installed in his memory. Thirty years later, such a window was made by Louis Tiffany.

### Fort Caroline, the Mayport Ferry, and the Kingsley Plantation

For tourists wishing to explore Jacksonville's scenic and historic hinterlands, a twenty-five-mile jaunt out to the Kingsley Plantation via Fort Caroline and the Mayport Ferry is highly recommended.

The route to the Fort Caroline National Memorial goes east from downtown on historic Atlantic Boulevard (Florida 13). The boulevard was built in 1910 as a one-lane oyster-shell roadway, enabling young Jacksonville picnickers in their Model Ts to sputter out to the beaches. Despite the road's primitiveness, it represented the beginning of Florida's highway system. Just after Atlantic Boulevard passes the Regency Square Shopping Mall, watch for Monument Road, which leads north to Fort Caroline.

### The Fort Caroline Massacre

Fort Caroline was built by a colony founded by French Huguenot Protestants in 1564, a year before the Spanish came to St. Augustine. Much of the fort has been reconstructed, with timber-and-earth ramparts, a moat, and sixteenth-century brass cannons. The Spanish attack in 1565 was such a surprise that none of the cannons could be fired in time. A hundred and forty French were massacred, sixty women and children spared. But did the Spanish have any other choice? They did not have enough food to feed such a large number

*The French built Fort Caroline in eastern Jacksonville in 1564. One year later the Spanish from Saint Augustine surprised and wiped out the garrison.* —P. H. Yonge Library of Florida History, University of Florida

*Timucuans worship Ribault's column erected in 1562. Drawing is by Jacques Le Moyne, who was based in the French colony at nearby Fort Caroline.* —P. H. Yonge Library of Florida History, University of Florida

of prisoners; furthermore, in the age of religious wars, they were convinced that the Huguenots were in league with the devil.

From the memorial, signs indicate the short drive to the Ribault Monument, which consists of a replica of the large stone column that French commander Jean Ribault erected when he stopped briefly at the mouth of the St. Johns River in 1562. Bearing the French coat of arms, it proclaimed the land as belonging to France. When the colonists arrived two years later, they found that the Timucuan Indians worshipped the column.

The current column was erected in 1924 by the Daughters of the American Revolution. It is atop the St. Johns Bluff, which commands a majestic view of the river and the grassy wetlands to the north. These wetlands constitute the forty-six-thousand-acre Timucuan Ecological and Historic Preserve, created in 1988.

Atlantic Boulevard can be regained via Mount Pleasant and Girvin Roads. Then head east, crossing the Intracoastal Waterway, and turn north on A1A.

### The Mayport Ferry

A1A skirts the Mayport Naval Station, a major installation and home of an aircraft carrier, destroyers, and other warships. The base and ships are often open to the public; call to find out when.

Approaching the hamlet of Mayport, A1A parallels the St. Johns, along which are scores of shrimp boats, deep-sea fishing vessels, and seafood restaurants. The car ferry to Fort George Island runs frequently. Usually the boat must fight the same fierce currents that made the mouth of the St. Johns so treacherous for early sailing vessels. These currents also laid a shifting sandbar across the river's entrance that forced some ships to wait days for the local pilot, who himself was waiting for favorable tide and wind conditions. The pilots were about the only people living here, and the settlement was known, with good reason, as Hazard. In 1895 a pair of jetties was completed several miles into the Atlantic and the sandbar vanished.

### The Kingsley Plantation: A Chilling View of Slavery

Once you're on Fort George Island, named after a vanished fortification built by English soldiers from Georgia in 1736, turn north on A1A/105 about a mile to the sign pointing to the Kingsley Plantation. The plantation is several miles into a rather wild area on a gravel road. A large savanna, consisting mainly of spartina grass and

*The bleak walls of slave cabins still stand at the Kingsley Plantation near Jacksonville.*

needlerush, can be seen through the trees that line the road. This savanna, part of the Timucuan Ecological and Historic Preserve, is home to wood storks, great blue herons, and many other exotic birds.

The Kingsley Plantation, a rather plain, two-story wooden home, was built in 1789 and reflects the lifestyle of frontier planters during the second Spanish and early American periods. On the dark side are the grim oyster-shell walls of twenty-three slave cabins, arranged in a neat arc that enabled the master and his overseers to better observe and regulate the activities of the two hundred or so slaves over whom they held the power of life or death. For disciplining, the nearby barn also served as a jail.

Entire generations of black families lived and died here, laboring in the dreary cotton and sugarcane fields that once existed around them.

Zephaniah Kingsley bought the plantation around 1813. He had made much of his money purchasing black men, women, and children in Africa and selling them in the Americas. With his profits he bought several other Florida plantations, at which he took many black women as his mistresses. His mistress at the Kingsley Plantation was a special lady named Anna Jai. His affection for her was so deep that he married her and gave her a home next to the main house. The pair had four children.

Though the two Kingsley daughters apparently married well, Kingsley was concerned about the boys' future in a region increasingly hostile toward people of color. Therefore, in 1835 he moved Anna Jai and the boys to a colony he established in Haiti. There the family must have prospered, for we know that one of the sons, George, eventually became a large landholder in Florida, though later he was lost at sea.

The other slaves did not fare so well. They remained chained to the soil after Kingsley sold the plantation in 1839. The plight of such slaves was vividly described by Frederick Law Olmsted in *A Journey in the Back Country, 1853–1854* (revised in 1970).

Although Kingsley had lived on-site, most owners of the larger plantations such as his resided in a distant city, where they could enjoy the pleasures of the wealth their plantations afforded them. Left in charge was an overseer, whose instructions were to produce the maximum crop. Beyond that, he was free to conduct himself as he saw fit. "No wonder he . . . presses everything at the end of the lash; pays no attention to the sick, except to keep them in the field as along as possible; and drives them out again at the first moment, and forces sucklers and breeders [women pregnant or nursing babies] to the utmost. He has no other interest than to make a big cotton crop"—so ran a Southern article that Olmsted quoted.

> The Negro cabins were small, dilapidated and dingy [Olmsted wrote in his book] . . . there were no windows. . . . The furniture in the cabins was of the simplest and rudest imaginable kind, two or three beds with dirty clothing upon them, a chest, a wooden stool or two made with an ax, and some earthenware and cooking apparatus. Everything within the cabins was colored black by smoke. . . . At the door of each cabin were literally "heaps" of babies and puppies, and behind or beside it a pig-stye and poultry coop, a lye-tub and quantities of home-carded cotton placed upon boards to bleach. Within each of them was a woman or two, spinning with the old-fashioned great wheel, and in the kitchen another woman was weaving coarse cotton shirts with the ancient rude hand-loom.

Leaving Fort George Island with its melancholy memories, you can drive west on Florida 105 across scenic wetlands back to central Jacksonville. However, it is also rewarding to continue eighteen miles north on A1A/105 to the quaint town of Fernandina Beach on Amelia Island.

*This handsome building, once the Carnegie Library, now houses the Black Archives at Florida A & M University.* —Florida A & M University.

# ~ 5 ~

# *Tallahassee*

## THE OLD SOUTH

### *The Ancient Mound Builders*

Long before the Europeans, long before the Seminoles, even before the Apalachees, the densely forested hills around Tallahassee supported a large Native American population. The later Indians called the area Tallahassee, meaning "the old town," for their ancestors had built half a dozen towering religious mounds around Lake Jackson, dating back to around A.D. 1000. These mysterious people were part of a cultural complex that extended into Georgia, Alabama, and Tennessee. Trade objects link them even as far west as Oklahoma.

### *The Triumph and Tragedy of the Spanish Era*

By the time Hernando de Soto and his men blustered into the "old town," the Lake Jackson culture had vanished. During the winter of 1539–40, the Spaniards camped on a low hill just southeast of the modern capitol, where they celebrated Florida's first Christmas.

Around 1633 Franciscan friars founded the mission of San Luis on the western outskirts of Tallahassee. As the largest of their thirty-one Florida missions, it became the capital of a holy fiefdom that encompassed twenty-six thousand Apalachee and Timucua worshipers.

The destruction of the mission system began in 1702, when James Moore, British governor of South Carolina, led a powerful force of Creeks against the Spanish. Moore's goal was to injure the Spaniards, with whom England was at war, and at the same time enrich himself and his friends with thousands of Christian Indian slaves. In both of these goals he was successful.

When the United States took over Florida from Spain in 1821, the Apalachee and Timucua were no more, and their place had been taken by a few thousand Seminoles and Miccosukees who had drifted down from the north.

## Exciting Life During Territorial Days

Tallahassee became Florida's capital solely because it was almost equidistant between the state's two main towns, St. Augustine and Pensacola. When William Duval, the first territorial governor, arrived in 1824, there was almost nothing here—just pine trees and a picturesque little cascade. Duval built his home on a hill near the cascade, and later the first legislature met in a log cabin in the otherwise deserted Capitol Square.

Settlers were reluctant to move to Tallahassee, for it was not only primitive but almost entirely cut off from the rest of the world. All luxuries and most necessities had to be imported from the pitiful little gulf port of St. Marks, twenty miles south. However, the village did have one big asset, and that was Duval himself. Jolly and informal, he went around in a tattered straw hat and deerskin trousers. His optimistic demeanor inspired confidence. But, though he was

*Florida's first territorial governor, William Duval, had to fight mud as well as Seminoles when he helped lay out Tallahassee in 1824.*
—P. H. Yonge Library of Florida History, University of Florida

*Between 1826 and 1839 this was Florida's capitol. It had replaced the log cabin where the first legislators met during the governorship of William Duval in 1824.* —Florida State Archives

a friendly person, he could also pack a wallop, as when he confronted the obstreperous Seminole chief Neamathla. In front of the chief's astonished warriors, Duval shook him by the throat and literally threw him out of the room where they were negotiating.

With the arrival of Duval's wife, Nancy, Tallahassee's society began to coalesce. The Duvals had a beautiful and flirtatious daughter named Elizabeth. One night two hot bloods fought a pistol duel on Capitol Square to see which most deserved her. Luckily, neither was seriously hurt. As for Elizabeth, she had just been toying with them and cared not a whit for either.

The duel was described by Lizzie Brown, who came to Tallahassee in 1828 as a girl of ten. Young Lizzie had her own adventures. Seminoles still roamed the streets, and one brave, named Tiger Tail, took a fancy to the bright red plume on the little girl's hat. He insisted that she give it to him, and when she would not, he sullenly followed Lizzie and her sister all the way from a Fourth of July celebration to their home at the top of the cascade. "This, of course, frightened me very much," Lizzie wrote in her memoirs. Fortunately, Tiger Tail was basically a friendly person, and when he left to join his comrades during the Second Seminole War, everyone was sad.

Lizzie's younger companion during the 1830s was Ellen Call. She was the first white child born in Tallahassee, and to announce the event the militia boomed the old Spanish cannons at Fort San Luis. Ellen became the darling of the little town, present at almost every event of importance—many of which she described in her colorful book, *Florida Breezes,* authored under her married name of Long.

In *Florida Breezes* Ellen describes the stagecoach as it came down the St. Augustine Road, the driver bellowing on a horn that announced what was often the biggest event of the week. And she recalled outings at St. Marks, where lovers would dance by moonlight. And how on very special occasions, like Mardi Gras, everyone would board a ship at St. Marks and sail all the way to the festivities at Pensacola!

There were picnics amid the evocative Spanish ruins atop San Luis Hill. And, of course, when the town was flooded with legislators there were constant rounds of parties and balls. The most special were the Feasts of Roses at Colonel Butler's fine mansion on Lake Jackson. The home was not far from the eerie Indian mounds that they liked to climb and then muse about the past.

Perhaps most of all, Ellen liked excursions along the romantic St. Augustine Road. Often there were as many as forty men and women in the party. The ladies rode in carriages, and the swains galloped and cavorted around them on spirited horses. "It was a joyous ride," Ellen wrote, "the air scented with the magnolia bloom, bay flower, and the grape blossom."

The way was past de Soto's ancient encampment, though all traces had been covered by the debris of three centuries. Neamathla's village was also on the route, but by this time the Seminoles had been forced out of the area and the site now was merely a convenient place to enjoy picnic lunches beside a stream.

In 1836 Ellen's father, Richard Keith Call, was appointed territorial governor by his friend, President Andrew Jackson. Somewhat earlier, Richard had built a spacious house north of town at a place called the Grove. Call grew increasingly wealthy, eventually owning an estate of 2,644 acres worked by up to 118 slaves. Some became beloved house servants, and one black lady cared for Ellen through most of her early years, virtually replacing Ellen's mother, who had died.

## Slavery

During the years preceding the Civil War, cotton plantations blossomed forth in Tallahassee's Leon County, which, along with

Jefferson County next door, produced almost as much cotton as the entire rest of the state. During the harvest months, the roads leading to Tallahassee were white with cotton bales hauled in mule wagons. The town itself was filled with planters and their families, who arrived in fancy carriages to trade their sale vouchers for the goods they needed on the plantation. While the women were purchasing clothing and household goods, the men often went to the slave pens to examine the latest arrivals from the port of St. Marks.

Plantation society had grown accustomed to slavery and, far from being shocked at it, considered slavery to be a normal condition of Southern life. The main auction house was at Jefferson and Monroe Streets (now the northeast corner of the capitol grounds), and here John Lloyd blandly announced that he attended to all kinds of sales, including "Real Estate, Negroes, Cotton, Furniture, Horses, Mules," etc. While the wealthy landowners were buying and selling blacks as if they were chattel, their wives could go next door to Clark's Fashionable Clothing Emporium and purchase the pretty frocks they would wear to the upcoming society balls.

The white inhabitants glibly made excuses for slavery: they claimed that their prosperity depended on it; that it had always existed and was a natural institution; that it was best for the Negroes; and that there was no way to change it, for to release the slaves from bondage would let loose an illiterate, untrained mass of people who would doom Southern white civilization as well as cause the blacks' own economic ruin.

Many others observers were not so tolerant of slavery. One of these was Frederick Law Olmsted, a young New Yorker who rode across the South on horseback and wrote his experiences in *A Journey in the Back Country, 1853–1854* (reprinted in 1970). Although Olmsted's travels did not take him to Florida, his observations clearly pertained to that state as well.

The slaves were herded into the fields long before dawn, Olmsted found. The men did the plowing, the women the hoeing, and the young children carried water pitchers and did other errands. They labored the entire day without rest, except for the noon meal, though they were often forced to work while eating, and they would continue working until it was so dark that they could no longer see. Then it was back to their one-room shacks, where they would prepare dinner before retiring early so as to be ready for the following day. They had Sunday off, but it was not a time for leisure: clothes had to be mended, cabins had to be cleaned, and work had to be done in their modest family gardens, as well as innumerable other tedious chores. Shirkers were treated harshly:

> The whip was evidently in constant use. . . .There were no rules on the subject that I learned; the overseers and drivers punished the Negroes whenever they deemed it necessary, and in such manner, and with such severity, as they thought fit. . . . "If you don't work faster," or "If you don't work better," or "If you don't recollect what I tell you, I will have you flogged," are threats which I have often heard. "Why, sir" [one overseer told Olmsted], "I wouldn't mind killing a [Negro] more than I would a dog."

### From Slave to Free to Slave Again:
### The Tragic Story of Nancy Proctor

Nancy was a slave girl belonging to the Mary Chandler family, who owned a plantation near Tallahassee. Evidently Nancy accompanied Mrs. Chandler on shopping trips to Tallahassee, for here she caught the eye of George Proctor, a free black man who was one of the town's foremost building contractors. George wanted to marry Nancy, but to do so he had to purchase her from the Chandlers—the sale price being $1,300. George arranged to pay $450 in cash to Mrs. Chandler, who agreed to accept the rest in the form of a note payable with interest in one year. As security for the note George was forced to mortgage Nancy herself!

In 1839 George and Nancy were wed in the St. Johns Episcopal Church. The two were happy together, and soon Nancy became pregnant with her first child. But the couple's joy was tempered by the fact that when the year was up George was unable to pay off his wife's mortgage. So Mrs. Chandler brought suit to recover her property. In addition to Nancy, Mrs. Chandler now claimed the baby, whose value she placed at $1,250!

Fortunately for George and Nancy, a friend apparently took over the note and its payments, so the foreclosure was postponed, though presumably not George's obligation to continue paying interest on his mortgaged wife.

During the next ten years the couple had five more children. Although George continued building houses, one of which, the Knott House, was one of Tallahassee's finest, he was never able to save enough money to pay off Nancy's mortgage—to say nothing of what he owed on their children. In desperation he joined the gold rush of 1849, hoping to make his fortune in California. After a tearful farewell, he set out.

Nancy and the children expected to hear almost momentarily that George had struck it rich, but the months passed and there was no word. Then it was more than a year. What had happened? Was he dead? Or had he just deserted them? They were never to know. He utterly vanished.

But the debt remained. With six hungry children, Nancy was unable even to meet the interest payments. Finally the friend must have decided he could no longer foot the bill, for the note ended up with Mrs. Chandler, who instituted foreclosure proceedings once more. This time there was no question what would happen. Nancy and the children were simply property, the same as cattle or a cotton crop.

They were probably held in the Tallahassee slave pens, for we know that they were soon put on the auction block. Here Nancy not only was forced back into slavery but had to watch as her four girls and two boys were individually sold.

However, Nancy and her children survived the ordeal and were eventually set free. Nancy continued to live in Tallahassee, where she probably lived to see her son John elected to the Florida legislature in 1872.

### The Civil War Comes to Tallahassee

Not all Southerners regarded slavery as a sacred institution that was to be protected at all costs. One of those people most opposed to secession was Ellen Call's father, Richard. Richard had given up his position as territorial governor in 1844, hoping to be elected Florida's first state governor when statehood was granted and an impressive new capitol constructed the following year. However, such was not the case. So Richard retired to the Grove, his large estate next to the governor's mansion, content to become an elder statesman. He was fiercely loyal to the Union, and when Florida declared secession in 1861, he was furious. Meeting a legislator outside the capitol, Richard Call, now an old man with less than two years to live, waved his big walking stick and roared, "You have opened the gates of hell, from which shall flow the curses of the damned!"

He was right, for the state suffered immensely from the federal naval blockade. With Union forces in control of Jacksonville, Pensacola, and the St. Johns River, Tallahassee was so isolated that the surrender of General Lee on April 9, 1865, was not known until two weeks later. Even so, wartime governor John Milton had long realized that the cause was lost; a week before the surrender, he had rigged his carriage, driven with his wife and son to his plantation outside Marianna, and killed himself there with a shot to the head.

In May, Union occupation troops marched into Tallahassee, and the Stars and Stripes once more fluttered atop the capitol. Ironically, the formal announcement of the Emancipation Proclamation was made from the steps of the Knott House, built by George Proctor.

### Touring Tallahassee

The old 1845 capitol still stands—although it is dwarfed by the spectacular twenty-two-story governmental tower built in 1978. Once the tower was operative the old building was restored, and it is now open to the public. The former chambers of the state supreme court, the senate, and the house of representatives are much as they were in years gone by. Many of the offices have been converted into museums, each devoted to a different period in the building's long history. There are exhibits on William Duval, Richard Call, and John Milton.

Tours are given of the new capitol, where the modern legislative chambers stand in plush contrast to those of the old capitol. A

*The pillared capitol where rabid secessionists withdrew Florida from the Union in 1861 is dwarfed by the twenty-two-story shaft of the new capitol, built in 1978.*

splendid vista of Tallahassee can be gained at the building's top, and an excellent view of the old capitol is offered from the snack bar on the tenth floor.

The 1882 Leon County Courthouse stood at Monroe and Jefferson, facing the old capitol. Recently the ramshackle edifice was replaced by a modern, glass-clad courthouse. But hardly was this building completed than mockingbirds began crashing into the reflective windows. The solution came not from state-of-the-art technology but simply from hawk cutouts stuck onto the glass.

The famed City Hotel was at Pensacola and Adams Streets—a site now occupied by the north wing of the new capitol, but which then was across Adams from the Square. Lizzie Brown's father, owner of the hotel, became so well known as a genial host that the people elected him governor in 1848. Lizzie herself developed into a great beauty, and former Governor Duval even wrote her a love poem.

Immediately west of the new capitol is the impressive 1948 Supreme Court Building. One block farther west is the Gray Building, home of the Museum of Florida History, with marvelous displays of everything from Spanish gold to a nine-foot-high mastodon skeleton.

The southeast side of town has many interesting locations. The parking lot at Bloxham and Gaines Streets is at the foot of a little ravine through which a stream once tumbled before railroad tracks put an end to it. This was Lizzie Brown's homeward path while the pouting Seminole, Tiger Tail, followed her as he demanded her red hat-plume.

Gaines turns into Myers Park Drive as it ascends the hill. The Duval family, including saucy Elizabeth, had their home on a site now occupied by tennis courts. Myers Park Drive weaves around to end at Lafayette Street. A block east is De Soto Park Drive, leading to excavations that are uncovering artifacts from the Spanish explorer's campsite. Continuing east, Lafayette merges with the old St. Augustine Road, down which you can enjoy a dreamy excursion beneath moss-canopied live oaks, along the route taken a century and a half ago by Ellen Call and her partying friends.

If you enjoy canopied roads, Tallahassee and Leon County have three hundred miles of them. One of the most interesting is Miccosukee Road, which runs northeast from the heart of town. During the antebellum era, nearly three dozen plantations used this route to and from Tallahassee. A highlight along the way is the Goodwood Plantation, at 1600, whose grand manor was built in the

1840s. Ellen Call and her friends were once guests of the first proprietor, Hardy Croom. Here they enjoyed fresh strawberries and cream on his flower-covered porch. After Croom and his family were lost at sea during a hurricane, his brother ran the plantation with the forced labor of more than two hundred slaves.

Returning to Capitol Square, go west on Pensacola Street to Florida State University. The site was once known as Gallows Hill, popular for hangings. Just before the Civil War, the gallows were replaced by a women's college. Not until after World War II did Florida State take in males.

A short distance south of the city center on Martin Luther King Jr. Boulevard is Florida A & M University. Founded in 1887 with just fifteen students, it now boasts more than ten thousand, nearly 90 percent of whom are black. It often surpasses Harvard University in the enrollment of National Achievement Scholars. The Black Archives building, impressive with its four Ionic columns, was once the Carnegie Library. Within, there are displays relating to the African American experience in America. Included are slave chains and a Ku Klux Klan robe.

To explore the north side of Tallahassee, take Monroe Street (US 27) two blocks beyond Capitol Square to Park Avenue, originally a two-hundred-foot area cleared of trees to prevent surprise Seminole

*The Knott House, one of Tallahassee's oldest and most handsome buildings, was constructed around 1843 by free black man George Proctor.*

attacks. It didn't work, however, for worshipers in the still-standing Presbyterian Church, built in 1835, sometimes had to barricade themselves within until help arrived. Picturesque homes and buildings abound along the avenue. One of these, the famed Knott House, built by free black man George Proctor, is at 301. Indeed, Park Avenue has so many vintage homes, churches, and other buildings that the entire area has been put on the National Register of Historic Places.

The governor's mansion is eight blocks north of Park, at Brevard and Adams. Built in 1957 and modeled after Andrew Jackson's hermitage, it is open only periodically to the public.

Next to the governor's mansion is the large estate known as the Grove. Mostly hidden by trees, the spacious home was built by Richard Keith Call between 1828 and 1836. His daughter, Ellen, resided in it during her long life and here wrote *Florida Breezes.* During her later years she was barely able to meet the mortgage payments. She died in 1904, and the home is now owned by the state and will eventually be open to the public.

The San Luis Mission is not far from the Grove. Drive west on Brevard Street to the linkup with US 90 (Tennessee Street), and continue west a short distance to White Drive, where there is a sign pointing north to the mission.

The old church foundations have been found, and the site is being further excavated. Some of the artifacts discovered during the diggings are on display in the 1938 Greek Revival Visitor Center. Here artists have provided large color sketches of what the mission and nearby fort must have looked like.

Lake Jackson Mounds State Archaeological Site is off Crowder Road, two miles north of I-10 via US 27. There are wooden steps leading up several mounds and many interpretive plaques.

St. Marks, Tallahassee's old port and a historic town in its own right, can be reached by way of a twenty-mile drive down Florida 363.

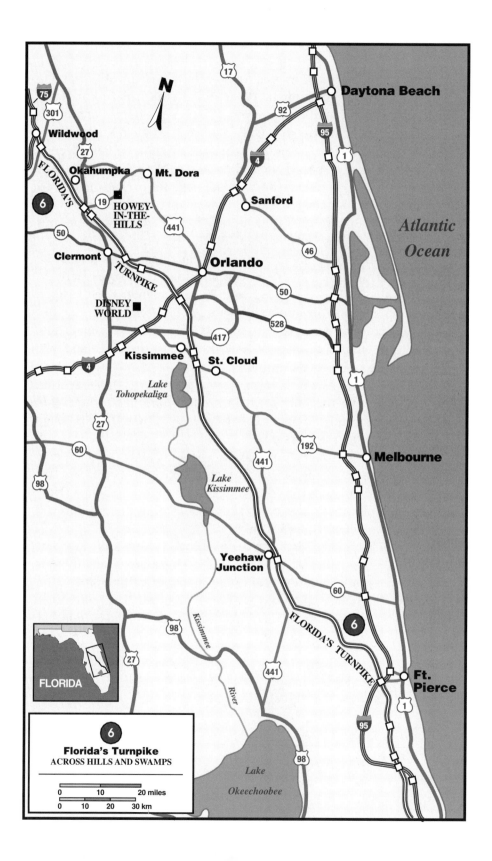

N

75
301
Wildwood
27
Okahumpka
FLORIDA'S
19
Mt. Dora
HOWEY-
IN-THE-
HILLS
441
50
Clermont
TURNPIKE
DISNEY
WORLD
Kissimmee
4
St. Cloud
Lake
Tohopekaliga
27
60
98

6

17
Daytona Beach
92
95
4
1
Sanford
46

Atlantic
Ocean

Orlando
50
528
417

192
441
Melbourne
1

Lake
Kissimmee

Yeehaw
Junction
60
Kissimmee
98
FLORIDA'S TURNPIKE
6
441
River
Ft.
Pierce
1
95
98

FLORIDA

6
**Florida's Turnpike**
ACROSS HILLS AND SWAMPS

0    10    20 miles
0    10    20    30 km

Lake
Okeechobee

# ≈ 6 ≈
# Florida's Turnpike
## ACROSS HILLS AND SWAMPS

Florida had long realized that the state's prosperity was directly related to its transportation facilities. Thus, when the automobile came into popularity, Florida was among the first to begin work on a network of good roads. The most important early road was the Dixie Highway, which ran from the Midwest to Miami. The Florida section of the Dixie Highway was all of nine feet wide and paved with bricks, making it a minor wonder, and it generally took the route now followed by US 1.

The primitive Florida roads were adequate until after World War II, when the increase of tourism required an entirely new type of road system—one that provided wide lanes and conveyed traffic past unimportant byways and the congestion of city streets. To create such a highway, Florida's Turnpike Authority was established in 1953.

The first turnpike segment, 118 miles from Miami to Fort Pierce, was completed in 1957 along a route that was acceptable to nearly everyone. But the route of the second segment was a matter of much debate. Many people assumed it would continue up the East Coast. But after pressure by influential Orlando citizens, the turnpike was bent toward the central part of the state to terminate at a virtually unknown locale called Wildwood. (It was several years before the I-75 interchange would link the turnpike with a nationwide system.)

The second turnpike segment, completed in 1964, played a crucial role in the development of Orlando and central Florida, for that very year Walt Disney flew over the state seeking a suitable location for the huge theme park he was planning. When he saw the turnpike crossing I-4, which itself was in the process of completion, he decided then and there that this deserted area was the place to build, since it had cheap land and good transportation.

# Wildwood — I-4
### 49 miles

## Wildwood

Wildwood received its name before its people. The story goes that a telegraph construction crew ran out of wire, and when the supply office asked where the men were, they looked around and replied, "in the middle of a wild wood."

Recently the town was the locale of a bizarre scheme. To take advantage of the highly visible site at the head of the turnpike, a group of speculators proposed a fifty-story pyramid, which would have been the second-tallest skyscraper in the state. The purpose of the hulking pyramid was to inter 1.3 million dead people! The idea was that many tourists would find it an ideal place for their deceased parents, for they could stop off and pay their respects while not taking much time out of their vacation. There was one problem, however. Sumter County had a two-story maximum height limit and refused to raise it by a mere forty-eight stories. So the project ended in the morgue.

## Okahumpka

Okahumpka, a few miles down the Pike from Wildwood, has one of those strangely distinctive Indian names that appears so often in Florida. *Oka* means "water" and *humpka* means "deep." The deep water refers to a spring whose source is lost within the porous limestone that underlies nearly all of peninsular Florida. Early American settlers called the bubbling water Bugg Spring, after a man who drowned in it. Eventually, though, the villagers concluded that the Indian name, awkward as it was, sounded better than the English one. Hence, Okahumpka. The spring is now part of a navy installation where divers use its mysterious depths to perfect their skills, but it is closed to the public.

# Howey-in-the-Hills

Howey-in-the-Hills is six miles north of the turnpike on Florida 19. It was founded by William Howey, who began buying land in 1914. Although he was a relatively young man of thirty-eight, Howey had already experienced successes and failures enough for several ordinary lifetimes. While still in his early twenties, he owned three insurance companies in his home state of Illinois. By the age of twenty-nine he had operated and closed an auto manufacturing plant, his total production being seven Howey cars. A year later he was off to Mexico, where he bought land for settlement by Americans. Although the Mexican Revolution of 1907 put a dismal end to that escapade, it did not dampen Howey's enthusiasm for financial adventure.

Howey arrived in Florida in 1908, at which time he accumulated a great deal of acreage around Lake Wales. This included Iron Mountain, the scenic prominence where Edward Bok would build his lovely bell tower two decades later. Howey sold out for a nice profit, then took his jackpot up to Lake Harris, where he bought land for eight dollars an acre, planted a smattering of forty-eight citrus trees per acre (modern groves run well over four hundred), and sold each "grove" for up to a thousand dollars an acre. Needless to say, the gold rolled in.

During the fabulous 1920s Howey built the seventy-five-room Hotel Floridian as well as the Floridian Country Club, which boasted a fine nine-hole golf course. Visitors came in droves—up to ten thousand a year. In addition to receiving huge profits from his hotel, country club, and land sales, Howey squeezed juicy profits from his private orange groves, which covered thousands of acres south and east from the town, of which he was mayor, naturally.

With his diverse sources of income, Howey was one of the few Florida developers not hurt by the bust of 1926. Indeed, in 1927 he built a mansion across from the country club. In it, he and his beautiful wife, Grace, had gala parties—once even hosting the entire New York City Opera Company. The living room was spacious enough for a full orchestra to play for Grace, who loved to dance.

Billy Howey, with his gift of gab, was a natural for politics. He revamped the Republican Party and ran for governor in 1928. Although he was publicly a strong supporter of Prohibition, he could bend his elbow with the best of them and even had a secret liquor vault in his

*The mansion of flamboyant William Howey is deserted now. Entire orchestras once performed for gala parties here.*

mansion. Despite losing the election in that year and again in 1932, he got double the votes of his Republican predecessors.

Howey passed away in 1938, at age sixty-two. About his only disappointment in life was that he and Grace never had children of their own, and of the two daughters they adopted, one died while still young. Grace lived on until 1982.

Although the Hotel Floridian was recently destroyed, it went down in a grand explosion after being doused with three hundred gallons of gasoline and filmed for use in Hulk Hogan's *Lethal Weapon 3*. Billy would have loved it.

The two-story Howey mansion still stands at Florida 19 and Citrus Avenue, where it is a decaying dowager crying for help; it's not open to the public.

Across Florida 19 is the Mission Inn Golf and Tennis Resort, which is a major draw throughout the region and the nation. Although Howey's smallish original building has been demoted to the Group Sales Department, next to it has arisen a large complex of Spanish-style buildings that include 187 deluxe hotel rooms and three public restaurants. There are also two eighteen-hole golf courses set amid the soft rolling hills of Florida's Central Ridge. One of the courses, Howey's own El Campeon, built in 1926, is not only one of the Southeast's oldest, but is rated among the top twenty of Florida's more than eleven hundred links.

Mission Inn has ten-seat pontoon boats that cruise nearby Lake Harris. The docking area is off Florida 19, a mile north of the main buildings.

# Mount Dora

From Howey-in-the-Hills take Florida 19 twelve miles north to Tavares, then 500A east into Mount Dora. Don't bother looking for a mountain, because in Florida even a low lakeside bluff, as is the case with Mount Dora, serves quite nicely.

The "Dora" part of the town's name dates back to a pioneer lady who lived here during the Second Seminole War. When a troop of tired solders came to her house, she gave them food and permitted them to camp on her grounds. Surveyors later named the lake in her honor.

### A Pioneer's Amazing Saga

One of Mount Dora's earliest settlers was J. P. Donnelly. When his doctor recommended Florida for his health in 1879, the twenty-year-old youth migrated to Jacksonville, where he signed on a St. Johns River steamer and worked his way to Sanford. At Sanford he heard about opportunities in Mount Dora, a day's tramp due west. So he jumped ship, bought a twenty-five-cent compass, and set out through the trackless forest.

Perhaps he should have gotten a better compass, for he had not reached the town by nightfall and the next morning emerged at Lake Apopka, south of his objective. The route to Mount Dora lay along a six-mile stream and a two-mile little lake. As his feet were now raw with blisters, he built himself a raft using an ax he borrowed at a turpentine camp. Then, with a board as a paddle, he set out down the narrow waterway, accompanied by almost every mosquito within biting distance. Eventually the bugs became so bad that he jumped into the water to escape them, pushing the raft before him. This worked fine until he realized that a large snake was swimming merrily along beside him. With the choice of a snake or the mosquitoes, he stayed with the snake, which soon went off on business of its own.

At last he found the entrance to Lake Dora. The channel here was shallow, perfect for the host of alligators dozing in the dappled sunshine. Back on the raft for safety, he inched past the huge beasts. Suddenly one rose beneath him, upsetting the raft and sending him into the water. As the gator lunged for him, he grabbed its snout and held it shut while man and beast thrashed in the water. Then he jammed his paddle into the gator's throat and ran for Lake Dora. Once in the lake, he swam the rest of the way to town.

Mount Dora was fortunate that Donnelly survived, for he became the town's first mayor. It was he who laid out most of the streets and who provided the town's central park, which he named for his beautiful wife, Annie. In 1893 Donnelly constructed the fanciest home in town, a three-story mansion with a garish gingerbread fringe. Painted brilliant white, it bespoke of the man's character: flamboyant and gregarious, a doer and a builder.

Over the years, Donnelly became a lovable character as he bounced around town in his 1920s Model T Ford or took guests out on Lake Dora in his private launch. In 1929, at age seventy, he threw the decade's most boisterous birthday party at the Lakeside Inn. He died the following year.

### Touring Mount Dora

Mount Dora is very proud of both its historical buildings and its remoteness from modern city life. This remoteness was solidified in the late 1950s, when the federal government made plans to modernize US 441, which meandered through town. Mount Dora residents insisted the new road be routed outside town. Though business suffered initially, most observers are convinced that this act saved the town.

The Donnelly home, now a Masonic Lodge on Donnelly Street near Fifth Avenue, is still Mount Dora's centerpiece. Annie Donnelly Park is across the street. Yet there is far more to see, for almost the entire downtown is a museum of old buildings, most of which, it seems, sell antiques.

The historical society museum has taken over the old city jail, in the quaint alley connecting Fifth and Sixth Avenues. The chamber of commerce is in the former railroad depot, at 341 Alexander Street.

Perhaps Mount Dora's most cherished building is the Lakeside Inn, at 100 Alexander Street. Completed in 1883, it was the brainchild of a triumvirate, one of whose members was the dynamic Annie Stone, who at twenty-seven had been deserted by her first husband and who later married J. P. Donnelly. In 1924 the hotel came into the hands of a group that included Charles Edgerton, whose son, Richard, managed the operation until he sold out in 1980. Among the inn's many notable guests, possibly the oddest was Calvin Coolidge, the dour

*Mount Dora's first mayor, J. P. Donnelly, built this ostentatious Victorian home in 1893.*

New Englander who had just retired from the presidency. When he walked to church, he insisted his wife keep five steps behind him out of respect.

Modern guests staying at the hotel or eating at the highly rated restaurant enjoy a fine view of Lake Dora.

### FLORIDA'S TURNPIKE
# I-4—Fort Pierce
**106 miles**

As Florida's Turnpike approaches I-4, it enters the environs of Orlando and the theme parks, attractions that are covered in chapter 1. Then, south of Orlando, the turnpike passes Florida 528, also called the Bee Line Expressway, which leads to Cape Canaveral, fifty-two miles east. Continuing south on Florida's Turnpike leads you into the Kissimmee area.

# Kissimmee and St. Cloud

Kissimmee (kis-SIM-mee) is best known as a sleep-over for Disney World visitors. However, the area has a long history, predating even the Seminoles. The Ais tribe made this part of Florida their domain—before wars and European diseases brought their extinction. To the Ais, *kissimmee* meant the "long water," presumably referring to the lake upon which the modern town is situated.

The settlement of St. Cloud is six miles east of Kissimmee. For a time the two communities' histories were intertwined by the career of a most unusual man, Hamilton Disston.

## The Doomed Visionary

Hamilton Disston, who had made a fortune as a tool manufacturer in Pennsylvania, loved Florida for the fishing. Often during the 1870s he would stop in Sanford to chat with the town's wealthy founder, Henry Sanford, about the opportunities in this virgin land. So when the state ran into financial difficulties and the governor approached Disston for help, he agreed to purchase nearly a third of southern Florida for $1 million. His down payment of $200,000 saved the state from its creditors.

Although the land was mostly swamp, Disston was confident that he could build a chain of canals that would drain it and permit the growth of such crops as sugarcane. In 1882 his steam dredge began

*Hamilton Disston, tragic developer of the 1880s and 1890s.*
—Florida State Archives

operations that eventually opened Lake Okeechobee to the Gulf of Mexico via a breakthrough of the Caloosahatchee River at Moore Haven. Then Disston, making his headquarters at Kissimmee, began to dig navigable drainage canals connecting nearly two dozen lakes of various sizes to the Kissimmee River. Thereupon he deepened the Kissimmee, so boats could reach Lake Okeechobee and from there link with oceangoing ships at Fort Myers.

As the land around Kissimmee began to dry out, Disston planted sugarcane in the rich former muck. The crop thrived, and many of his plants reached a height of fifteen feet. He also built a large mill at his St. Cloud plantation, located almost precisely at the turnpike exit. Samples of his sugar won first prize at an important New Orleans exposition in 1884. Soon he had some thirty cane varieties under observation at his St. Cloud experimental station. He also grew rice, potatoes, peaches, and vegetables of all kinds.

When prosperity came, Disston opened two hotels on East Lake Tohopekaliga. Among his many prominent visitors was John Jacob Astor and his bride. Disston, himself, enjoyed staying aboard his own luxury yacht. That way he could distance himself from his four hundred tenant farmers, mainly immigrant Italians imported from Tampa during the harvest season.

*Portions of Hamilton Disston's 1880s canal can be seen from Sexton Park near Kissimmee.*

But the end came swiftly. Disston paid less and less attention to operations. Then cane borers appeared, followed by several years of excessive rain, which overextended his canals. Next there was the financial panic of 1893. Finally Florida was hit by disastrous freezes in 1894 and 1895. Disston was ruined. He returned to Philadelphia in 1896. Then one evening in April, Disston filled his bathtub, eased into the warm water, held a pistol to his head, and pulled the trigger.

Almost everything Hamilton Disston did has disappeared. However, you can drive along St. Cloud's beautiful Lakeshore Boulevard through what was once Disston's plantation, now occupied by homes and a long waterfront park.

To see one of his canals, take US 192/441 to Sexton Park, which is about half a mile east of the turnpike interchange. The old canal is choked by duckweed and water hyacinths, and only with difficulty can you picture it during Disston's times: twelve feet wide, six feet deep, with free-flowing water that carried the cargo boats Disston dreamed would increase his fortune and make his name known through the ages.

## The Kissimmee Valley

Beyond St. Cloud, the turnpike crosses a broad canal of the South Florida Water Management District. The waterway runs along much the same route as an old Disston canal.

The turnpike has now entered an enormous wetland drained by the Kissimmee River. It is bounded by the Citrus Ridge, twenty-five miles west, and by low Atlantic beach ridges the same distance east. This country is so sparsely populated that for the entire ninety miles between St. Cloud and Fort Pierce there is only one exit. It is a world unto itself. The land is so flat that you can see a circling buzzard miles away. The landscape passes endlessly by: a succession of meadows of grasses and saw palmetto interspersed with pine forests. At intervals are large clumps of cypress growing in domes. The reason for the domes is that cypress, loving water, thrive in shallow sinkhole depressions—the taller cypress growing in the center. Don't be concerned if in the winter the cypress appear dead: they will bear bright green foliage in the spring.

## The Kissimmee Controversy

Because this environment is apparently so inhospitable to humans, it is strange that it has roused so much controversy between conservationists and sportsmen. The problem is the Kissimmee River.

Left alone, the Kissimmee, which is around fifteen miles west of the turnpike, would meander sleepily across the landscape until it found its sluggish destiny in Lake Okeechobee. Hamilton Disston tried to change it in the 1880s, but he had no long-term effect. It was different when the Army Corps of Engineers got into the act in the 1960s. The corps decided the Kissimmee should be disciplined the military way. So they routed the river into a three-hundred-foot-wide, thirty-foot-deep channel that was as straight as a rifle barrel. Thus the 103-mile Kissimmee disappeared, and in its place appeared a fifty-six-mile ditch called Canal 38.

Boaters and fishermen loved Canal 38, because they could speed along it to their favorite haunts on Okeechobee or even continue to Fort Myers on the gulf or Stuart on the Atlantic. Conservationists, however, were horrified, for they claimed hundreds of species of birds, animals, and plants were becoming endangered. So they began agitating to bring the river back.

But it is easier to destroy than to re-create. There were river bends to cut, meanders to restore, watersheds to plan. It would be the largest such program ever attempted in the history of the world. The cost would approach $1 billion! When sportsmen were told about meetings to discuss the river's restoration, few came, for, as one told a reporter, the whole idea was "preposterous": the money was needed for schools and housing, not to save wood storks or something called snail kites.

Yet the "preposterous" bill was passed, and in 1994 work started on a thousand-foot experimental section just north of Lake Okeechobee. If the restoration proves successful, the main job will continue over a fifteen-year period. But by then, who knows? The boaters may have gotten enough support to begin efforts to restore Canal 38!

# Yeehaw Junction

*A Must-Visit for Name-Droppers*

The Seminoles called this desolate area "Yeehaw" after the wolves that stalked their prey across the wetland prairie. Later, when Henry Flagler in his waning years decided to run a rail line from near Titusville through the deserted interior to Lake Okeechobee, Yeehaw became a watering station for his steam-driven locomotives.

*Yeehaw Junction's Desert Inn, built in the 1930s, has actually made the National Register of Historic Places!*

But the Okeechobee Division was never successful and, after it was abandoned, the minuscule settlement took on a more descriptive name, Jackass Junction, after the local breeders. Jackass Junction's main activity centered around the filling station/cafe built where US 441 and Florida 60 crossed. By the mid-1930s some tourist cabins had been added.

Locals may have thought Jackass Junction had now reached its pinnacle, but when the turnpike came through in the late 1950s, a refueling place was needed, hence the name Yeehaw was resurrected and soon a thrilling array of service stations graced the turnoff.

Those who scorn a stop at Yeehaw Junction will miss a visit to the weather-worn filling station at US 441 and Florida 60. Not only does the station have a cafe/bar typical of the 1930s, but some ancient motel units still exist. What is more, the Desert Inn, as it is called, actually made the National Register of Historic Places in 1994.

People still disdaining Yeehaw Junction should heed the remarks of a sophisticated traveler: "Anyone can say he's been to Paris. But to Yeehaw Junction? Try dropping *that* name at a party!"

Five miles beyond Yeehaw Junction is the Fort Drum Plaza. Shortly, the turnpike bends gently toward the east, and a few citrus groves announce civilization is beginning. As the highway approaches Fort Pierce, it intertwines with I-95 from the north.

## FLORIDA'S TURNPIKE
# Fort Pierce — Miami
### 118 miles

Florida's Turnpike and I-95 run on parallel routes to Miami. The turnpike is a toll road and the interstate is free. But I-95 is far more crowded, especially around rush hour. You'll have to make your own choice which to take. The locations they pass are identical. They are described in chapter 13 and include such colorful and historical cities as Palm Beach, Boca Raton, and Fort Lauderdale.

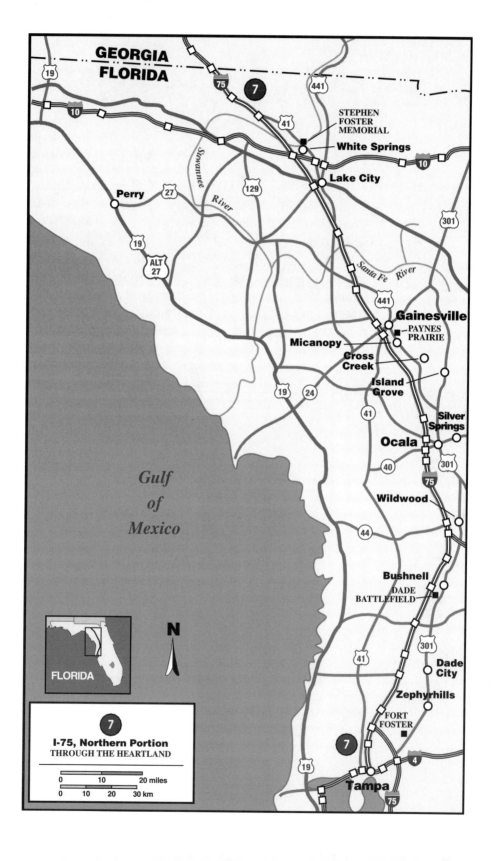

GEORGIA
FLORIDA

19

75

7

441

41

STEPHEN
FOSTER
MEMORIAL

White Springs

10

10

Lake City

Perry

27

*Suwannee*

129

*River*

19

ALT
27

301

*Santa Fe River*

441

Gainesville

PAYNES
PRAIRIE

Micanopy

Cross
Creek

Island
Grove

Silver
Springs

19

24

41

Ocala

40

301

*Gulf*
*of*
*Mexico*

75

Wildwood

44

Bushnell

DADE
BATTLEFIELD

301

Dade
City

41

Zephyrhills

N

FORT
FOSTER

FLORIDA

7

7

19

4

Tampa

75

7

**I-75, Northern Portion**
THROUGH THE HEARTLAND

0        10        20 miles

0    10    20    30 km

# ≈ 7 ≈
# I-75, Northern Portion
## THROUGH THE HEARTLAND

I-75 is the gateway to Florida from the Midwest as well as from most southern states. It runs almost the entire length of the state as it skirts Gainesville in the north and Tampa on the gulf coast to its end just above Miami on the Atlantic. It is Florida's longest expressway—about five hundred miles—and as such passes through areas with a tremendous variety of geographical and historical interest. Accordingly, I have divided the highway into three sections.

This chapter on the northern portion, "Through the Heartland," describes old-time Florida—the land of farmers, timbermen, and horse and cattle ranchers. The land is rolling and often forested. This is a fertile area, and during part of the year the roadsides are pink tapestries of phlox, which the state began planting in 1963 as part of its wildflower program.

The northern area was the haunt of the Seminoles after they had been expelled from the area around Tallahassee by Andrew Jackson as a result of the First Seminole War. The Indians' spirit had not been broken, however, and under Osceola they turned this area into a bloody cauldron during the late 1830s. This Second Seminole War became the longest and most costly of all America's Indian conflicts.

Along the southwestern portion of I-75, described in chapter 8, "To Paradise Beaches," the winters are milder than in upper Florida, for this area is generally below the frost line. Many famous people have been lured here by the weather and the beaches. The Ringling Brothers found Sarasota ideal for their famed circus's winter quarters. Both Thomas Edison and Henry Ford spent their winters in Fort Myers. Today, vacationers still love the white sands of the gulf towns.

In the southeastern, "Alligator Alley" portion of I-75, which you can read about in chapter 9, "Through Cypress and Saw Grass," the expressway turns east to cross the awesome Everglades. Since there are no historical turnoffs, you may opt to take the Tamiami Trail (US 41) as an alternative route replete with Miccosukee villages, airboat rides into Everglades National Park, and a fascinating construction saga dating back to the early twentieth century.

I-75

# Georgia Line—Florida's Turnpike

140 miles

South of the Georgia border, I-75 passes through a gently undulating countryside. The deepest bedrock was formed during the early Paleozoic era, when Africa collided with North America and a line of volcanoes rose in a wide belt from St. Augustine through Ocala to Cedar Key and beyond.

During later eons, Florida rested beneath the sea, and the shells of countless mollusks accumulated in a thick sediment. When the sea retreated, the sediment turned into the limestone that lies close to the surface throughout northern Florida. This limestone forms the basis of a rich soil that supports corn as well as pastures for horses and cattle, all visible from the highway. It also allowed cotton plantations to flourish during the antebellum decades—a period immortalized by composer Stephen Foster. The plantations, dependent on slave labor, were largely abandoned after the Civil War.

Although this section has a feeling of being bypassed by progress, there is a special flavor here. In a time when 70 percent of Floridians were born someplace else, it is a pleasure to hear the native twang in the towns off the expressway.

## White Springs

*Stephen Foster: A Study in Contradictions*

At exit 84, Florida 136 leads east three miles to the village of White Springs. Here the Stephen Foster State Folk Culture Center consists of a twenty-story carillon tower that chimes out Foster melodies, a museum with dioramas illustrating the settings of many Foster songs, and a craft square where artisans create rustic goods for sale.

*The Suwannee River at the Stephen Foster Memorial in White Springs. Before the Civil War steamboats transporting cotton plied these waters.*

Although the Florida legislature designated "Old Folks at Home" ("Suwannee River") the state song in 1935, it was not until 1950 that the park opened.

There are many oddities about the site, the song, and about Foster's life itself. Foster never visited Florida and probably had no idea what the Suwannee looked like. The original song lyrics eulogized South Carolina's Pee Dee River, until Foster and his brother stumbled on the more melodious Suwannee in an atlas. Far from the gentle sentimentalist, an image with which we have grown so familiar, Foster was moody and unstable. His wife, Jane, could not get along with him, and they were constantly separating. Not even Foster's beautiful love song to her, "I Dream of Jeanie with the Light Brown Hair," could induce a permanent reconciliation.

Born in Pittsburgh in 1826, Foster spent some of his formative years in Cincinnati, across the Ohio River from slave state Kentucky. From local blacks he heard sketchy tales of plantation life. He adapted and sweetened these stories in his songs of the antebellum South.

Foster's songs were immensely popular during the 1850s. But, though royalties came in, he never learned to handle money, and toward the end of his life he became overwhelmed with debt. By then he had turned to alcohol, to the detriment of his composing. In 1860 he moved to New York City, where he lived alone in a run-down boardinghouse. Growing ever more lonely and despondent, he died in 1864, burned-out at the age of thirty-seven.

Although Foster had little direct influence on Florida's history, his importance lies in his portraits of plantation life. Foster's picture of slaves singing happily in the cotton fields helped publicize the false idea that they were contented with their lot in life. His descriptions became part of a mythology that enabled Southern whites to justify their repressive system. They also influenced millions of white Northerners and helped account for the fact that far more Americans voted for Stephen Douglas and two other presidential candidates in 1860 than for antislavery Lincoln. It was only because he captured the electoral college that Lincoln became president.

The village of White Springs has some history of its own. Atop a Suwannee River bluff, it marked an important stop on the ancient Spanish trail connecting St. Augustine with missions all the way to Tallahassee. The spring waters had long been sacred to Native Americans, who believed they healed warriors' wounds. During the Civil War the area became known as Rebel's Refuge—a place to which many plantation owners fled to escape Union forays.

# Lake City

Hernando de Soto, his army, and his chained Indian captives trudged through the Lake City vicinity in 1539. Directed by local tribesmen, they turned west along a route now followed by I-10 to spend their first winter on the site of Tallahassee. When Americans founded the town three centuries later, they called it Alligator, after a Seminole chief. But the name discouraged new settlers, and a change was decided on. One impish legislator moved to substitute Crocodile, but Lake City was finally adopted.

## The Santa Fe Missions

Twenty miles south of Lake City, I-75 crosses the Santa Fe River, the name meaning "holy faith" to the gentle Franciscan friars who founded several missions nearby. The Santa Fe missions thrived during much of the seventeenth century but were destroyed by English and

Creek raiders from the north between 1702 and 1706. Their existence has become a virtually forgotten period of Florida history.

For people who would like to get a small feeling for the mission era, get off I-75 at exit 81 just south of Lake City. Ten miles south on Florida 47 is Ichetucknee Springs, "the pond of the beaver" to Native Americans, where seventy-two-degree spring water gushes for six miles through an oak-and-pine forest to join the Santa Fe River. Franciscan holy men and their Indian converts once lived here, for the remains of an early Spanish mission have been found along the stream. It is now a state park where visitors can enjoy hiking trails and picnic areas. Swimming, too, is permitted.

Now continue down Florida 47 a few miles to US 27, then seven miles southeast on 27 to the Santa Fe River Bridge. Here canoes can be rented for an easy expedition along one of Florida's prettiest and least-spoiled rivers.

The village of High Springs is just beyond the river. It is a fascinating little world in itself. Once an important part of the Henry Plant railroad empire, and later of the Atlantic Coast Line, it had repair shops and tobacco warehouses. Today the depot and the two-story opera house, both nicely restored, as well as many other vintage homes and buildings, remind visitors of bygone days. But the village is a vital place, with its antique stores, specialty shops, and quaint restaurants.

Easy access to I-75, seven miles east, can be gained on US 441.

## Gainesville

Gainesville is the home of the University of Florida, which until 1947 was for men only. (Women went to the college in Tallahassee that has become Florida State University.) Today, the University of Florida, with more than thirty-five thousand students and eight hundred buildings, is among the twenty largest such institutions in the United States. To reach the campus, turn east at exit 76, which becomes University Avenue.

The city's current name, in honor of General Edmund Gaines of Seminole War fame, was acquired in 1853. Prior to that it had simply been "Hog Town," which seemed good enough to the British traders who were here between 1763 and the return of the Spanish twenty years later.

In 1774, thirty-five-year-old William Bartram, business failure and nature lover from Pennsylvania, joined a small group of Brits heading westward over the old Spanish Trail to trade with Seminoles who

*An Atlantic Coast Line train chugs down Gainesville's West Main Street in the 1920s.*
—P. H. Yonge Library of Florida History, University of Florida

*Paynes Prairie is an unusual grassland near Gainesville. When William Bartram was here with a group of British traders in 1774, Seminole horsemen were galloping across it in pursuit of wild Spanish cattle.*

were living beside a fertile depression, fifty miles in circumference, on the southern outskirts of the future Gainesville. In Bartram's time the depression was known as the Alachua Savanna, but today we call it Paynes Prairie.

The thick grasses that grew in the savanna provided sustenance for bountiful numbers of deer, turkeys, and other game animals. The grasses also supported the largest of the more than thirty Spanish cattle ranches in this part of Florida. From here in the 1600s, Spanish cowboys drove herds to St. Augustine, where the beef helped feed the colony and the hides provided a much-needed export. But English and Creek rustlers from the Carolinas ended the ranches in the 1700s.

By the time Bartram arrived, the savanna was home to Seminole huntsmen, whom Bartram described with admiration as "painted, fearless, uncontrolled, and free."

Today the area is a state wildlife preserve. A scenic wayside park beside I-75 overlooks the wide prairie from the north rim. But, because scrub willows often obscure the view, many travelers prefer taking US 441, on which there is a turnoff with a raised walkway leading to an observation platform. An interpretive center is a few miles south on 441.

## Micanopy

The site of Micanopy (mi-can-OP-y) was once occupied by Cuscowilla, an important Seminole settlement of about thirty lodges. In 1774 William Bartram and four English traders visited Cuscowilla,

*Downtown Micanopy is mostly antique shops. But long ago it was an active Seminole village. In 1774 William Bartram and British traders were treated to a feast of bull's belly here.*

where Chief Cowkeeper, eager to have European trade goods, gave them what he regarded as a sumptuous feast. The pièce de résistance was bull's belly spiced with its half-digested stomach contents. "The dish is greatly esteemed by the Indians, but is, in my judgment, the least agreeable they have amongst them," Bartram wryly wrote in his journal.

Later, Americans named their village after Chief Micanopy, a direct descendent of Cowkeeper and one of the leaders of the Dade Massacre during the Second Seminole War.

The modern settlement seems to dwell yet in a prior time, as more than a dozen antique shops poke out through dusty old buildings. The main street is shaded by spreading live oaks draped with Spanish moss—still reminiscent of days when mission bells summoned Timucuan men, women, and children to worship here.

## Cross Creek

Cross Creek, home of author Marjorie Kinnan Rawlings, is nine miles east of Micanopy on County Road 346, then south on County Road 325. It is almost impossible to get a feeling for northern Florida's past without reading Rawlings. Certainly *The Yearling* brings home

*Marjorie Rawlings often moved a table into the front yard of her Cross Creek home to do her writing.* —Florida State Archives

the rigors as well as the pleasures of life on the late nineteenth-century farm frontier.

Marjorie's early years did not prepare her for Florida. Born in 1896, she spent her first eighteen years in Washington, D.C., where her father worked in the Patent Office. In 1919 she married Charles Rawlings, a fellow writer, and moved to Rochester, New York, where for the next eight years her undistinguished column, "Songs of the Housewife," appeared daily in the local newspaper.

When she was thirty-two, she and Charles traveled to Florida, as the result of which they bought a small house at a sparsely populated location called Cross Creek. Her most productive years began here in 1930, when she sold her first short story for a goodly sum to the nationally prominent magazine *Scribner's.* Encouraged, Marjorie began to study Florida lore. The next year she went to live for a few weeks with a farm family in the Big Scrub, a desolate region of low-growing sand pine thirty miles east of Cross Creek. Thereupon she began working on *The Yearling,* a coming-of-age novel based on life in the Scrub.

In 1933 the Rawlingses divorced. But, despite Charles's departure, Marjorie stayed on. It was an act of great fortitude, since few women—particularly those who were city-bred and rather pretty—lived alone in the country. She was not even deterred when she fell from a horse and broke her neck—she just spent some time in a Tampa hospital, then she was back at Cross Creek in a metal brace that "gave me the noble look of Joan of Arc in armor."

*The Yearling,* published in 1938, received immediate acclaim and eventually earned her the coveted Pulitzer Prize. Within months the movie rights had been sold to MGM. Production on the film began in 1940, but it was delayed by World War II. It finally came out, starring Gregory Peck and Jane Wyman.

In 1941 Rawlings completed *Cross Creek*, a nonfiction account of life around her tiny Florida community. Once again she had a national bestseller. That same year she married Norton Baskin and moved into his accommodations at St. Augustine's luxurious Castle Warden Hotel, which he managed. She did not know it, but with that change her halcyon writing days were over. Though she kept the house at Cross Creek, it was only to visit, and as a result the inspiration of rural Florida began to leave her.

Just as disruptive was a lawsuit filed in 1943 by Zelma Cason, the chief character in "The Census" chapter of *Cross Creek*. The issue was invasion of privacy, involving one specific passage in an otherwise laudatory account of the hardy lady and the days the two of them spent on horseback conducting a county census: "Zelma is an ageless spinster resembling an angry and efficient canary. . . . I cannot decide whether she should have been a man or a mother. She combines the more violent characteristics of both and those who ask for or accept her manifold ministrations think nothing of being cursed loudly at the very instant of being tenderly fed, clothed, nursed or guided through their troubles."

Zelma and Marjorie had been close, perhaps closer than Marjorie realized. The author had identified 121 of her neighbors in *Cross Creek*, and she took great care that the important ones were aware of how she characterized them—this included Zelma, to whom Marjorie gave an autographed copy of the book when it first came out. But it did nothing to alleviate Zelma's ire, which may have related as much to Marjorie's friendship with Dessie Smith as to the unflattering passage. Smith was the young woman with whom Rawlings took an idyllic boat trip down the St. Johns River, which the author described in the chapter "Hyacinth Drift."

Whatever the cause of Zelma Cason's fury, the lawsuit seemed to go on interminably, for when the jury found in favor of Rawlings, Cason sued a second time, taking the case all the way to the Florida Supreme Court. There the decision was reversed in 1947, and Rawlings was directed to pay Cason damages of one dollar plus court costs.

The trials put a severe strain on Rawlings. For months after, she suffered from nervous exhaustion. The experience was probably the second major element contributing to the decline in her literary output during the last decade of her life. In 1953, she died of a cerebral hemorrhage at Crescent Beach and was buried near the village of Island Grove, not far from her beloved Cross Creek.

## The Yearling: *A Florida Classic*

Rawlings's best-known work, *The Yearling*, is set in the Big Scrub, a wild region that is now the Ocala National Forest. The story takes place in the 1870s or 1880s and concerns a frontier farmer, his wife, and their twelve-year-old son, Jody, who is the hero of the tale.

Rawlings's vivid prose enables us to share the dangers surrounding the family, as when Pa is struck by a rattlesnake and almost dies. We hear with them the alligators bellowing in the swamp and feel the damp coolness of the deep sinkhole where they get much of their

*Cracker farmers had a hard life. Here one laboriously grinds sugarcane one stalk at a time.* —P. H. Yonge Library of Florida History, University of Florida

drinking water. We learn how they tell when the rain is coming by the fiddle of the tree frogs. We are almost at their dinner table as they enjoy the sweet cores of the palmetto, which Floridians call swamp cabbage.

Growing up with no playmates, Jody is very lonely. Thus he makes a pet of a just-orphaned fawn. As the months pass, the fawn develops into a yearling buck. When he eats much of the family's precious field corn, Jody's parents are forced to make an agonizing decision: "Take the yearlin' out in the woods," his father says sadly but firmly, "and tie him and shoot him."

The order has a near-catastrophic effect on Jody. But it must be done. As the story draws to an end, Jody's father tells him, "Ever' man wants life to be a fine thing, and easy. 'Tis fine, boy, powerful fine, but 'tain't easy. Life knocks a man down and he gits up and it knocks him down again." So it was on the frontier.

### The Farm at Cross Creek

It is easy to relive the days when Marjorie Kinnan Rawlings resided at Cross Creek, for her home and grounds are administered by the

*Marjorie Kinnan Rawlings and her husband bought this little farmhouse at Cross Creek in 1928. It was here, after they divorced, that she wrote her masterpiece,* The Yearling.

state park system. Tours of the home are given, and one can linger on the front veranda where she did much of her writing.

The big magnolia tree she could see from her kitchen window, which gave her a lift during days of melancholy, remains as stately as before, and even taller. The old road where she took evening walks with her dog is there, though now it is paved. Beside the road are fence posts similar to the one beneath which she stashed a small hoard of gold—and had a frustrating time finding again.

The farmyard is much the same as it was the time Charles sold a story to the *Atlantic Monthly* and to celebrate the couple uncorked the corn whiskey and turned all the chickens loose to chase them with .22 rifles. The orange grove where Marjorie and her dog played and danced in the moonlight has been replanted.

At the far end of the modern parking lot is Orange Lake. Marjorie often mused on its shore as she looked across the water to the decaying tower of a plantation house. "When I am an old woman," she wrote with a twinkle in *Cross Creek,* "I mean to build a tower like it on my own side of the lake, and I shall sit there on angry days and growl down at anyone who disturbs me."

*A Passing Vignette*

Every road has little stories particular to it and to the few people involved. I-75 is no exception.

When the state government began purchasing land for the future highway in 1963, one of the farms it was to transverse belonged to Julius James, whose family had occupied the farm since 1868, when James's grandparents had been freed from slavery. It was on a remote portion of the state, served only by County Road 326. Thus, when the government offered James eleven thousand dollars for a portion of his holdings, he was glad enough to accept it.

But a controversy arose thirty-two years later, when the state decided to expand the County Road 326 interchange, six miles north of Ocala, and turn it into a major truck stop. For this, all of Julius James's remaining twenty-one acres were needed. This meant that James, now 108 years old, would have to move.

The proposed eviction of the virtually helpless old man, to whom the $2.3-million purchase price meant nothing, made the national wire services. Such an outcry ensued that a new agreement was worked out, whereby James could remain on a three-acre plot in one corner of the property and a memorial to James and his grandparents would be put up at the truck stop.

# Ocala

The velvet hills around Ocala are among the most fertile in Florida. The area boasts well over six hundred horse farms, many of which, with their rustic wooden fences, can be seen from I-75.

For a closer look at horse country, a ten-mile drive south from Ocala on Florida 474 is highly recommended. It is a two-lane road, often shaded by live oaks. Horse farms are everywhere, with their neat wooden fences and miles of green pastures. Most of the horses are thoroughbreds raised for racing. They often come to the fences to gawk at the tourists as they pass. A few of the farms welcome visitors.

Many tourists regard Ocala merely as a place to pass through on the way to Silver Springs. But the town center has been laboriously upgraded to meet the strict standards of Florida's Main Street program, and it is well worth a visit.

Ocala was the site of the decisive incident that began the long and bloody Second Seminole War. The story goes like this:

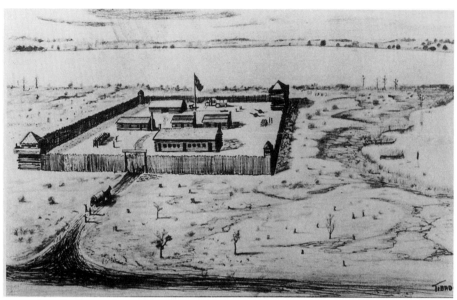

*A typical army fort of the Second Seminole War. Fort King, where Osceola murdered the Indian agent and began the Second Seminole War, may have looked like this.* —P. H. Yonge Library of Florida History, University of Florida

*A sketch of Seminole leader Osceola, done in 1857. Osceola was only part Indian and grew up in white society, where he was known as Billy Powell.*
—P. H. Yonge Library of Florida History, University of Florida

### The Murder of Wiley Thompson

In 1827 Fort King had been built on a knoll three miles east of downtown Ocala. The fort's purpose was to protect the Indian agent, who was established here in accordance with the Treaty of Moultrie Creek. In this treaty the tribesmen, having been defeated by Andrew Jackson in the First Seminole War, agreed to abandon upper Florida and settle in central Florida on a large reservation reaching from Fort King south to the Kissimmee River. The U.S. government, for its part, promised to pay the Indians an annuity each year and supply them with agricultural equipment and livestock, as well as with the services of a blacksmith and gunsmith. Supervising these operations would be the duty of the government's Indian agent. This agent was Wiley Thompson.

Thompson, a tall, muscular man experienced at Indian fighting, arrived at Fort King in 1833. He knew the Seminoles were seething at the provisions of a brand-new treaty that eliminated their reservation and demanded that they migrate beyond the Mississippi by 1835. The Indian unrest did not bother Thompson, for he was a blustery fellow, confident that he and his soldiers could protect themselves from any mischief the Seminoles might provoke. Thus he completely underestimated the warrior who was rising within the Seminole ranks. His name was Osceola.

Osceola was a man of many contrasts. Born to an English father and a Creek mother, he was neither a chief nor even a Seminole. He was shorter than average, and his face often showed a mild expression. He could be quite charming with his friends, white and red alike. But he was a natural leader and could also be forceful and dramatic— as when he shouted at an American general that he would sign no paper promising the tribe's migration. "The only treaty I will ever make is this!" he roared, plunging his knife into the document and leaving a gash that remains to this day.

Thompson was not cowed by Osceola's tactics. When the warrior became unruly at Fort King, Thompson had him seized and put in chains until he cooled down. But to an Indian, such action demanded vengeance. Furthermore, the 1835 removal deadline was now at hand, and Osceola and his tribesmen had no intention of leaving their homeland. It would be war!

Osceola and his braves planned their actions carefully. Upon learning that a reinforcement under Major Francis Dade was marching up from Fort Brooke (Tampa), they decided to ambush it. At the same time, Osceola would kill Thompson, thereby securing his vengeance while disorganizing the American response to the ambush. The main body of warriors moved out to meet the Fort Brooke troops, leaving Osceola and a few braves to handle their part of the plan.

Late in the afternoon, Thompson and a dinner companion emerged from the stockade for a stroll about the grounds. Osceola waited behind some trees. As Thompson approached, Osceola took careful aim with a rifle that Thompson himself had given him just days earlier. When the agent was squarely in sight, Osceola and his men fired. Thompson spun to the ground, riddled with fourteen bullets.

In jubilation, the Seminoles ripped off Thompson's scalp and cut it into small pieces, so that each warrior could have a trophy. Osceola personally severed the head and carried it off. Then the Indians vanished into the forest, hoping to join the main Seminole force fifty miles south, not knowing that already the warriors were methodically eliminating Dade's soldiers, who were huddled behind an inadequate log barricade.

Today nothing remains of Fort King, although a plaque off Florida 40 at Southeast Thirty-ninth Avenue and Southeast Fort King Street marks the site. The locale is wooded and quiet and, some say, still haunted by the spirit of Osceola, who himself was soon to meet a strange and tragic fate when he was captured at St. Augustine.

### Silver Springs

At famous Silver Springs Park, a mile east of Ocala, glass-bottom boats take visitors on intriguing journeys over some of the fourteen major springs flowing up from underground rivers. The water is crystalline, and one can easily see silver shells dancing in the current more than eighty feet below.

Prehistoric natives built burial mounds beside the springs, and the Seminoles lived in a village here until they were evicted in 1844, after losing the Second Seminole War. By the 1870s steamboats were carrying hundreds of tourists to the site from Jacksonville and Palatka. Soon a railroad and a three-and-a-half-story wooden hotel, both now gone, made ugly appearances beside the sparkling waters.

But the springs had an essence that could not be denied, and Marjorie Kinnan Rawlings's *The Yearling* was filmed here in 1946. Eventually the springs became a registered national landmark. In 1993 the state of Florida purchased the site and now leases it to the operator for nearly $1 million a year. When the lease ends in 2008, the state has the option of closing Silver Springs as a tourist attraction and preserving it in its natural beauty.

The Ocala National Forest, which in frontier days was known as the Big Scrub, begins five miles east of Silver Springs.

**I-75**

# Florida's Turnpike—I-4 (Tampa Turnoff)

**61 miles**

South of Ocala, I-75 passes Florida's Turnpike, built before the interstate. When the turnpike opened it had no major connection, and its beginning was a place called Wildwood, which was simply that: a wild wood. Fourteen miles beyond the turnpike is the exit to Bushnell.

## Bushnell

*The Dade Battle: Indian Victory or Defeat?*

Two miles south of the Bushnell exit on US 301 is the site of the battle that, along with the murder of Wiley Thompson, marked the beginning of the Second Seminole War, the longest, most expensive Indian conflict in American history. At issue was the federal government's decision to force all the eastern Indians to relocate west of the Mississippi. No tribe relished this, the Seminoles least of all.

Most military experts at the time believed that the four thousand Seminoles and their Miccosukee allies posed little problem for the army, since the the Indians had already lost an earlier war with Andrew Jackson. But the experts did not consider the fact that the timid chiefs of that time had been replaced by aggressive men like Osceola and other determined leaders.

When Major Francis L. Dade and 107 well-trained soldiers set out from Fort Brooke to reinforce Fort King in late December 1835, they felt they could handle anything Osceola and his braves could attempt against them. Their route was over the Fort King military road, built seven years earlier, following the same Indian trail Hernando de Soto had taken three centuries before.

*Traces of the old military trail still remain at the place where Seminole warriors ambushed and virtually wiped out Major Francis Dade's command in 1835.*

By the evening of December 27, Dade and his men had covered two-thirds of their hundred-mile journey. They had passed the most dangerous ambush places and were now dreaming about their belated Christmas celebration when they reached Fort King. They had no scouts to probe the underbrush, and their ammunition was covered up and difficult to get at.

Suddenly, 180 hidden braves let forth a sheet of bullets that caught the troops completely off guard. Dade and half his blue-coated men fell with the first volley. The remaining officers rallied the survivors and hurriedly threw up a low log breastwork.

The Seminoles, better supplied than the troopers, maintained a withering fire all day. They charged once but were beaten back. Then Dade's men kept them at bay with their single cannon, whose roar was distantly heard by an American army of 750 soldiers searching for hostile Indians—but they thought it was thunder and did not respond!

Finally the troops ran out of ammunition, and by late afternoon it was all over. Nearly the entire column had been wiped out. Several days later, two survivors stumbled back to Fort Brooke with the dreadful news. One of these men died two months later.

Was the battle a victory or a defeat? Although it was a defeat for the army, it enabled opponents of the Seminoles to marshal the maximum government support for their removal from Florida. And although it was a victory for the Seminoles, it marked the beginning of the end of their way of life.

The state historic site of the battle features a small visitor center with some good displays. The log breastwork has been reconstructed. It is only about three feet high and shows how little protection the soldiers had. A portion of the Fort King road is immediately beyond the breastwork.

# US 301: A Historic Trailway

An alternate to I-75 is US 301, which generally follows the ancient Indian trail that ran between northern Florida and Tampa Bay. The soldiers of both Hernando de Soto and Major Francis Dade followed this same route, past the sites of Zephyrhills and Thonotosassa.

### *Zephyrhills: De Soto's March, 1539*

De Soto and his six hundred men had landed at Tampa Bay near Bradenton in May of 1539 and marched toward Ocala, which local tribes had falsely told them was a large city shimmering with gold. By the time they reached the Zephyrhills area it was July, and the torrid Florida climate broiled the Spaniards in their armor. Water was so scarce in the sandy ridges that at least one man died of thirst. When they emerged into the wetlands beyond, other men fell to Indian archers who contested almost every stream crossing.

But de Soto responded with a force that the Indians could not match. Mounted soldiers with steel weapons accompanied by attack dogs cut through the Indians and enabled the Spaniards to force their way ever northward.

### *Thonotosassa: Fort Foster, 1836*

Crossing the rivers also caused Major Dade and his 107 troopers problems in 1835, as they followed the southern bank of the Hillsborough out of Fort Brooke. When they reached the army bridge near the modern US 301 span, they found it burned. Rafting over the river made the force vulnerable to a sudden attack—though none came. A few months later, military authorities decided to fortify the strategic location and Fort Foster was erected. Although the fort was abandoned at the conclusion of the Second Seminole War, it has now been reconstructed and is garrisoned by personnel wearing replica uniforms. The fort is off US 301, seven miles north of the hamlet of Thonotosassa—an Indian word denoting the place where arrowhead flint was found.

### The Wahoo Swamp

I-75 passes through the once-notorious Wahoo Swamp, now the Chinsegut National Wildlife Refuge, five miles south of Bushnell. Shaded by cypress, this was a favorite rendezvous of Osceola and his Seminole warriors. They had wild festivities here in December 1835, celebrating the murder of Indian agent Wiley Thompson and the victory over Major Dade. Such festivities were not warranted, however, for these two events set off the Second Seminole War, which resulted in Osceola's death and the relocation of most of the Indians west of the Mississippi.

Continuing south, I-75 leaves the central uplands and enters the gulf plain. Travelers going to Tampa should take the I-275 cutoff, for I-75 veers left and skirts Tampa Bay. At this point you are crossing the Peninsular Divide, a subtle hump of the land that separates the rivers flowing north in this part of Florida from those flowing south.

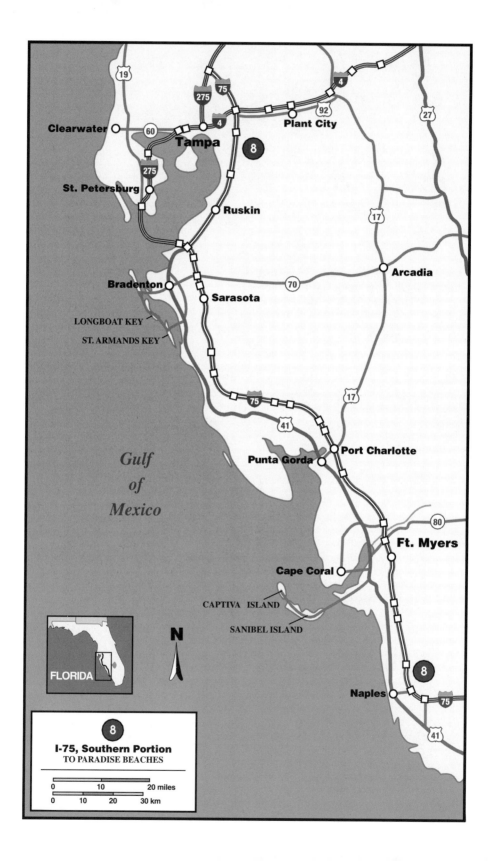

US 19

I-275

I-75

US 4

US 27

Clearwater

60

US 4

92 Plant City

Tampa

8

St. Petersburg

275

Ruskin

17

Bradenton

70

Arcadia

Sarasota

LONGBOAT KEY

ST. ARMANDS KEY

Gulf
of
Mexico

I-75

41

17

Punta Gorda

Port Charlotte

80

Ft. Myers

Cape Coral

CAPTIVA  ISLAND

SANIBEL ISLAND

N

FLORIDA

8

I-75

Naples

41

8

I-75, Southern Portion
TO PARADISE BEACHES

0        10        20 miles

0    10    20    30 km

# ☙ 8 ☙

# I-75, Southwestern Portion

## To Paradise Beaches

# Tampa—Naples

### 165 miles

South of Tampa, I-75 leaves the predominantly Democratic, native-born counties of upper Florida and enters the more Republican counties inhabited by newcomers from the northern states. Greetings here are not "How yawl?" but "Where are *you* from?" There is also a significant topographical change at this point as the gentle landlocked hills of upper Florida are replaced by sandy flatlands from which roads lead to gulf beaches.

*Guarded by an alert bull, a cattle herd grazes on a southwest Florida prairie.*

*This pre-Civil War plantation home of Robert Gamble near Bradenton was the finest on Florida's gulf coast. It is open to the public.*

The land south of Tampa is excellent for raising vegetables, and Ruskin is a major source of the nation's winter tomatoes. From 1934 through 1950 the town was well known for its annual tomato fairs—highlighted by ripe-tomato-throwing contests.

Fifteen miles farther along the expressway, exit 43 leads to the Gamble Mansion, a beautiful antebellum plantation house that in 1865 was refuge to former Confederate Secretary of State Judah P. Benjamin as he made his successful flight to England.

# Bradenton

### *Hernando de Soto: March Toward Oblivion*

Bradenton is the probable landing site of Hernando de Soto. The location has become a national monument, with a museum containing Spanish weapons, armor, and a model of a Spanish ship. The museum shows a well-done movie depicting de Soto's horrendous four-year search for gold.

De Soto's venture was launched from Spain with great fanfare. Men from all parts of the country vied to be chosen for his expedition, since everyone was convinced that the dashing young veteran of Francisco Pizarro's awesome Inca conquests was exactly the sort of man to discover new riches. De Soto's fleet left Spain to the cheers of a huge crowd and the blare of trumpets.

*Hernando de Soto and six hundred fighting men landed at Bradenton in 1539. De Soto's search for golden cities to match those he had helped loot in Peru would lead him through Ocala and Tallahassee.*
—Florida State Archives

De Soto landed at Tampa Bay on May 25, 1539. Disembarking from his nine ships were around six hundred men, amply provided with guns, war dogs, and more than two hundred horses. The horses, in particular, proved decisive in giving the Spaniards a military advantage over the natives.

De Soto marched around the Manatee River marshlands and made camp at the deserted Indian town of Ucita, which was probably at modern Terra Ceia, a tiny settlement at the southern foot of the spectacular I-275 Sunshine Skyway Bridge. Then, on July 15, de Soto and his men left Tampa Bay to begin their trek northward toward the rich cities the local tribes had glibly led them to believe existed. There was a festive mood. Little did they know that unbelievable hardship, privation, and, for nearly half of them, death lay ahead.

To reach the De Soto National Memorial from I-75, take the Florida 64 exit west to Seventy-fifth Street West. Then follow the sign north to the memorial, from which there is a wonderful view of Tampa Bay.

While on Florida 64 you will pass through central Bradenton and over the Braden River. If you turn north on Twenty-seventh Street East, in a short distance you will come to a marker and a few low walls surrounded by piles of shells and rocks. This was once the two-story Braden Castle, built in 1851, home of Dr. Joseph Braden, founder of Bradenton. In 1856, during the Third Seminole War, it was successfully defended when attacked by a small party of Indians.

## The Scenic Route to Sarasota

Florida 64 going west from Bradenton ends at Anna Maria Key, on the Gulf of Mexico. From here, a three-mile jaunt north will take you to the tip of the key, where a picturesque 1911 wooden wharf juts more than seven hundred feet into Tampa Bay.

The key's history dates back to Juan Ponce de León, who is supposed to have named it in honor of his sponsor's wife. The island was platted in 1912 by the gentlemen who invented the Fig Newton and made a fortune when they sold it to Nabisco.

Sarasota is nineteen very pleasant miles south from the Florida 64 junction on Florida 789. The route passes quaint ocean homes and seafood restaurants. At Bradenton Beach the road is close to the sandy shore, and there are public beaches.

The aspect changes abruptly crossing the bridge to Longboat Key, where the wealthy have elegant homes, play at fine golf courses, and stay at fancy resorts. Some of these resorts are open to the public, like the Hilton, where you can enjoy a meal or just a snack while looking out on the gulf.

During World War II, Longboat Key was not so tranquil. Then it was used as a bombing range for planes operating out of Tampa and Sarasota. Gates at either end of the island kept civilians away during daylight hours. A tall-range control tower directed the planes, and a landing strip mid-island accommodated aircraft in distress.

Another bridge leads to St. Armands Key, famous for its premier shopping circle. Everything sparkles here. There are flowers year-round, but especially in the spring, when masses of oleanders lead their own fashion parade of reds, pinks, and whites.

The key's first white settler was Charles St. Armand, who established a homestead on this then-isolated barrier island in 1885. John Ringling, wealthy circus baron, attempted to end its isolation in 1926 when he built a causeway from the mainland. Ringling had ambitious plans for a casino, resorts, and upper-income homes. But the excitement ended abruptly with the Great Depression and Ringling's ensuing financial problems.

St. Armands Circle is highlighted by the Circus Ring of Fame, created in 1988 to honor Ringling. In and around it are gardens, statuary, bronze busts, and mementos of famous personalities of the big top. From St. Armands the Ringling Causeway leads across the bay to downtown Sarasota.

# Sarasota

Sarasota is a bustling little city of fifty-five thousand. It had a slow beginning, and it was not until after the Civil War that a small cluster of homes appeared. The settlement was initially called Sara Sota, though even its earliest residents didn't know where the name came from. In jest they said it was from a mysterious daughter of Hernando de Soto, the one called Sara.

Although the first railroad reached the village in 1903, it was the arrival of the Tamiami Trail in the early 1920s that brought the village to life. At that time, the chief architect of its fame was entertainment magnate John Ringling.

### The Ringling Brothers Circus

The story goes that when John Ringling and his gorgeous wife, Mable, told their architect what they wanted in their Sarasota mansion—the turrets, the colored-glass windows, the curling stairs,

*John Ringling began as a circus clown and ended owning the fabulous Ca'd'Zan mansion in Sarasota. But after his beautiful wife died in 1929, the sparkle drained from his life.* —Florida State Archives

*John and Mable Ringling's fabulous home, Ca'd'Zan, built in 1926, is now a Sarasota showplace open to the public.*

and the tower borrowed from Madison Square Garden—that he gulped and went pale. But he did draw up the plans.

The garish home was called Ca'd'Zan, or House of John, and the couple moved into it in 1926. It was a delightful place, with a lovely living room looking out on a marble terrace and beyond to the pier on Sarasota Bay, where Mable tied the gondola she brought all the way from Venice.

Ca'd'Zan was a fitting crown to a fantastic career. John Ringling began as an itinerant clown performing with his four brothers in little Wisconsin towns during the 1880s. The group prospered, and eventually the Ringling Brothers Circus became the largest circus in the country. At its height it took more than a hundred railroad cars to move it from town to town. The parade from the railroad yards to the circus ground was the highlight of any town's summer. There were gaudy bands, bright wagons with snarling beasts, costumed ladies on prancing horses, chains of lumbering elephants, and cavorting clowns.

Then came the thrill of watching the huge canvas tent go up—the "big top"—and suddenly there was an Aladdin's city in what had been only an empty field. The magic of it all! No wonder a lad's greatest dream was to run away with the circus.

John and Mable's own dream was to live the happy life in Sarasota. But it was not to be. Lovely Mable contracted Addison's disease, with its accompanying weakness and constant vomiting. Although the disease is easily controlled today, such was not the case then.

When Mable died in 1929, John was devastated. "The party is over," he mourned. Indeed it was, for the Great Depression hit him at the same time. He suffered severe financial difficulties and even lost control of the circus before dying in 1936.

Though John and Mable Ringling have departed and their circus no longer winters at Sarasota, the grounds are almost as lively as in the past. The fabulous Ca'd'Zan is on display, with guides conducting tours of the incredible home. Ringling Brothers' huge winter storage building is now a museum, amply stocked with colorful memorabilia, including a group of circus wagons painted bright red

*Colorful wagons and other displays at the Ringling Museum in Sarasota make circus memories come alive.*

and blue, some with wooden figurines of lions and tigers and others of beautiful women in shimmering gold.

Across from the museum is the colorful Banyan Cafe, offering sandwiches as well as full meals. If the weather is right, you can eat outdoors beneath the wide-spreading banyan tree, a gift to the Ringlings from Thomas Edison, who raised it from a seedling at his Fort Myers home.

South of, and separate from, the Ca'd'Zan and the Circus Museum is the Ringling Museum of Art, with more than one thousand paintings, including works by Peter Paul Rubens, Frans Hals, Thomas Gainsborough, and Paolo Veronese.

To see more of Sarasota, take US 41, the Tamiami Trail, south from the Ringling grounds to downtown. On your way you will pass the Van Wezel Performing Arts Hall. Built in 1969 on spacious grounds overlooking beautiful Sarasota Bay, it is an eye-catching asset of which any city would be proud. Farther south is the Quay, a bayfront complex with shops and restaurants of many shapes and sizes.

(For more on the Tamiami Trail, see chapter 10.)

# Venice

### I-75: Not Wanted by Everyone

Interestingly, not everyone was happy when the expressway was being built. Local merchants of the resort towns it would bypass—Sarasota, Fort Myers, Naples, and others—were resentful. Opposition to I-75 helped delay its completion in this area until the 1980s.

One of the towns bypassed by I-75 was Venice, sixteen miles south of Sarasota on the old Tamiami Trail (US 41). Although this coastal area had a few settlers as early as the 1860s, its real beginning did not occur until 1925, when the Brotherhood of Locomotive Engineers selected Venice as its retirement settlement. The union, wanting its members to while away their remaining years in paradise, hired a well-known city planner, who decided that all the buildings should conform to the northern Italian Renaissance style.

Although Venice went through hard times as I-75 bypassed it and shoppers turned away from the central business district, it has resurrected itself admirably as a Main Street City. Now palms, pines, and silver trumpet trees grace the downtown, and a beach renourishment program has re-created three miles of the gulf front, famous for its abundant fossilized sharks' teeth, some up to three inches long.

## Punta Gorda

In early times, Punta Gorda was known to Spanish fishermen as the "fat point" of land that projected into the water. Americans did not become established here until 1886, when the railroad's arrival gave the region access to northern markets. At this time, the huge Hotel Punta Gorda was built between Marion Avenue and the Peace River. The hotel enjoyed a distinguished career, but it had been in decline for many years before a fire of suspicious origin burned it to the ground in 1959.

Punta Gorda's civic spirit survived the fire. With choice riverfront property now available, a fine mall went up. Then the town brightened, bordering Marion Avenue (US 17) with brick planters, quaint street lamps, benches, and shade trees. The buildings were also spruced up, and soon the entire town began to sparkle. Thus Punta Gorda came to the attention of *Money* magazine editors, who in 1996 awarded it the coveted honor of the nation's best small town in which to live.

*There is always activity at Punta Gorda's Fishermen's Village.*

Visitors to Punta Gorda usually drive four miles west on Marion to Fishermen's Village, built in 1970 on the site of an earlier wharf. The village, an appealing mixture of forty specialty shops and six restaurants, has become a popular drawing card up and down the coast.

It has become a late-afternoon tradition in Punta Gorda to head west on Marion until it ends at the Ponce de Leon city park. Here, appreciative crowds clap while the setting sun turns the Gulf of Mexico to fire.

Upon returning from the park or the village, be sure to turn north on McGregor Street to Retta Esplanade. The Esplanade is graced by several blocks of towering royal palms, while on one side of the street are vintage homes, constructed mainly during the 1890s, and on the other is Gilchrist Park, with a splendid vista of the Peace River.

# Fort Myers

## *The Mighty Calusa Tribe*

The site of Fort Myers has been a populated place since the Calusa people built large ceremonial mounds in the vicinity. The Calusas probably chose Fort Myers as their chief settlement because of its location on the river, which led far into the interior. This waterway, known as the Caloosa Hatchee, or "River of the Calusa," linked with Lake Okeechobee and gave the Calusas access to the Atlantic coast and the tribes there from whom they collected tribute.

When the ominous sails of Ponce de León's two large ships materialized out of the river mist in 1521, the Calusas were not awed, though Ponce de León had two hundred fighting men with armor and guns. Hardly had they landed when Calusa arrows greeted them. The ensuing battle lasted for hours. But when an arrow pierced Ponce de León's armor, the Spaniards retreated and soon were on their way back to Havana. There, the would-be conquistador, who may have dreamed he would find immortality in the land he named Florida, found death instead.

## *A Fort Is Built*

In the following years, Spain laid claim to the entire Florida peninsula, though efforts to subdue the Calusas were futile. Nonetheless, by 1821, when Florida passed to the Americans, the once-mighty Calusa people had vanished—possibly victims of European diseases. Ultimately in their place were bands of Seminoles and

Miccosukees, who had been pushed down from the north as a result of the First and Second Seminole Wars. There were less than six hundred of them, and their leader was a cautious man named Beaulieu. Whites found "Beaulieu" difficult to pronounce, so he became Billy Bowlegs—it was close enough.

As Americans began moving into the area, the inevitable murder of a trader occurred, resulting in the demand for troops. In 1850 impressive Fort Myers was built, named on a whim for the fiancé of a general's daughter. There were fifty-seven buildings, including a bowling alley and a separate house for the groundskeeper who tended the ornamental palms and the white-shell walkways. A wharf extended nearly a thousand feet into the river, where supply steamers unloaded.

## The Third Seminole War

Fort Myers's presence was enough to keep the Seminoles cowed— that is, until a group of unruly soldiers willfully trampled Billy Bowlegs's garden. The Indians retaliated, though they knew their plight was desperate, and raiding bands went on a burning and pillaging rampage that terrorized the frontier as far north as Bradenton, where they attacked the home of Joseph Braden, the town's founder. After three years of American harassment, Billy admitted defeat. In the spring of 1858, he and most of his followers reluctantly trudged to the fort and boarded ships for resettlement in Arkansas. The third and final Seminole War was over.

## The Giants Come: Thomas Edison and Henry Ford

One of the more important events in Fort Myers's post–Civil War development was the arrival of Thomas Edison in March 1885. He had not intended to vacation this far south, but bad weather in St. Augustine had altered his plans. The quaint little place with less than four hundred inhabitants instantly appealed to his semireclusive side, and he purchased a thirteen-acre estate, where he built a winter home to which he would return more or less regularly for the better part of half a century.

The following March, Edison brought his new bride, twenty-year-old Mina Miller. The honeymooning couple were soon serenaded by the village brass band, whose concerts some citizens called a "hideous noise." This was not Edison's first marriage. Fifteen years earlier he had wed Mary Stilwell, only sixteen years old. His love must have cooled quickly, for he spent most of his wedding day in his lab. Eventually the poor girl suspected that his objective may have been more to secure a housekeeper than a wife. In any event, she began to suffer periods of mental derangement and eventually died of something that was called "brain congestion."

Mina was a wife of a different sort. Although she had agreed to marry Thomas after receiving his proposal via Morse code on the telegraph, she had no intention of becoming subservient to his science. She worked on him, and gradually he became a more conventional husband. She even got him to donate a pair of lots to the Congregational Church, although religion played little part in his routine. Yet despite Mina's efforts, Edison continue to be so absorbed in his experiments that, when asked when he would retire, he retorted, "the day before the funeral."

In his later years, Edison became enthralled with the idea that he could make commercial rubber from goldenrod. Even his wife and their three children became involved. "We talk rubber," Mina complained, "think rubber, dream rubber. Mr. Edison refuses to let us do anything else." Thus Edison was severely disappointed when his goldenrod experiments produced rubber so wildly expensive no manufacturer would buy it.

In 1916 Henry Ford and his wife, Clara, bought the house next door and began spending their winters with the Edisons. Though

*Thomas Edison, naturalist John Burroughs, and Henry Ford (L to R) pose for a photo in 1914 on the grounds of Edison's winter home in Fort Myers.* —Florida State Archives

Edison had been 90 percent deaf for most of his life, the two men were able to communicate through their mutual interest in mechanical things. Soon they even took camping trips together, accompanied by Harvey Firestone, the famous tire tycoon. The trips attracted considerable public interest, and by 1924 the trio was accompanied by such an obtrusive pack of reporters and general gawkers that Firestone called it a traveling circus, and the three regretfully ended their outings.

When Ford first began coming to Fort Myers, he was a friendly fellow who would roll up the rugs at his Fort Myers home and call out square dances. He was in his prime and had just perfected assembly line production, which was to revolutionize industry around the world. His Model T was by far the world's top-selling car. And he was idolized by most of his workers for establishing their base pay at five dollars a day, nearly twice the average.

By 1931, the year Edison died and Ford stopped wintering in Fort Myers, Ford was a changed man. Angered by the fact that he was being outsold by both Chevrolet and Plymouth, he had turned on his workers, who now hated him. The public found the quixotic old man hopelessly out-of-date and generally ridiculed him.

### Modern Fort Myers

During the early 1900s, downtown Fort Myers became a popular shopping, financial, and recreational attraction. First Street boasted an impressive array of buildings, and many are still there, such as the Bradford Hotel (1905), the Earnhardt Building (1915), and the U.S. Post Office (1933), now the county courthouse. On the courthouse grounds are plaques locating the original fort, whose stockaded perimeter enclosed most of the business district and whose wharf was at the foot of Hendry Street.

Although the erection of outlying malls, as well as the long-dreaded completion of I-75, brought the virtual collapse of downtown Fort Myers as a shopping area, a good deal of work and planning is going into its revival. The area along the waterfront between the Caloosahatchee Bridge (US 41) and the Edison Bridge (Business Route 41) is a good beginning. At one end is the Harborside Convention Hall, built in 1981, and at the other is the handsome Sheraton Harbor Place Hotel, built a few years after. From the second-floor dining room, the Sheraton offers a nice view of the Yacht Basin and the river beyond.

*The Fort Myers Historical Museum is in the 1924 railroad station.*

The waterfront park contains a life-size statue grouping called Uncommon Friends, which shows Ford, Edison, and Firestone during one of their camping trips.

Fort Myers has a fine historical museum in the 1924 former railroad station at Jackson and Peck Streets, three and a half blocks south of the center of town. The Edison and Ford homes, a few blocks west of downtown on McGregor Boulevard, are two other attractions well deserving a visit. Tours are conducted throughout the day.

### Sanibel and Captiva Islands

Once in Fort Myers, you may want to drive out McGregor Boulevard to the bridge that leads to Sanibel Island. McGregor alone is worth the trip. It is lined with majestic royal palms for many miles. The first palms, which have since been replaced, were donated by Thomas Edison in 1907.

Originally, McGregor Boulevard was a cow path leading to Punta Rassa, the "flat point," near the foot of what would become the Sanibel Bridge. Cattle baron Jake Summerlin had one of his homes here. Now the only reminder of this once-busy port is the 1884 lighthouse across the bay on Sanibel, built to guide the cattle ships to and from Summerlin's docks.

*Tough old Jake Summerlin and his cowpokes often drove their cattle down Fort Myers streets on the way to his shipping dock at Punta Rassa, near the modern Sanibel Bridge.* —Orange County Historical Museum

Sanibel is a popular destination—so popular, in fact, that sometimes the bridge is closed to sight-seers after 11 A.M. The beaches are famous for shells and draw hundreds of visitors daily. If you wish to spend more time here, there are many fine resorts, most beside the sugar-sand beach, where you'll view some of the finest sunsets anywhere.

Legend has it that the fearsome pirate Jose Gasparilla was headquartered at Sanibel, which he named for a Spanish queen he sanctified as Santa Isabella. The lusty pirate and his men also used nearby Captiva as a tropical prison for the beautiful women they captured. (Why let the pesky fact that Gasparilla is probably fiction spoil the story?)

The two islands are very small—Sanibel is only twelve miles long and Captiva a quarter of that. Before the bridge to the mainland was built in 1963, both were sleepy little places accessible solely by ferry. The economy revolved around growing coconuts and key limes— and one of the buildings from this era can be seen at Captiva's lovely South Seas Plantation resort.

But the bridge changed all that. The flood of tourists and the accompanying building boom made the people of Sanibel so uncomfortable that in 1976 they adopted a land-use plan that severely restricted future development. The plan came just in time to help protect the wild and scenic areas that still existed. Foremost was the "Ding" Darling National Wildlife Refuge on Sanibel, named in honor of the political cartoonist and 1942 Pulitzer Prize winner who helped establish more than three hundred animal sanctuaries across the nation. The five-mile auto tour through the five-thousand-acre park offers delightful glimpses of such native birds as ospreys, brown pelicans, various types of herons, and colorful roseate spoonbills. Altogether, 291 species of birds, as well as 50 types of reptiles and amphibians, have been spotted in the park.

### The Scourge of the Melaleucas

Between Fort Myers and Naples, I-75 passes through dense stands of melaleuca trees, conspicuous with their gray-white shaggy bark and greenish gray leaves. Although they may have an appealing beauty, they are regarded by environmentalists as one of the greatest threats to the Everglades. Indeed, they were introduced from Australia in the early 1900s with the specific purpose of drying out the wetlands, for just a single acre of the trees transpire as much as twenty-two hundred gallons of water in a single hour!

The melaleucas have few natural enemies and can invade fifty acres of wetlands a day. So serious is their menace that they have been called the "Everglades's Terminator." Various proposals have been considered to control them, and it is hoped that a breakthrough is close at hand.

# Naples

From its inception in 1887, Naples has been a winter retreat for well-off folks. The founding father, Walter N. Haldeman, was the owner of the *Louisville Courier Journal.* In 1888 he constructed the Palm Cottage, close to the beach, for the editor's pleasure. At the same time, in order to accommodate the influx of vacationers, the main building of the Hotel Naples complex went up and a six-hundred-foot pier was constructed at the foot of Twelfth Avenue South.

But Naples did not really take off until the railroad and the Tamiami Trail reached it in the 1920s. At that point, tourism and a modest fishing industry developed.

Despite rapid changes, Naples clings to its past. Though the lordly Hotel Naples is now a humble parking lot along Gordon Drive at

Twelfth Avenue South, the Palm Cottage, nearby on 137 Twelfth, is well preserved and is occupied by the historical society. The original wharf down the street was a hurricane casualty, but it has been replaced and is once again a recreation center.

The town's traditional shopping area along Third Street at Twelfth has been refurbished and repainted in a most pleasant array of pastel greens, pinks, whites, and off-oranges. Although the town has a population of only twenty thousand, the upscale shops of Olde Naples rival those of Sarasota's St. Armands Key.

Naples also has links with its fishing past at Tin City, beside the US 41 bridge, where gift shops and waterfront restaurants are housed in converted clam and oyster processing plants.

From Naples, I-75 turns abruptly east to cross the Everglades, on the stretch of four-lane highway nicknamed Alligator Alley, as it heads toward Miami.

*The Naples pier has been an attraction ever since the first one was built in 1887.*

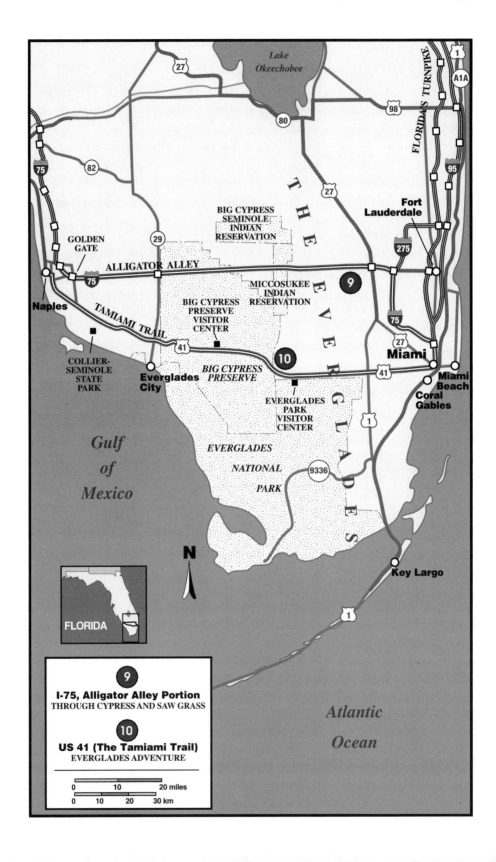

# ≈ 9 ≈
# *I-75, Alligator Alley Portion*
## THROUGH CYPRESS AND SAW GRASS

*The Birth of the Everglades*

The Everglades was born as the floor of a shallow sea. When the sea vanished, the flat limestone bedrock, dipping ever so slightly to the south, provided a wide spillway for excess water from Lake Okeechobee. The water was not stagnant, for it was filtering southward ever so slowly; this movement explained why saw grass was the predominant plant rather than swamp-loving cypress. Where the land did turn swampy, along the western border of the Everglades, the cypress grew tall and massive. But in both environments the quiet water provided ideal breeding places for a tremendous variety of wildlife.

A land route across the Everglades had been discussed ever since the days of the Spanish. But the way was barred by wetlands, alligators, mosquitoes, and lances of saw grass that could rasp through skin as well as clothing. The completion of the Tamiami Trail in 1928 was a tribute to human perseverance and ingenuity.

**I-75**
# Naples — Miami
**118 miles**

## Crossing the Everglades: I-75 vs. US 41

For some travelers, a trip through the Everglades is a dreary chore. They will appreciate I-75, a rapid throughway that means business. On it, the Everglades flits past rapidly. For others, seeing the Everglades is an exhilarating experience that requires a leisurely pace. US 41 (the Tamiami Trail) is for them. However, you should be aware that it is only two lanes and often filled with sight-seers. If you opt for that route, turn ahead to chapter 10.

### Alligator Alley

The road now designated as I-75 came much later than the Tamiami Trail to the south. It had its inception in the 1960s as a two-lane highway designed to take the pressure off the Tamiami Trail. Its opponents dubbed it "Alligator Alley" in derision. Rather than object, proponents found the name had an appealing resonance—so Alligator Alley it became.

Ever so slowly the road was broadened into the four lanes required by the interstate system, and it wasn't until the early 1990s that the road finally met federal regulations.

The western end of Alligator Alley begins at Golden Gate. Golden Gate Estates started as a huge development in the midst of the Big Cypress Swamp in 1962. It became a fiasco, as ill-planned canals and overbuilt roads caused a calamitous loss of water that resulted in drought and wildfires. Nevertheless, the developer's pressure tactics rushed inexperienced individuals into purchasing almost worthless lots. Eventually the scandal grew so large that the developer was cited in the congressional hearings that resulted in the Interstate Land Sales Full Disclosure Act of 1968.

Passing through the Big Cypress Swamp, the expressway follows the canal that was dug to provide material for the roadbed. A barbed fence prevents boaters as well as wild animals from mingling with the traffic.

Soon cypress domes appear. These are stands of cypress growing where the underlying bedrock has dipped in the form of a broad saucer. The trees in the deeper, more nutritious middle are higher. Cypress lose their needles in the winter, so don't assume they are dead if you see them at that time of year.

After about forty miles, the cypress give way to the Everglades. The vista is impressive as "the miracle of the light pours over the green and brown expanse"—to quote from Marjory Stoneman Douglas, poetic historian of the Everglades. Nowhere on earth is there such a natural saw grass area. There are frequent turnouts where you may want to stop and enjoy the awesome world surrounding you.

At exit 14 a road leads seventeen miles north to the Seminole Reservation, where the tribe has just erected a museum with a five-screen orientation movie theater and some 5,000 exhibits of Seminole cultural and military artifacts, many on loan from the Smithsonian Institution. In addition, a one-mile nature trail leads to a living Seminole village and ceremonial grounds.

Quicker than you'd expect, the seventy-eight-mile Alligator Alley ends and I-75 turns south. In twelve miles it crosses Florida's Turnpike, which heads toward the Keys. Five miles farther on it ends, at the Palmetto Expressway (Florida 826), from where there is direct access to downtown Miami via the Dolphin Expressway (Florida 836).

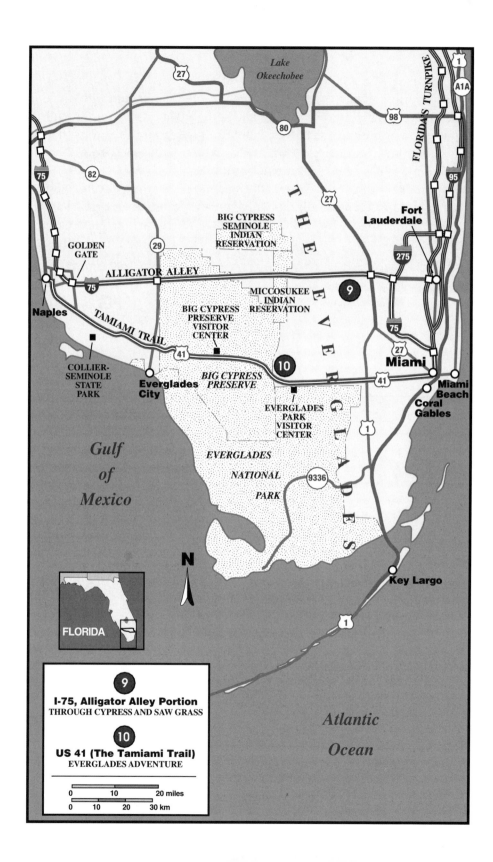

# ≈ 10 ≈
# US 41 (The Tamiami Trail)

## EVERGLADES ADVENTURE

# Naples—Miami

**107 miles**

*Wild Idea: A Road through the Everglades*

In the 1910s the idea of running a road from Tampa down the gulf coast and across the Everglades to Miami seemed impossible, for the forests along the coast and the wetlands around Tampa Bay and in the Everglades would offer almost insurmountable challenges to the road-building techniques that were just beginning to evolve.

But in 1914, as the Dixie Highway was being built along the Atlantic coast to Miami, residents of the western coast began agitating for a road between Tampa and Miami. They called it the Tamiami Trail. But the idea was ridiculed by experts, and the name was scoffed at as sounding "like a bunch of tin cans tied to a dog's tail." However, the concept caught on, particularly after it was decided that each town along the route, not the state, would secure the financing and do the building along its section.

Miami had no trouble. In 1916 bonds were sold, and work started on the portion of the trail that would run forty-two miles west to the Dade County line. By 1922 the Dade section was almost completed.

Construction on the much longer gulf coast segment started out about the same time. By 1921 a long bridge enabled motorists to reach Punta Gorda. Three years later, the trail penetrated dense pine forests to enter Fort Myers, 130 miles south of Tampa. But south of Fort Myers the only populated location was tiny Naples, clearly unable to finance anything. A narrow road paved with seashells

*187*

*This photo, taken in 1926 near what would become the Everglades National Park Visitor Center, shows a service boat, drill barge, and dipper dredge working on the Tamiami Trail.* —Historical Museum of South Florida

staggered south from Naples, but even that ended outside the hamlet of Everglades City. Beyond was a hundred miles of trackless cypress swamp and saw grass until the Miami segment was reached.

This area was the domain of the Miccosukee people, who had retreated there during the Seminole Wars, finding it their only place of refuge.

### A Tragic Saga

Once a powerful tribe, only four hundred or so of the Miccosukees remained. They resided mainly on hammocks, land slightly higher than the wetlands, where they lived in palmetto-thatched shelters called chickees. About their only contact with the outside world was at posts in Miami and Fort Myers, where they traded the pelts of deer, panther, and other Everglades animals for tools and the cloth from which they fashioned their colorful costumes.

The Miccosukees relished their isolation and refused to show whites the way through the Everglades. Thus the area remained a huge unknown that not even the master railroad builders of the late 1890s and early 1900s dared challenge.

*A Miccosukee family poses beside the Tamiami Trail in the 1920s.*
—P. H. Yonge Library of Florida History, University of Florida

## Eleven Horrible Days: The Trail Blazers of 1923

As interest in the Tamiami Trail developed, the Indian agent at Fort Myers convinced a pair of his Miccosukee friends to act as guides for a group of local businessmen who wished to make the trek across the Everglades in order to show that the trail could actually be built.

It started as a lark. There were nine autos carrying twenty-six tenderfoots, including a youngster named Russell Kay, who later wrote about the experience. The motorcade assembled at Fort Myers on April 4, 1923. A festive crowd gathered, and none other than Thomas Edison, making his winter home in the town, handed Kay a bottle of grape juice to present to William Jennings Bryan when he reached Miami. Then they were off.

Following the route now taken by US 41, they bounced along the shell road, having to take out their shovels only once, to fill a place where rain had washed out the bed. By dusk they made camp just east of Everglades City, having traveled nearly seventy miles.

When they rose at sunrise, they found before them no road at all, just a few surveyors' stakes and a limitless vista of devilish saw grass. Undaunted, the first car started out. But after about a hundred yards it became mired. A second car followed, and it became mired, too. It took a tractor from Everglades City to drag the entire procession to higher ground before it could continue. Now the seriousness of the enterprise dawned upon them, for beyond here they would be out of contact with civilization. They must rely on their two Miccosukee guides for survival.

Oddly, most of the time the trailblazers had problems with water—not from too much, but from too little! Since this was the dry season, much of the way was through the muck that overlay the coquina bedrock. To get drinking water they had to scoop a hollow in the muck and let the dirty brown water ooze in. Although it tasted horrible, at least no one got sick.

The going was far slower than they had expected. After three days their supply of food ran out, and they were forced to eat cattail roots, swamp cabbages, and an occasional deer that the Miccosukees brought in. Eventually the bottle intended for William Jennings Bryan fell prey to the thirsty explorers, and Kay remembered it as the "the best grape juice I ever tasted."

Never had they expected such a rugged trip. About the only pleasant occurrence was the lack of mosquitoes, which the dry season held to a minimum.

As the days passed and the party did not emerge, newspapers began headlining them as the "lost convoy." At one point they saw a circling plane obviously looking for them. But they were obscured by the saw grass. So the stories grew: they were captives of the Miccosukees, or they were fighting for their lives with wild alligators, or they were starving and almost dead.

Eventually gas began running out. They kept going by draining the tanks of certain cars that they then abandoned. On the eleventh day, when they were five miles from the completed portion of the trail, the last cars caved in, and they tramped the remaining distance on foot.

The fact that some of their cars had actually crossed the Everglades—or at least almost crossed it—made headlines in America and Europe. Public support for the project grew and its success was assured.

### Barron Collier and the Completion of the Tamiami Trail

Completion of the western end of the trail was largely the accomplishment of Barron Collier, a wealthy eastern businessman who had vast landholdings in the area that was soon to become Collier County.

Barron Collier knew that the value of his real estate would skyrocket when the gulf coast was linked with booming Miami. Thus he took hold of the project with vigor and money, establishing his base at Everglades City, a waterlogged hamlet he helped create out of river dredgings. Making this settlement the seat of his namesake county, he built port facilities, a machine shop, and a sawmill. Collier owned almost all the houses in town, and nearly every citizen was one of his employees.

Under Collier's firm hand, work on the western portion of the Tamiami Trail moved ahead rapidly. He had road building down to a science. First came the crew to clear the path, for much of this part of the trail was through large clumps of cypress. Then came the drillers, using one-and-a-half-story derricks with bits that cut into the bedrock. Next, blasters set dynamite in waterproof casings into the holes and exploded the rocks. Then the dredge arrived to scoop up the rock fragments and deposit them to one side. Finally work crews formed the rocks into a nineteen-foot-wide roadbed.

The workers lived in bunkhouses on wheels that were constantly towed to the most forward position. At night they slept under nets for protection against the mosquitoes. But during the day just palmetto fans stood between them and the voracious little vampires. The heat and humidity were often stifling.

The dredge crawled forward at the rate of just eighty feet a day. Finally on April 26, 1928, the road from the gulf met that from Miami. A gala ceremony at Everglades City marked the trail's formal opening. It had taken nearly thirteen years!

## Collier-Seminole State Park

Although the Tamiami Trail runs from Tampa to Miami, the scenic part begins at Royal Palm Hammock, seventeen miles south of Naples, where Collier-Seminole State Park is located, on land that was once part of Barron Collier's imperial domain. Although Collier died suddenly of a heart attack in 1939, he had made plans to set aside acreage for the park, and in 1947 the land was deeded to the state.

Of major interest is the huge dredge that was actually used in the road's construction. The park also offers canoe rentals as well as narrated boat tours of the bordering mangrove swamps.

*This dredge at Collier-Seminole State Park was used to create the Tamiami Trail. The bucket scooped out the muck and previously blasted limestone and piled it to one side to form the roadbed.*

Back on the trail, the way is through flatlands where water-loving saw grass and cattails alternate with the pines and cabbage palms that grow where the elevation is slightly higher. The two-lane road is very straight, as there are no natural obstructions in this level, virtually uninhabited world. Turnouts are provided in places, most with picnic tables.

In sixteen miles you come to the Florida 29 junction, location of the official Welcome Station. This was once known as Carnestown. Here a lone warehouse stood beside the short railroad line that brought cypress logs to Everglades City, where they were sawed into planks used on the trail's construction.

## Everglades City

Everglades City, port of entry for workers and material, is a few miles south on Florida 29. Its present population of less than five hundred gives no indication of the town's importance in the days of Barron Collier. But some relics remain. The old railroad depot at Collier Avenue and Broadway has become a riverside restaurant. The colonnaded building that was the courthouse when Everglades City

*This impressive building was to have administered Barron Collier's south Florida empire. Now it administers only Everglades City, population five hundred.*

was the seat of Collier County is on the circle formed by Broadway and Copeland Streets. This building was demoted to city hall after the county government moved to Naples in 1962. On the main floor are vintage photos of Tamiami Trail construction.

East on Broadway is the Rod and Gun Club, built in 1850. It was later purchased by Barron Collier both for his personal use and as a recreational attraction for visiting dignitaries. Over the years, the club has hosted many famous people, including Theodore Roosevelt, Herbert Hoover, Dwight Eisenhower, and Richard Nixon. Today it is a popular restaurant. It, too, has interesting trail memorabilia.

Modern Everglades City receives most of its tourists by way of the overflow from the gulf-coast branch of Everglades National Park, down Copeland Avenue from the circle. Here, sightseeing boats go into the "mysterious mangrove wilderness," as the park leaflet proclaims.

## Big Cypress National Preserve

From Everglades City, the Tamiami Trail heads eastward into the Big Cypress National Preserve. Although the preserve is associated with the Everglades, it is very different. Big Cypress is a swamp, where the water has no natural outlet, whereas water in the Everglades moves slowly south down the Shark River Slough. The road is good, though drivers should take note of the sign that warns of limited car service for the next sixty miles.

There is also a sign announcing panther crossings. But if you should see one you are extremely lucky, for it's estimated there are fewer than fifty in the entire state—so few, in fact, that a dozen or so closely related Texas cougars have been released around there to alleviate inbreeding.

Big Cypress Preserve has a beauty all its own. The cypress stands often appear as domes, with the center trees the tallest and their size diminishing as they radiate out. The reason for this is that cypress, which crave the deeper swamp, congregate in depressions in the bedrock. On the depression's rim, where the water is shallower, the trees are stunted. (Cypress are strange members of the pine family, for they lose their needles during the winter. And though they are brown at that time, by spring they are verdant once more.)

Where the road has been cut directly through a cypress stand, you will notice spiky balls growing from many tree limbs. These are bromeliad air plants. Late in the winter they sprout red shafts that bear purple flowers.

Set amid the trees are occasional Miccosukee thatched-roof villages, most supporting the usual gift shop and offering tours for a fee.

A narrow canal runs beside the road, and in places you can see large rocks that were blasted from the underlying limestone in the 1920s. They contain fossils from the time when southern Florida lay beneath a shallow body of water known to geologists as the Pamlico Sea.

The Big Cypress Preserve has a visitor center and museum twenty miles beyond Everglades City.

## The Everglades

Big Cypress Preserve ends with startling abruptness eighteen miles beyond the visitor center. At this point, the majestic Everglades grassland stretches out as far as one can see. This is the great "river of grass," to use the words of Marjory Stoneman Douglas, whose book, *The Everglades: River of Grass,* is must reading for an appreciation of the area.

Here there is a dam that attempts to control the massive sheet of water, usually less than twelve inches deep, that silently glides southward beneath the saw grass at the leisurely rate of a hundred feet a day. Historically this water came from overflows of Lake

*Dams like this beside the Tamiami Trail regulate the Everglades's water flow.*

Okeechobee. But in 1937, as the result of earlier hurricane-induced Okeechobee floodings that killed two thousand people, the government ringed the lake with a huge dike. Then, to provide water for the 'Glades, fourteen hundred miles of canals and levees were extended throughout much of the upper saw grass country. The water flow was maintained by control dams.

Along the canal bank that runs on the north side of the Tamiami Trail are Miccosukee airboats. Driven by old airplane propellers, they send guests skimming through the saw grass on unforgettable explorations.

Originally the Everglades continued to the very outskirts of Miami, nearly thirty miles to the east of where it ends now. But dikes and ditches have converted much of this rich land into agriculture. Indeed, the soil is so fertile that farms around Homestead provide the nation with fully half its winter vegetables. And to the north, the former Everglades has become acre after acre of lush sugarcane fields. Many farmers contend that using the Everglades for food production serves a better purpose than leaving it an idle expanse of saw grass and alligators.

## Everglades National Park

The land along the south side of the Tamiami Trail is part of Everglades National Park. Park trams transport visitors through the

*The lofty observation walkway at Everglades National Park offers an inspiring view.*

saw grass and past dozing alligators to a five-story observation tower. If you like magnificent distances, you will find the view from the tower truly inspiring. Here you can appreciate Marjory Stoneman Douglas's description of the Everglades: "Nothing anywhere else is like them: their vast glittering openness, wider than the enormous visible round of the horizon." She also notes the "massive winds, under the dazzling blue heights of space."

### Marjory Stoneman Douglas: Voice of the Everglades

Marjory Douglas, with her epochal book *The Everglades: River of Grass,* was instrumental in preserving the Everglades as we know it today. Douglas was a character to match the unusual water world that she helped save. Though small in stature, she was not afraid to voice her opinions, so much so that sometimes she seemed unduly stubborn. Beautiful she was not and was perhaps the only girl at Wellesley to go through college never being asked to a dance, as she admitted in her autobiography, *Voice of the River.*

She married Kenneth Douglas, thirty years her senior, more out of curiosity than for real love, she claimed. When he was sent to the penitentiary for forgery, she took the train to Florida, where her father, Frank Stoneman, had started the newspaper that would develop into the high-flying *Miami Herald.* When her father made her society editor in 1915, her writing career began.

For many years she was content with her column and with writing short stories. However, by the early 1940s she was ready for something more ambitious. The book that became *The Everglades* started out as a project about the Miami River. Yet soon Douglas was complaining to her editor that the river was hardly longer than good spitting distance. To get any kind of book she must include the Everglades. So the 'Glades were tossed in as a kind of afterthought. But quickly her interest in the Miami River dried up and the 'Glades became her entire focus.

Douglas had trouble choosing a title, for she knew very little about the Everglades—who did in the 1940s? About her only experience there had been cruising through a small portion of it on a luxurious houseboat, where the main activity was hooking fish. So she went to the state hydrologist and asked the basic question: Just what were the Everglades? From him she learned that the vast field of saw grass was growing not in stagnant water but in an immensely wide, slowly moving flow of fresh water. Stretching the definition, she decided that it could be called a river—a "river of grass." The title was inspired, for until that time most people, if they thought of the Everglades at all, pictured it as a smelly, unhealthy swamp. And who saves swamps? But a freshwater river—that was different.

It took Douglas four years to complete the book, which begins with the limestone rock of an ancient seabed being exposed as the ocean receded during the Ice Age, includes the era of Napoleon Bonaparte Broward, Florida's flamboyant governor who won the election of 1904 vowing to drain the Everglades, and continues to what she called the "reckless" levee and canal building of the 1930s and 1940s.

While writing *The Everglades,* Douglas became active with the committee to turn a portion of the 'Glades into a national park. One of her proudest moments came when she, now a woman of nearly sixty, watched as President Harry Truman inaugurated the park in 1947. It was the same year her book came out, to national acclaim that surprised the publisher.

Douglas's work still was not done, however. She became an active public speaker, quickly identified by her distinctive horn-rimmed glasses and broad-brimmed hat, horribly out-of-date. When she was seventy-eight, she founded the Friends of the Everglades, which

*Marjory Stoneman Douglas (right) autographing books in 1958.* —Florida State Archives

spearheaded efforts to protect and restore the threatened region. A major result of the efforts by the Friends and other environmental groups was the passage of Florida's Everglades Forever Act in 1994. Under this law, a twenty-year program was established to control pollutants discharged by the sugar mills around Lake Okeechobee, from which the Everglades receives most of its water.

Douglas continued to remain active, for a great deal was still to be done to save the Everglades. There was the matter of the dikes and canals dug by the Army Corps of Engineers. These dikes and canals disrupt the water flow upon which the saw grass and other plants depend. Then there was the monumental problem of the melaleuca trees, imported from Australia many years ago, gobbling away the 'Glades at the rate of fifty acres a day.

As the years went by, Douglas became partially blind but asserted, "No matter how poor my eyes are I can still talk." And talk she did, although she admitted that "sometimes I tell them more than they wanted to know."

Even past the age of a hundred, Marjory Douglas kept active in the movement, though she had never learned to drive and had to be chauffeured to events from her tiny home in Coconut Grove, near Miami, where she lived alone with her cats. She had no children, as she had not married again, nor even had sex after 1915 (so she stated in her autobiography). But she was happy. She had helped saved one of the earth's most unique and endangered ecosystems. Few humans can leave such a legacy.

### The Everglades and the ValuJet Crash

Although environmentalists view the Everglades as "fragile," to look upon it as weak and helpless is to miss its essence. Even Marjory Douglas preferred not to venture far into its tangled, essentially hostile recesses. "The naturalist in the Everglades must usually appreciate it from a distance," she warned. Just how hostile the Everglades can be was illustrated by the crash of a ValuJet airliner on May 11, 1996.

Fire and deadly gas fumes doomed the plane just minutes after it left Miami. Diving out of control into the Everglades near the L-67 canal along the eastern border of the Miccosukee reservation, the aircraft vanished into the muck and saw grass. In effect the Everglades had swallowed the large plane with its 110 passengers and crew "with one gulp," wrote a newspaper reporter.

Officials from the National Transportation Safety Board were onsite almost immediately, hoping to learn from the wreckage what went wrong. But they found no wreckage—and no bodies, to the dismay of the victims' friends and relatives. There was only the dark water and the everlasting saw grass moaning in the wind.

A command post was set up on the one-lane dirt road that was the only access to the crash site. Motorists looking north from the Tamiami Trail could see the power trucks, the fuel tankers, the police cars, and the vans from the Dade County morgue. Communication antennas spiked above the grass, as did the tops of the shelter tents, which were air-conditioned against the muggy heat that hung over the area like a wet cloak.

The Florida Marine Patrol ferried searchers to the crash site, where they dressed in sweltering wet suits to probe the chest-high water for the debris and human remains that might be lodged in the six-foot-thick gooey layer of peat and rotting plant matter that overlay the bedrock. Sharpshooters were posted nearby to watch for alligators and poisonous snakes. The saw grass loomed about the waders like butcher knives, their serrated blades able to rasp through leather. "It certainly makes everybody rethink the idea that man is all powerful," remarked one searcher. "That is not true out here. The Everglades rule."

The days went on. Only the barest fragments of the plane were found. As for human remains, arms and legs often floated past, but soon the body parts began putrefying in the blood-warm, soupy water, leaving only a stomach-churning odor. Experienced salvagers said it was more difficult to recover a plane here than on a distant mountain.

After eight days of intensive probing, only 10 percent of the plane had been recovered. Now a series of summer storms roared across the 'Glades, stabbing the water with dangerous spears of lightning. But the search continued. Where was the rest of the plane? From radar it was learned that there was a pit in the limestone bedrock 175 feet long, but still no plane.

At last the waders had to give up, and heavy equipment was brought in. A large backhoe was placed on pontoon barges and towed to the site, but ironically the operators had to wait for an emergency permit from the Army Corps of Engineers before dredging in this environmentally sensitive area.

Work continued on into June using the big equipment. When at last 70 percent of the plane had been recovered, the National Transportation Safety Board had to give up. The bodies and the rest of the plane had forever become part of the Everglades.

The Tamiami Trail continues into Miami, where it becomes bustling Eighth Street, or Calle Ocho to its Cuban residents. After crossing I-95, it ends just south of the city's colorful waterfront entertainment district.

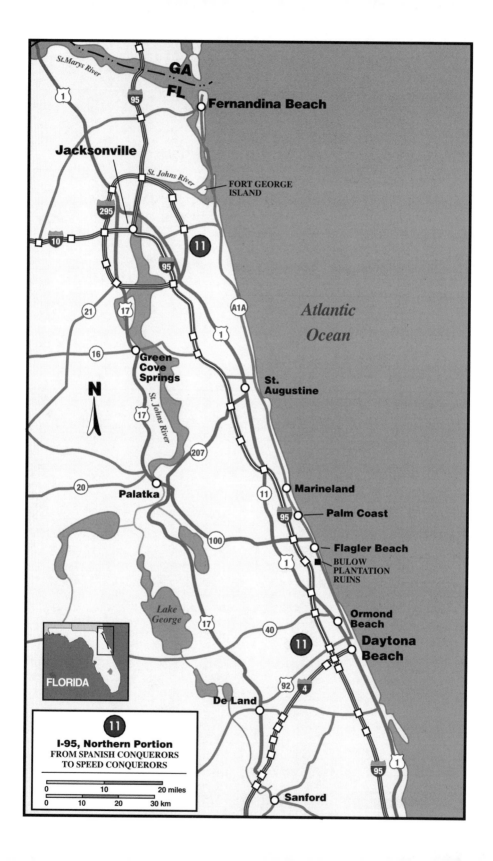

St.Marys River

**GA**

**FL**

① 1

95

○ **Fernandina Beach**

**Jacksonville**

St. Johns River

FORT GEORGE
ISLAND

295

10

95

❶ 11

21

17

A1A

*Atlantic*

*Ocean*

16

○ **Green Cove Springs**

St. Johns River

17

① 1

**St. Augustine**

**N**

207

20

100

○ **Palatka**

11

○ **Marineland**

95 ○ **Palm Coast**

① 1 ◇ **Flagler Beach**

■ BULOW
PLANTATION
RUINS

*Lake George*

17

40

❶ 11

○ **Ormond Beach**

**Daytona Beach**

92 4

**De Land** ○

① 1

95

**Sanford** ○

FLORIDA

❶ 11

**I-95, Northern Portion**
FROM SPANISH CONQUERORS
TO SPEED CONQUERORS

0        10        20 miles

0    10    20    30 km

# ≈ 11 ≈

# *I-95, Northern Portion*

## FROM SPANISH CONQUISTADORS
## TO SPEED CONQUERORS

# Georgia Line—St. Augustine
### 62 miles

*The Bloody St. Marys River*

I-95 crosses into Florida over the St. Marys River. Nowadays we have grown accustomed to Florida's northern border at this river, but for a long time the exact limits of Florida with regard to the British colonies up the coast were hotly disputed. Spanish influence reached far north of the St. Marys (named for a mission on the river) into Georgia. Only when the British and their Indian allies wiped out the missions in the early 1700s did the Spanish reluctantly accept the St. Marys as Florida's limit.

I-95 travels along what Floridians call the First Coast, between the Georgia line and St. Augustine. The name relates not only to the fact that St. Augustine is the oldest continuously occupied town in the United States, but to the very early Spanish and even earlier French activities in this area.

## Fernandina Beach and Amelia Island

Ten miles south of the Georgia line, I-95 comes to the A1A turn-off. This is a fine highway leading eastward fourteen miles to Amelia Island and the town of Fernandina Beach. The route parallels Florida's earliest cross-state railroad, opened in 1861, which ran between Fernandina and Cedar Key. The railroad was the project of David Levy Yulee, a colorful Jewish promoter and U.S. senator. Yulee, scorning Jacksonville, believed that Fernandina, with its protected, easily accessible harbor, would become north Florida's principal port.

Fortunately for those who have come to cherish the little town's quaint isolation, Yulee's vision was faulty.

Nonetheless, the coming of the railroad initiated Fernandina's greatest prosperity. Between 1875 and 1900 Fernandina grew wealthy from tourism, as well as from a lucrative trade in lumber and phosphates. During this period, dozens of commercial buildings were constructed along Centre Street, many of which still stand.

But when Henry Flagler's East Coast Line diverted tourists to Palm Beach, Miami, and finally Key West, Fernandina began a long decline that did not end until the mid-1970s, when the southern portion of the island, with its luscious sand beach, was transformed by an upscale resort known as the Amelia Island Plantation. Other major developments followed, and today the island is a highly regarded vacation getaway.

A fifty-block area of downtown Fernandina Beach has been placed on the National Register of Historic Places. Just to stroll down Centre Street is to relive the late nineteenth century. There is the Palace Saloon, reputedly Florida's oldest watering hole, which serves sandwiches as well as booze. Nearby is the 1878 Steak House. Farther along is the old Nassau County Courthouse, with its Byzantine pillars. The railroad tracks still run along the waterfront, where the old train depot is now occupied by the chamber of commerce.

Just north of town off A1A is Fort Clinch, construction of which began in 1847. Impressive with its moat and strong walls, it was occupied during the Civil War by Union forces. Today, park rangers dressed in federal uniforms explain garrison life of the 1860s. Nature trails lead through a coastal hammock frequented by wading birds.

Traveling south from Fernandina Beach, people with historical and environmental interests may prefer to take highway A1A rather than I-95. The road leads down Amelia Island, across the Nassau River, and along the beaches and coastal marshes of Fort George Island. For details of this trip, see chapter 4. Suffice it to say here that a side trip can be made to the old Kingsley Plantation, with its unforgettable ruins of former slave cabins.

Once you have taken the ferry across the St. Johns River, named for a vanished Spanish mission near here, you can head into Jacksonville on Florida 10, which connects with I-95, or you can continue south along the coast on A1A to St. Augustine. One of this highway's special attractions is the new high-rise bridge over the Intracoastal Waterway, just north of St. Augustine. The spans provide excellent

*Historic Fernandina slumbers in the late afternoon sunshine.*

*Fort Clinch on Amelia Island was begun in 1847. Union troops occupied it during the Civil War. It is now open to the public.* —P. H. Yonge Library of Florida History, University of Florida

*Ponce de León first sighted Florida in 1513 during the holiday known as the Festival of Flowers, hence the name "Florida."*—Florida State Archives

views of the ancient towns as well as of rivers, ocean, and forest. You may also enjoy a stroll on the bridge's lofty walkway.

# St. Augustine

## Juan Ponce de León

Although St. Augustine's population is less than fifteen thousand, its importance far exceeds its numbers, for Florida's recorded history began when Juan Ponce de León went ashore at or near here in 1513. Ponce de León told the native peoples, in a language they fortunately did not understand, that their homeland was now a possession of Spain and that it was henceforth to be known as "La Florida," after the Christian Festival of the Flowers, or Easter—for it was then that the would-be conquistador made his fateful landing.

Ponce de León was thirty-nine at the time and was seeking a site for colonization, though if he could have located the mythical fountain of youth, he would not have refused to partake of its waters. In any event, he soon sailed south to explore the Keys and the gulf coast, where, on a second voyage eight years later, he received the arrow that ultimately caused his death.

## Pedro Menéndez de Avilés: The Misunderstood Butcher

The actual colonization of St. Augustine fell to Pedro Menéndez de Avilés, who arrived in 1565 with eight hundred men. He hastily

*Pedro Menéndez lands on the site of Saint Augustine. History knows Menéndez as a butcher for his killing of unarmed French soldiers in 1565.* —Florida State Archives

constructed a fort, since French soldiers had already established Fort Caroline at the mouth of the St. Johns River, just forty miles to the north. Hardly had Menéndez secured himself than the French set out to destroy him. But a hurricane blew the attackers' fleet past St. Augustine and on down the coast. Menéndez, realizing that Fort Caroline was now virtually undefended, conducted a daring attack against the post, whereby he surprised and killed most of its garrison. Then, upon learning that the French ships had been wrecked by the hurricane, Menéndez captured large groups of survivors on the beaches south of town. Once they were in his power, he executed around three hundred men at a location that from then on was called *matanzas,* or "the slaughtering place."

Menéndez has been denounced as a butcher, and his actions have become part of the "black legend" of Spanish cruelty. But did he have any real choice? He could not send the French back to rebuild Fort Caroline and renew their threat to St. Augustine. Nor could he keep them as prisoners because he had so little food that almost a hundred of his own men would die of starvation the coming winter.

St. Augustine maintained a precarious existence during the Spanish period. Several times the king considered abandoning it, for the swampy environs were not suitable for farming, and there were no rivers to give it good communication with the interior. In addition, the too-shallow harbor was of little use in its main purpose— to protect and shelter the treasure fleets. The Spanish remained here mostly from concern that another power would occupy the site. But an additional factor was the Franciscan friars.

### The Spanish Missions

The Franciscans valued St. Augustine as headquarters of the mission system that they had extended over much of northern Florida. These missions were connected by a road that led westward from St. Augustine, crossed the St. Johns River at Picolata, where the Spaniards built a fort, and continued on to a settlement bordering the great Alachua Savanna near Gainesville. Then it headed north to the missions on the Santa Fe River, and from there west past more missions to reach San Luis de Talimali, the largest mission of all, near Tallahassee.

At its height in the late 1600s, there were thirty-one missions teaching Christianity to upwards of twenty-six thousand Timucuan and Apalachee Indians. Not only do these numbers attest to the Franciscans' success, they demonstrate the falsity of another legend: that Hernando de Soto, marching through Florida in the prior century, had introduced diseases that virtually wiped out the early Florida tribes.

### The Dickinsons' Heroic Trek

Most of the days at St. Augustine were boring; there was almost no commerce, and sometimes three years would pass before the appearance of the so-called annual supply ship from Mexico. But on November 15, 1696, an unusual event livened things up for a while. This was the arrival of Jonathan and Mary Dickinson and the other English survivors of a shipwreck three months earlier. They made a pathetic sight—emaciated from hunger, their naked bodies almost blue with cold, their feet swollen and bloody from their grueling, 230-mile trek up the coast from the locale of modern Jupiter.

Governor Laureano Torres had had many conflicts with belligerent English ruffians from Charleston, and were it not for a just-negotiated truce, he probably would have imprisoned the Dickinsons

*The Governor's House at Saint Augustine in 1764. The British ruled east Florida from here for twenty years.* —P. H. Yonge Library of Florida History, University of Florida

and their companions. But now, being a kindly man at heart, he accepted them hospitably.

Mary Dickinson, guest of the governor's wife, immediately took to bed with a high fever. But Jonathan had time to explore the town. "It is about three quarters of a mile in length," he later wrote in his journal, "having large orchards in which are plenty of oranges, lemons, pome-citrons, limes, figs, and peaches: the houses [are] old buildings and not half of them inhabited. The number of men being about three hundred. . . . At the north end of the town standeth a large fortification." Aside from fruits, the chief foods of the monotonous Spanish diet were pumpkins and boiled corn, though every so often tough beefies arrived from the ranches beyond the St. Johns River.

Governor Torres enjoyed the Dickinsons' company but knew they wished to get to the English colonies. Thus he provided them with canoes and Spanish oarsmen for their trip to Charleston. He also gave them such provisions as corn, peas, and salt. Astonishingly, Jonathan Dickinson offered to pay him in the form of two of his slaves who had been shipwrecked with him. But the governor said he'd accept instead Dickinson's promise to pay him later in much-needed

*The Castillo protected the Spanish at Saint Augustine for many decades after it was completed around the end of the seventeenth century.* —P. H. Yonge Library of Florida History, University of Florida

coin. Then he accompanied the couple to the dock, where he embraced them and implored them not to forget him when they were again among their own people.

Jonathan and Mary Dickinson arrived in Charleston twenty-seven days later.

### The Fort

The Dickinsons had reached St. Augustine just as the Spaniards had completed the great stone fort that they called Castillo de San Marcos. It had been started more than two decades earlier as a response to a raid by English pirates.

The Castillo proved its mettle in 1702, when James Moore, British governor of Carolina, was unable to take it. (Torres was no longer at St. Augustine.) Instead he had to satisfy himself by burning the town. Two years later Moore, not as governor but as a simple plunderer and slaver, descended on the Franciscan missions and virtually destroyed the entire system that the Franciscans had labored a hundred years to create and that conceivably could have become the core of a Native American state.

## The Strange Demise of Osceola

After Spain ceded Florida to the United States in 1821, St. Augustine remained an important town and, as such, was headquarters for army units during the Second Seminole War.

In October 1837, Seminole leader Osceola camped with a band of warriors near Moultrie Creek, several miles south of town. This was the site where a treaty had been signed fourteen years earlier, apparently giving the Seminoles a huge reservation in central Florida. But a later treaty nullified the Moultrie Creek treaty and called for the Seminoles to leave Florida entirely. This angered the Indians and led directly to the Second Seminole War, which began in 1835.

Although the Seminoles had some spectacular initial successes, it was soon apparent that they could not win the conflict. Thus, Osceola sent word to General Thomas Jesup that he wanted to parley under a truce arrangement. Although Jesup agreed, he dispatched General Joseph Hernandez with contrary instructions. Hernandez easily found Osceola's camp, marked by a white flag. As the men talked, American troopers secretly surrounded the Seminoles. At a signal from Hernandez, they closed in, guns at the ready. Osceola and his seventy-one followers had no choice except to surrender.

Though they had been taken in violation of the truce, the Seminoles were marched through St. Augustine as prisoners of war—with the entire populace turning out as if for a circus. Then they were

*Seminole leader Osceola was captured under a flag of truce here at Treaty Park, Saint Augustine.*

*Henry Flagler opened Saint Augustine's fanciest hotel, the Ponce de Leon, in 1888. It boasted electric lights—and even private toilets in some rooms! Today it is Flagler College.* —P. H. Yonge Library of Florida History, University of Florida

herded into cells in the Castillo. Shortly, Osceola was transferred to Charleston. Being ill when he was captured, he died in January 1838, probably of complications from malaria.

But the tragic story does not stop here. The physician attending Osceola was none other than the brother-in-law of Wiley Thompson, the Indian agent Osceola had killed and beheaded at Fort King (modern Ocala). Upon Osceola's death the doctor, Dr. Weedon, severed the Seminole leader's head and took it with him to his St. Augustine home, where he preserved it with embalming fluid. Whenever one of his sons was disobedient, he would force him to sleep with the head atop the bedpost.

The gruesome trophy had a series of owners and is believed to have been burned in a New York museum fire several decades later. But no one knows for sure. Perhaps it still exists . . . somewhere.

### Advent of a Titan

When fifty-three-year-old Henry Flagler and his second wife, Alice, arrived at St. Augustine in 1883, the town had long since been bypassed by progress. Its ancient homes and churches were decaying, and its only attraction was the crumbling Spanish fort. Nonetheless, Flagler believed that this sleepy place with fewer than two thousand inhabitants had possibilities as a resort. It would be a challenge, but Flagler thrived on challenges.

Flagler had been born to poor parents in 1830, and when he was in his early teens his father had drifted off. The next year, Flagler quit school and went to live with a cousin in Ohio. There, he got a job in a country store for five dollars a month. Energetic and quick-witted, he was soon store manager. By the time he was twenty-two he had saved enough money to invest in a small distillery. One of his suppliers was an equally ambitious young man named John D. Rockefeller.

When petroleum was discovered near Cleveland, Flagler and Rockefeller formed a partnership and got into oil refining. They were as close as two men could be, even having their desks in the same room. Rockefeller, introverted and serious, was the master of details. Flagler, extroverted and imaginative, was the master of strategy. Their goal was simple: to control the oil business throughout the entire country.

They pursued their goal ruthlessly. Flagler had a motto pasted to his desk: "Do unto others as they would do unto you—and do it first." Forcing the railroads to give them huge, but secret, rebates, they were able to undercut all other producers, thereby forcing them to sell out or face bankruptcy. In 1882 Flagler was instrumental in organizing the Standard Oil Trust. By then their goal of utter dominance had been fulfilled. Although Flagler would stay on as director, he began looking for new enterprises. St. Augustine was one of these.

In 1885 Flagler purchased tidal marshland just west of the main part of town. Into it he dumped many tons of sand, which he firmed with hundreds of pine pilings. Then he began work on a landmark hotel called the Ponce de Leon. He wanted to create a personal monument, "something to last all time," he told a friend. As a result, its walls were of poured concrete and were so massive that the overall effect was as much of a fortress as a hotel.

The hotel had its own water, which was stored in tanks within its large twin towers. Electricity, still a novelty, was supplied by Edison dynamos. Many rooms even had their own toilets, although they were not in the original plans. Louis Tiffany was the interior decorator, and the stained-glass windows he put in helped found his reputation.

Even before it was completed, the Ponce de Leon was the talk of the nation. It opened January 10, 1888, to the brassy fanfare of a twenty-one-piece military band. Over the years, many notables enjoyed the hotel's hospitality, including presidents Grover Cleveland, Theodore Roosevelt, and Warren Harding.

In addition to the Ponce de Leon, Flagler built the Alcazar Hotel across the street. It was originally designed as a shopping arcade, with moderately priced rooms on the second floor. But its popularity was such that the shopping area was converted into the lobby, and the Alcazar quickly developed into an attraction to rival the Ponce. Particularly well attended were diving exhibitions in the indoor swimming pool, which was the world's largest.

But Flagler soon realized that St. Augustine was too far north to become the real winter playground that the wealthy craved. For true subtropical weather, he turned to Palm Beach, 240 miles south. Although construction of an entire rail system would be required to transport tourists there, such a challenge was like an elixir to Flagler. By 1894 he had laid tracks to West Palm Beach. And, as Flagler's empire moved south, the glory days of St. Augustine began to fade.

### Touring St. Augustine

Although the time has long passed when St. Augustine was a premier winter tourist resort, it is still one of Florida's most popular places to visit.

The frowning Spanish fortress has survived the centuries. Views from the bastions are inspiring, and inspections of the dank cubicles beneath the walls, in one of which Osceola was imprisoned, are disquieting. It is believed that Osceola's cell was on the west side closest to the wells. The Indian leader used to climb up to the window to watch the clouds and muse upon the freedom that had been his.

North of the fort is Ripley's Believe It or Not, located in the former Castle Warden Hotel. Famed writer Marjorie Kennan Rawlings lived in the penthouse during the 1940s with her husband, the hotel's manager. Nearby is the site of Nombre de Dios, keystone of the Franciscan mission network, now sanctified by the Shrine of Nuestra Senora de la Leche.

Immediately west of the fort is a portion of the old city wall. It faces the information center, where there is public parking. The City Gate leads to St. George Street, the town's main thoroughfare ever since the days of the Spanish and English. A stroll down St. George leads past restored buildings that turn the ages back. In four blocks you come to the plaza, with the old governor's mansion and the

Spanish cathedral, now raised to the status of a basilica. It was here that the hardship saga of the Minorcan colony, whose story is told in chapter 12, ended when the survivors found sanctuary at St. Augustine in 1777. The basilica contains a mural over its main portal showing the Minorcans.

A block west of the plaza on King Street is the former Ponce de Leon Hotel. The building had a long decline and actually became a public eyesore until it was renovated as Flagler College, which opened in 1968. The Alcazar, across King Street, was rescued from dilapidation and eventual destruction by Otto Lightner, the man known as "America's Hobby King." Lightner died of cancer just two years after turning the building into a museum displaying his multitudinous collection. A particularly interesting use has been made of the Alcazar's swimming pool, which now houses a colorful arcade of antique shops.

Just as Flagler's Florida adventure began at St. Augustine, so did it terminate here. A block north of the former Ponce de Leon Hotel is the Flagler Memorial Church, which he built in 1890 and in which he always occupied pew number twenty. When he passed on in 1913, he was interred in the adjoining mausoleum beside his first wife, Mary, and his daughter, Jennie, who died unexpectedly of childbirth complications while on the way to visit her father in Florida.

For tourists wanting to return to I-95, take Florida 207 and watch for Wildwood Drive when you are in sight of the expressway. This road leads a mile south to Treaty Park, site of the Treaty of Moultrie Creek. There are hiking trails and a short boardwalk over ponds and wetlands. The trees are dense, and it is easy to imagine how Osceola and his followers were surprised and captured in this vicinity in 1837.

**I-95**

# St. Augustine — Daytona Beach
**53 miles**

## An Alternative to I-95

*A1A: The Scenic Route South*

People wanting a more scenic and historic road than I-95 between St. Augustine and Daytona Beach should drive east from the plaza over the Matanzas River to Anastasia Island. A lighthouse dating from

1874 is near the site of a sixteenth-century Spanish watchtower. Nearby is a state recreation area, with quarries where the Spanish cut stones for the Castillo.

Taking A1A down Anastasia Island, in ten miles you will reach Crescent Beach. Marjorie Kinnan Rawlings, author of *The Yearling*, owned a cottage at 6600 Broward Street. Among her guests were Ernest Hemingway and Zora Neale Hurston. It was in this home that Rawlings had a fatal cerebral hemorrhage in 1953.

Next, in quick succession, you come to Fort Matanzas, Marineland, and Washington Oaks State Gardens.

Fort Matanzas was erected in 1742 to guard St. Augustine's southern water approach. It was in this vicinity that Spanish commander Menéndez de Avilés executed approximately three hundred shipwrecked French soldiers and sailors in 1565.

Marineland opened in 1938 as the world's first underwater motion picture studio and is now on the National Register of Historic Places.

Washington Oaks State Gardens was once part of the Belle Vista Plantation, owned by General Joseph Hernandez, the one who captured Osceola. His daughter, Louisa, married a relative of George Washington. The plantation, which extended from the Matanzas River to the Atlantic, has nature trails with markers describing the native plants that grow along the coast. There is also a fine overlook onto the deserted beach where Atlantic breakers roll in, slowed only slightly by the artificial reefs Florida has placed far out along much of its coast to provide habitats for game fish. These reefs are an odd, even bizarre, assortment of twentieth-century artifacts ranging from obsolete bombing planes to worn-out auto tires and broken toilets. One can only wonder what historians from a different planet might make of these items. We only know that the fish like them.

# Palm Coast

*The Metropolis That Almost Was*

Travelers on I-95 are impressed by the Palm Coast Parkway interchange, with its attractive display of flowers, ponds, and landscaped terraces. Actually, the interchange is an artful contrivance designed to entice visitors into the town of Palm Coast, which is one of the larger planned communities in the nation. It is beautiful now. But that is not what it started out to be.

Megacorporation ITT began developing Palm Coast in 1969. The area involved was bigger than Philadelphia, and ITT's plans called for a population of 750,000, which would have made it Florida's largest city. ITT bulldozers knocked down trees and scooped out canal beds, leaving the land as scarred as if it were a strip mine. Environmental laws were largely ignored.

But by 1976, conservationists' clamor had become so great that the U.S. Department of Housing and Urban Development forced ITT to halt the sale of lots while it looked into the numerous complaints. Ultimately ITT's project director was indicted by a grand jury. This made ITT realize that not even a multibillion-dollar corporation could flaunt state and federal laws with impunity. So the company radically changed its plans for Palm Coast. Environmental protection was given high priority, and the project was scaled down so drastically that the current population is only around thirty thousand.

Today many environmentalists are still angered because the company was permitted to construct a bridge across the Intracoastal Waterway to a once-wild island that is being converted into the upscale development of Hammock Dunes. This conversion resulted in the removal of five precious miles of seacoast from public access.

Nevertheless, Palm Coast is a pretty community. Its modest marina is certainly one of the most appealing in Florida. The Harborside Inn has a charming public restaurant overlooking the boat slips. If you get a hankering to stay longer, why not buy a waterfront residence in exclusive Hammock Dunes? You can get a nice one for a million dollars.

# Flagler Beach

Flagler Beach, a small, friendly place, is four miles east of I-95—or if you are on A1A, it is the traditional wide place in the road. The town pier juts more than eight hundred feet into the Atlantic, and fishing poles can be rented here.

The Topaz Hotel/Motel, across from the pier, was built in 1923 for well-known architect Dana Fuquay. Fuquay was among those agitating for an oceanfront road, and in 1927 what was to become A1A was constructed between St. Augustine and Daytona. Sometime thereafter, Charles Lindbergh was Fuquay's guest—and to this day his quarters are called "The Lindy Room."

### Death of a Dream: The Bulow Sugar Mill

The Bulow Plantation Ruins State Historic Site is near Flagler Beach. It can be reached on either A1A or I-95 via Florida 100. Take

*The ruins of John Bulow's sugar mill stand as gaunt today as when the structure was burned by the Seminoles in 1836. John James Audubon stayed briefly with Bulow in 1831.*

that highway to the old Kings Road, which is just east of I-95. Then go three miles south to the ruins.

During the British era, many sugar plantations were established along the Halifax River and were connected on the land side by the Kings Road, which the British built between Jacksonville and New Smyrna. The number of plantations multiplied under the Americans, until eventually there were sixteen of them. One of these plantations was acquired in 1821 by Charles Bulow who, with the aid of his three hundred slaves, planted nearly half with sugarcane. At harvest time the slaves would cut the cane and cart it to Bulow's large mill, where steam-driven rollers crushed the stalks and extracted the juice. After the water was evaporated from the juice, sugar and molasses remained. These products were loaded into barrels and boated down the Halifax River to oceangoing schooners waiting at Ponce de Leon Inlet—just south of modern Daytona Beach.

Charles Bulow died three years after he came to Florida, leaving the plantation to his only son, John. Still a minor, John returned from Paris, where he was being educated, to run the plantation. His wealth increased until Bulowville, as the group of buildings was called, became the showplace of the region and attracted many guests. One of these was John James Audubon, who spent some time there in 1831 while on his way to Key West. The great painter enjoyed Bulow and called him his friend. No doubt Audubon also appreciated Bulow as a bon vivant, for so great was his penchant for entertaining that his boat slips were lined with innumerable discarded wine and ale bottles.

Young, rich, and with many aristocratic friends, Bulow, the amiable bachelor, must have thought the good life stretched endlessly before him. But he was distressed by the outbreak of the Second Seminole War in 1835. When the St. Augustine militia decided to use his facilities as headquarters, Bulow tried to warn them away with cannon fire, for he had amicable relations with the Seminoles, who often supplied his plantation with fresh meat. Despite his efforts, the militia took over his mansion and Bulow was actually held prisoner. When the militia abandoned the plantation, Bulow was forced to accompany them, leaving all his possessions.

The Seminoles arrived soon thereafter. Determined to destroy all the Halifax River plantations, they put Bulowville to the torch. It is said the burning buildings cast a bloody glow on the horizon that could be seen from St. Augustine, forty miles away.

John Bulow never recovered. Despondent, he returned to Paris, where he died a few months later at the age of twenty-six.

The sugar mill's two-story stone walls are still charred from the Seminole fire. On the park grounds are stones from the mansion at which Audubon was once a guest. A marker indicates the location of the forty slave cabins, which were well equipped for the time. The boat slips remain, and some of Bulow's many liquor bottles are on display in the small, state-administered museum.

## A Trip Along the Old Kings Road

From the Bulow ruins, there are three choices: (1) go back to I-95, (2) proceed down scenic A1A, or (3) continue down the Kings Road ten miles to Ormond Beach.

The Kings Road is an experience one does not soon forget. Although the road is paved, in many places it runs through a countryside nearly as wild as when the British constructed it between 1771 and 1777. Bronze warriors padded along the road during the fury of the Seminole War. A century later, Americans constructed the Dixie Highway

*The Kings Road dates back to the British era, when its main use was to connect the string of sugar plantations along the Halifax River. This photo was taken in 1916.* —P. H. Yonge Library of Florida History, University of Florida

over some of the same route, at which time it clanged with the jalopies of get-rich-quick hopefuls during the 1920s boom.

Today the highway is quiet. Live oaks laden with Spanish moss overhang the right-of-way. Some of the oaks are huge, with trunks more than six feet thick and spreading branches that could shade half a football field.

The road passes Damietta, site of the plantation of James Ormond, for whom Ormond Beach was named. The plantation was one of the most prosperous in the area until the Seminoles burned it.

Tomoka State Park is located on the site of yet another plantation, this once owned by Richard Oswald. In 1764 Oswald, highly influential in Great Britain, received a grant of twenty thousand acres, from which he founded four large plantations along the Halifax River. Later, Oswald was a British negotiator at the conference granting American independence.

The park museum has many Indian displays, for the Timucua tribe had a large village here during Spanish days, and previous tribes inhabited the site as early as 5000 B.C.

# Ormond Beach

Ormond Beach became one of Florida's major vacation destinations after the railroad arrived in 1886. Henry Flagler bought the little Ormond Hotel four years later and enlarged it into a spectacular showplace. The hotel stood on the east bank of the Halifax River at the Granada Boulevard (Florida 40) bridge—a site now occupied by condominiums.

### The Twilight of the World's Richest Man

So great was Ormond Beach's allure that when John D. Rockefeller, reputed to be the wealthiest person in creation, was selecting a winter home in 1918, he purchased a mansion across from the Ormond Hotel.

Rockefeller was seventy-eight years old when he moved into the Casements, as he called his Ormond home. Gone were the days when he and Henry Flagler had trampled all adversaries as they erected the mighty Standard Oil Trust. Rockefeller had been a feared robber baron then. Now he was just a wizened old man who gave out newly minted dimes to children as he tried to refurbish his tarnished image.

Rockefeller had almost no close friends, for he had always been a distant man. His family did not like the relatively modest Ormond

*John D. Rockefeller's home during his twilight years. A lonely man, he often sat in the gardens from which this picture was taken to watch boats on the Halifax River. His family rarely visited him.* —Florida State Archives

*John D. Rockefeller attends an Ormond Beach social gathering in 1926.* —Florida State Archives

Beach home, and rarely did any of them visit him. Although he had four guards, three chauffeurs, and a household staff of twelve, he was essentially alone.

So, as the years moved relentlessly on, Rockefeller lived a routine devoid of intimacies. His favorite pastime became sitting in his garden across from the Casements watching the Halifax River. At these times, he must have pondered if he would achieve his goal—to live to be a hundred. But this was to be one of his few failures, for in 1937 he died at the Casements. He had reached ninety-seven.

## Daytona Beach

The history of Daytona Beach began with Mathias Day, who purchased land along the west side of the calm Halifax River in 1870—even though he complained that there were "ten million fleas to the square yard." Fleas or not, he built a hotel facing the river, and eventually the settlement that followed was named in his honor.

It was not until the turn of the century that speed nuts began to run their horseless contraptions over the hard-packed sand that extended south from Ormond Beach fourteen miles to Ponce Inlet.

This activity started as a whim in 1902, when Ransom Olds and Alexander Winton, guests at the Ormond Hotel, challenged each other to a race. Although there was no winner—for both sped over the sand at 57 mph—the event caught on. Two years later, William K. Vanderbilt set a world record at Daytona Beach of 92 mph. Then in 1906, daredevil Fred Marriott caused the world to gasp as he went more than two miles a minute! Marriott was also involved in one of the beach's most spectacular crashes the following year. Upon hitting a sand ripple at 197 mph, his car flew high in the air, overturned, and broke in two. Miraculously, Marriott was not seriously injured.

### *The* Bluebird: *Faster than the Wind*

The beach achieved its greatest renown in the 1930s with the arrival of Malcolm Campbell, a charismatic Briton with an insatiable hunger to be the fastest man alive. Having made a fortune as an insurance underwriter for Lloyd's of London, Campbell enjoyed ample time and funds to indulge this passion.

But luxury was not enough. Campbell had always been fascinated by speed. As a youngster he had been fined for riding his bicycle so fast that he frightened two old ladies. During World War I he had zoomed around the battlefront on a motorcycle as a dispatch rider. Later he had barnstormed over the English countryside in a home-made airplane.

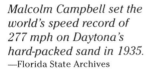

*Malcolm Campbell set the world's speed record of 277 mph on Daytona's hard-packed sand in 1935.*
—Florida State Archives

Campbell had a strong romantic streak: "I never grew up," he once admitted. He named his racer the *Bluebird,* after a famous play about children seeking the bluebird of happiness. He was also superstitious, and he kept a shiny dime Rockefeller had given him for good luck.

In 1931 Campbell was ready to try for the speed record. The nine-mile course began at the foot of Daytona's Main Street Pier. Heading toward Ponce Inlet, the *Bluebird* needed four miles to build up speed. The mist and sea spray made vision difficult, even though the track had been delineated by a line of thick oil laid on the sand. A black-and-yellow marker indicated the start of the measured mile, where Campbell's speed would be timed. He covered the mile in less than a dozen seconds, then he needed the remainder of the beach to slow down. At Ponce he stopped, changed tires, and roared off to run the measured mile once more. On the return, he shot through the pier pilings that in those days had a forty-two-foot space just for such bravado.

He achieved his ambition by setting a record of 246 mph. It was such a feat that he was knighted by King George VI.

Sir Malcolm was back in three of the next four years, each time upping the record until he topped out at 277 mph in 1935.

By then Campbell desperately wanted to break the 300-mph barrier. Although the beach at Daytona was good, the hard-baked western salt flats were better, and in 1936 Campbell was successful in Utah.

Campbell never raced again at Daytona. With the advent of World War II, he turned his talents to the military, and it was rumored that the information he learned from his *Bluebird* races was used to help perfect the Spitfire fighter planes that helped win the Battle of Britain.

After the war, Campbell developed glaucoma, impairing his eyesight and preventing him from racing. An operation for the disease resulted in a heart attack. Game to the end, on his last day alive he drank a farewell champagne toast to his family.

## Big Bill and the Daytona Speedway

One of the spectators watching Malcolm Campbell on his final beach run in 1935 was William France, a six-foot-five, 220-pound giant of a man who friends felt justified in calling Big Bill. France and his wife had come to Daytona with less than seventy-five dollars in the bank. Taking a job as an auto mechanic, Bill eventually saved enough to buy a gas station. During World War II there was no racing at Daytona, but in 1947 Big Bill decided to stage a stock-car race on the beach. It was a great success, and his new career took off.

*Racing on the beach at Daytona in 1956.* —Florida State Archives

At first, France used an oval track on the sand, but it was too hard on the cars; furthermore, there was no way to keep out non-paying spectators—despite posting innumerable "Beware of Rattle-snakes" signs near the track. Determined to build a real racetrack, France formed the Daytona Beach International Speedway Corporation and raised money by selling shares to his friends and neighbors. In 1958 he built the speedway in what had been a swampy area on the outskirts of town.

France died in 1992 knowing that his brainchild had become one of the world's premier racetracks.

## Seeing Daytona Beach

Although Daytona Beach is a modern city of over sixty thousand, visitors see little of it as they rush to the Atlantic shore, billed as the "world's most famous beach." The beach is almost as wide as the ballyhoo claims. And cars can indeed drive on it, though for a fee.

The beach's focal point is the Adam's Mark high-rise hotel. The hotel opened in 1989 as an upscale Marriott. Perhaps influenced by the legacy of Fred Marriott, the Marriott company desired a presence on the beach. But they grossly overestimated the rates they could

*Daytona Beach in the 1940s. The clock tower and band shell were built by the WPA during the Depression.* —P. H. Yonge Library of Florida History, University of Florida

charge, and occupancy was not enough to meet the mortgage requirements. Thus the hotel was sold under foreclosure proceedings in 1994. The current owners charge more enticing rates.

On the ocean side of the hotel is the landmark clock tower, erected in 1935 by the Works Progress Administration (WPA) and recently dedicated to Malcolm Campbell. The hotel's Clocktower Plaza has nearly a dozen casual restaurants, as well as various specialty shops.

To the north is another WPA memento: an open-air band shell, from which concerts enliven many evenings. In the other direction is the Main Street Pier, dating back to 1925. Campbell began his speed runs at the southern base of the pier and on his return usually coasted between its supports.

Daytona's other major attraction is the International Speedway, one mile east of I-95 on US 92. The visitor center, open seven days a week, has been recently enlarged with exciting displays, vintage photos, and other memorabilia. A star attraction is Malcolm Campbell's 1935 *Bluebird* racer, sleek as a bullet. Tours of the famed racetrack are also offered, featuring the incredible thirty-one-degree embankments.

The area slightly east of the speedway on US 92 was originally occupied by a sugar plantation with eighty slaves, until it was destroyed by the Seminoles in 1836. The site now contains the brick buildings of Bethune-Cookman College. The institution was founded by Mary McLeod Bethune in 1904 to provide educational opportunities for the female children of African American workers on Henry Flagler's Florida East Coast Railway.

Mrs. Bethune eventually became one of the nation's most prominent black women, being appointed to various governmental posts by presidents Calvin Coolidge, Franklin Roosevelt, and Harry Truman. The college currently has over two thousand students, both men and women. Mrs. Bethune's home, at 641 Pearl Street, is now a museum.

Amid the hoopla of the famous beach and the equally famous speedway, many tourists skip downtown Daytona. This is unfortunate, for the area has just undergone one of the most pleasing streetscape alterations of any of Florida's smaller cities.

To reach downtown, turn from US 92 onto Beach Street. You will find yourself driving along a tall, feathery, palm-center strip. The street intersections are of reddish bricks with large designs in green and blue. Antique-style streetlights and brick sidewalks add to the effect. The early twentieth-century stores have been renovated in most pleasing ways. For further enlightenment on Daytona's development, view the displays at the historical society, located in a converted 1910 bank building at 252 South Beach Street.

Mathias Day built his hotel on the Halifax River at South Beach Street and Loomis. The hotel is long gone, but the area has many spacious homes constructed in the town's early years. Across Beach Street is a large marina.

*Eleanor Roosevelt and Mary Bethune at a social function in 1937.* —Florida State Archives

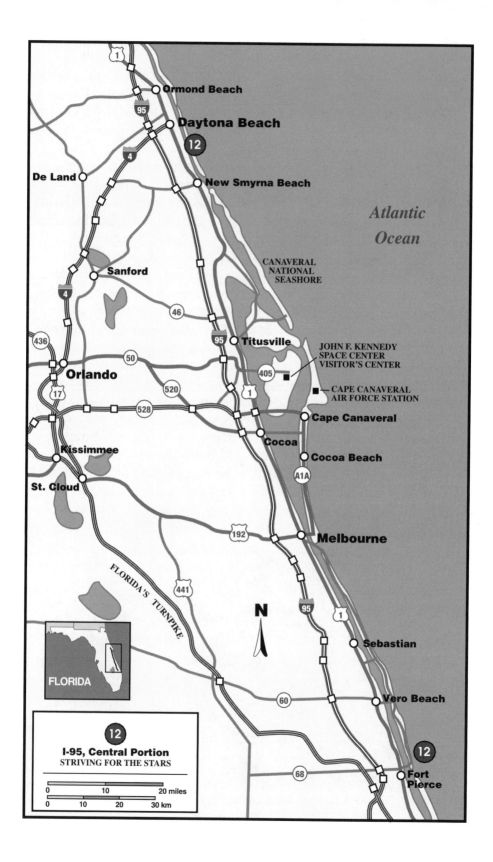

Ormond Beach

95

Daytona Beach

12

4

De Land

New Smyrna Beach

*Atlantic*

*Ocean*

Sanford

CANAVERAL
NATIONAL
SEASHORE

46

436

50

95

Titusville

JOHN F. KENNEDY
SPACE CENTER
VISITOR'S CENTER

405

Orlando

17

520

528

CAPE CANAVERAL
AIR FORCE STATION

Cape Canaveral

Cocoa

Kissimmee

Cocoa Beach

St. Cloud

A1A

192

Melbourne

FLORIDA'S TURNPIKE

441

N

95

1

FLORIDA

Sebastian

60

Vero Beach

12

12

I-95, Central Portion
STRIVING FOR THE STARS

68

Fort
Pierce

0          10          20 miles
0     10     20     30 km

# ❧ 12 ❧
# *I-95, Central Portion*
## STRIVING FOR THE STARS

# Daytona—Kennedy Space Center
**56 miles**

Going south from Daytona, I-95 travels along what geologists call the Pamlico Terrace, a sandy platform that developed during an interglacial period when the ocean was twenty-five feet higher than it is today. This terrace runs parallel to the coast for nearly two hundred miles.

## New Smyrna

New Smyrna began as a commercial venture in 1768, when Florida was a British colony. George Grenville, British prime minister well known in America for his hated stamp tax, and prominent physician Andrew Turnbull formed a company whose purpose was to reap profits from the families they planned to send to Florida. The company would furnish the transportation and initial food and supplies, but the farmers would be indentured to the company until they paid for these services and earned the shareholders ample returns on their investment.

Turnbull and Grenville recruited settlers from southern Europe—people accustomed to working under hot conditions. In order to attract such people, Turnbull named the colony New Smyrna, after the Greek town where his wife, Maria, was born. Eventually fifteen hundred Greeks, Italians, and Minorcans signed on.

Grenville tended company affairs while the Turnbulls went to Florida to supervise the settlers. Once there, Andrew and Maria, picturing themselves as feudal lords, began building a mansion that overlooked the Indian River. At the same time, they became almost dictatorial toward the indentured settlers. Andrew not only ordered the deportation of an obstreperous priest, but the execution of two unruly farmers. Moreover, his harsh overseers forced the people to work on company land rather than tend the private vegetable plots that could have kept them from starving. In the first year alone, 450 people died of diseases and malnutrition—a third of them children.

Finally, in 1777, the settlers were unable to continue. They convinced the British governor at St. Augustine of the desperation of their plight, and he released their indenture. When he did so, the colony collapsed, and the six hundred mostly Minorcan survivors resettled in St. Augustine—where today upwards of two hundred descendant families still worship at the Catholic basilica on Cathedral Place.

The Turnbulls never completed their mansion, whose massive stone foundations still stand on the riverfront at Julia Street and North Riverside Drive. Andrew and Maria, losing nearly all they had on the poorly managed venture, migrated to Charleston, where Andrew resumed his medical practice.

*The massive foundations of the Turnbull mansion, and perhaps of an earlier Spanish fort, overlook the harbor at New Smyrna.*

# Titusville

Titusville was a virtually unknown village until NASA began its massive operations on Merritt Island, across the Indian River, in the mid-1960s. Old Henry Titus would have been astonished at the worldwide fame of his little settlement, for it became a favorite location from which to watch the rocket launches. Many of the modern onlookers are Yankees, whom Colonel Titus would have viewed with utter disdain, being such an ardent Confederate that even after the conclusion of the Civil War he once battered a man so badly for supporting President Andrew Johnson that the man required hospitalization.

Rocket launches have now become so routine that it is easy to park near the foot of Florida 50 and obtain a good view. Even if there is no launch, a brief visit to Titusville's commercial section, spruced up as part of its Main Street program, is pleasurable.

# Canaveral National Seashore

Cape Canaveral is one of the major landforms on the Florida coast. When the Spanish began cruising the area, they discovered the jutting cape to be a convenient landmark and called it *canaveral,* after the

*The beaches are pristine along the Canaveral National Seashore.*

dense canebreaks that covered its extensive marshlands. Thus it became one of the first named places in the United States.

NASA began buying up land around Cape Canaveral for its moon project in the mid-1960s. It accumulated a wide area to prevent the public from being injured in case of a launch disaster. However, management of the land not essential to rocket facilities was given to other government agencies, and it has now been set aside as the Canaveral National Seashore and the Merritt Island National Wildlife Refuge.

To get to the seashore from I-95, take Florida 406 east to Florida 402, then 402 ten miles farther east to the beach. The drive is through wetlands supporting more than three hundred species of birds. After about ten miles you will pass the shuttle landing strip, just out of sight on the south. Farther on are turnouts where you get excellent, although distant, views of NASA's Complex 39, from which the shuttles blast off. However, this area is closed during the actual launches and landings.

At Playalinda Beach on the Atlantic, the road runs along the dunes for several miles before it dead-ends at a smallish area that is off and on reserved for nude bathing. The largest portion of the long beach is for people who prefer some attire. There are rest rooms and changing facilities all along the road, but otherwise the area has been kept primitive, with no food or other commercial establishments.

## The Kennedy Space Center

Although modern rocketry had its beginning in the early 1900s, with the experiments of American Robert H. Goddard and Russian Konstantin Tsiolkovsky, such missiles had no use at the time. The earliest significant use of long-range rockets was by the Germans in World War II, when the infamous V-2s bombed London. At the war's end, more than a hundred German rocket scientists fled to the American forces. The group, led by Wernher von Braun, was promptly installed at Huntsville, Alabama, where they began turning the V-2s into Redstone rockets for the U.S. Army.

Because the Redstone's range was too great for the missile testing grounds at White Sands, New Mexico, government leaders began searching for a better location. Their first choice was El Centro, California, with a firing range over Baja California and the Pacific. But negotiations with the Mexican government were unsuccessful, so Cape Canaveral was chosen.

*First launch from Cape Canaveral:* Bumper, *1950. The main rocket is a German V-2 similar to those that bombed London in World War II.* —45th Space Wing History Office, U.S. Air Force

Despite being a second choice, Cape Canaveral had about everything that was needed, including a firing range of ten thousand miles over water, where malfunctioning rockets would not endanger human life. Furthermore, the cape's isolation made it ideal for security purposes.

In 1949 President Harry Truman authorized activation of the cape testing grounds, and the following year a German V-2 was hauled over the primitive roads to the tip of the cape. There, the rocket was placed on a concrete slab and topped with a smaller rocket, called a WAC Corporal. The combination was given the inelegant name *Bumper.* The rocket was serviced from a painter's scaffold, and the control center consisted of an old tar-paper bathhouse protected by sandbags. Although *Bumper* traveled only ten miles, the firing was hailed as a success.

In 1953 Dr. Kurt Debus, a von Braun associate, was given charge of the army missile launches. There was almost nothing on the cape at this time except a pair of concrete slabs. Each launch meant that

*Missile Row, Cape Canaveral, 1964. Only two of these complexes are still in use, including Complex 36 directly below.* —45th Space Wing History Office, U.S. Air Force

Debus and several dozen scientists and technicians had to pick up a Redstone missile in Alabama, truck it down to the cape, erect it, launch it, and drive back to Alabama to wait for another Redstone to come off the line.

During the next few years, facilities at the cape remained minimal. Army and air force rocket men shared a Quonset hut office. A converted oil derrick became the service structure. Many of the permanent staff lived nearby in trailers and rode bicycles home for lunch.

An industrial building was eventually put up, but operations were still chancy. Two especially unnerving incidents involved misfiring rockets. The first incident occurred when a Redstone turned over just as it lifted from the pad and skimmed directly toward the industrial building—to the accompaniment of shouts and panic. Luckily it thudded to the ground while still a few hundred yards away. Later, a navy Polaris veered off course and zeroed in on the village of Cape Canaveral. Although a safety officer blew it up, some fragments of the missile plummeted into a trailer court while others exploded above the cape, igniting the scrub. For several days thereafter, guards were kept busy disposing of rattlesnakes displaced by the burning bushes.

The U.S. space program proceeded at a rather leisurely pace until October 1957, when the Soviet Union launched *Sputnik,* the world's first satellite. The shock was compounded as the Soviets quickly orbited a second, eleven-hundred-pound satellite. This was so much bigger than anything the United States even had on the drawing board that it was obvious the Americans lagged seriously behind. The fact that the Debus team successfully launched the two-pound *Explorer I* satellite early the next year did little to alter what was bemoaned as the "missile gap." Since it was obvious that atomic warheads could be transported by rockets, the seriousness of the situation was readily apparent.

In 1958 a nervous Congress passed the Space Act, which set up the National Aeronautics and Space Authority, or NASA. When NASA took over testing at Cape Canaveral, there were only 281 government workers on location. Nonetheless, they had managed to launch a pair of monkeys three hundred miles into space. Though both monkeys were recovered alive, one died later, and his preserved remains made it to the Smithsonian Institution as the first U.S. space traveler.

Under NASA the cape expanded. Project Mercury, designed for one-man flights, began on May 5, 1961, when Alan Shepard, riding a Redstone rocket, made a fifteen-minute suborbital excursion into space. Soviet Premier Nikita Khrushchev joked maliciously that it was only a "flea jump," for his own cosmonaut had just spent hours in actual earth orbit. But President John F. Kennedy was not amused. He had based his campaign on ending the missile gap and was determined to do just that. Buoyed by Shepard's flight, Kennedy made a declaration three weeks later that galvanized all Americans: "I believe that this nation should commit itself to achieving the goal, before this decade is out, of landing a man on the moon and returning him safely to earth." It was a direct challenge to the Russians. The "space race" was on.

## The Race for the Stars

The Soviet Union was still apparently far ahead, despite Kennedy's bold pronouncement, for in August 1961 a cosmonaut circled the earth seventeen times, while the best that Debus and his team could do was to send a chimp up for two orbits.

The United States so craved any success that in 1962, when John Glenn became the first American in orbit, he was treated as a hero. Ignored was the fact that the mission had been called back prematurely after three orbits when an errant warning light signaled a malfunction. Glenn had reentered the atmosphere with chunks from his spacecraft flying past his window. But he splashed down safely at the proper ocean rendezvous, and that was all that counted.

Glenn was flown to West Palm Beach, where he met an elated President Kennedy. With Kennedy were his wife, Jackie, and their young daughter, Caroline. "Caroline obviously expected something else," Glenn wryly admitted, "because when she was introduced to me, [she] looked all around, looked at me and asked, 'Where's the monkey?'"

Now the immense economic power of the United States began gearing up as NASA mobilized much of the nation's formidable scientific community. Over the next few years, NASA footed the education bill for five thousand graduate scientists and engineers. It constructed new laboratory facilities on thirty-two university campuses and gave research grants to fifty more institutions of higher learning. When the Apollo moon program peaked, more than four hundred thousand people were working on some aspect of it!

Much of the activity was centered on Cape Canaveral. Blastoffs to the moon required rockets infinitely larger than those that were tossing Mercury astronauts into low earth orbit. And not only larger rockets, but a whole new launch complex would need to be constructed. Also needed would be many new buildings to test the rockets, to assemble the space capsules, to train the personnel, and to store the tons of equipment. In addition, shipping wharves and railroad facilities would have to be provided.

It had long been apparent that the strip of land that made up the cape was too small. Merritt Island, separated from the cape by the Banana River and from the mainland by the Indian River, had to be utilized. So in 1961 a land acquisition office was set up in nearby Titusville. There were around 140,000 largely unpopulated acres to be acquired; a third were donated by the state, and four thousand different individual owners sold the rest—some unwillingly. Once the land was in government possession, NASA's contractors went to work. Chief among the new structures was the cavernous, fifty-story Vehicle Assembly Building, which was started in 1964.

Putting up a high tower on such a sandy base concerned the architects, who feared it might blow over under one of the fierce Florida hurricanes. Thus, to anchor the structure, engineers bored through the sand and the petrified remains of a twenty-five-thousand-year-old forest to limestone bedrock 160 feet below. It took six months to drive more than four thousand steel pilings down to the bedrock. Then the pilings, surrounded by wet, salty sand, took on an electrical charge that had to be neutralized. Otherwise, the joke went, NASA would just have made the world's largest wet-cell battery!

While the Vehicle Assembly Building was going up, work was being done on Launch Complex 39, designed especially for the great Saturn V rockets that would hurl the Apollo spacecraft to the moon. Pad A was completed in 1965 and Pad B one year later.

A sense of urgency was felt by NASA scientists, for Kennedy had promised the world that America would have a man on the moon by the end of the decade, and this time was fast approaching.

In 1965 Project Mercury was supplanted by Gemini, which involved launching pairs of men into earth orbit. The Gemini capsules were launched by Titan rockets, more powerful than the old Redstones.

As anticipation grew, the demand arose for public access to the cape. Prior to 1963 security had been so tight that not even the wife of the secretary of defense could accompany her husband onto the cape. But Secretary Robert McNamara relaxed the rules, and in 1964 Merritt Island was open Sundays for public drive-throughs. Two of the early visitors were Walt and Roy Disney, who noted the cape's obvious ability to attract tourists. This visit helped cement their decision to erect their theme park not many miles away.

Indeed, the cape quickly became so great a public magnet that NASA put some model rockets and a minimal assortment of photos in an unused warehouse that served as a museum. Eventually a temporary visitor center was set up on the mainland. From there, buses began taking guests on guided tours.

Meanwhile the Soviet Union had been active. In 1963 it sent a three-thousand-pound spacecraft within a few thousand miles of the moon in what many Westerners believed was a failed attempt at a soft landing. Three years later, a Russian satellite orbited the moon. By 1968 the Soviets had launched seven more unmanned spacecraft to the moon.

In October 1968, with only fifteen months until Kennedy's deadline expired, the United States launched the first manned Apollo, which carried three astronauts into earth orbit. Two months later, another Apollo actually took astronauts around the moon. There was plenty of drama here, for on Christmas Eve astronauts Frank Borman, James Lovell, and William Anders broadcast a message of peace to earth as they read from the Book of Genesis. Inspiring as it was, the world was waiting for the Really Big Show: the actual moon landing!

### The Moon at Last

The launch of *Apollo 11,* designed to carry astronauts to the moon, was scheduled for July 16, 1969. The Russians, resigned to losing the race, launched a Luna moon probe two days earlier. Hoping to thereby dilute the American victory, all they succeeded in doing was to cause the telephone hot line between Washington and Moscow to burn a little hotter as the Americans raged at what might happen if the Luna collided with the Apollo when they were both in orbit. But such an event was infinitely improbable, and few people paid any attention.

For days before the Apollo launch, the roads around Titusville were jammed with an estimated 1 million spectators, who crowded into Titusville and along the Indian River to watch Complex 39 across the water. All night, floodlights illuminated the thirty-six-story Saturn V rocket and the umbilical tower that supported it. On the grounds of

*Astronauts Neil Armstrong, Michael Collins, and Edwin Aldrin pose for a photo in 1969. Behind them is the rocket that will take them to the moon.* —Florida State Archives

the Kennedy Space Center, a large grandstand had been set up for the several thousand dignitaries and reporters from around the world.

Astronauts Neil Armstrong, Edwin Aldrin, and Michael Collins rose at 4:00 A.M., shaved, and had breakfast. Then they donned their space suits. With their helmets on, silence surrounded them. "I hear only the squish of my awkward yellow rubber galoshes and the hiss of the oxygen," Collins wrote, re-creating the epochal flight in his book *Carrying the Fire.* Just before entering the spacecraft, Collins took a final look around: "If I cover my right eye, I see the Florida of Ponce de Leon. . . . If I cover my left eye I see civilization and technology . . . and a frightening array of wires and metal."

Then came the wait. Collins was well aware of what he called the "monster" beneath him—the Saturn V rocket. As the final count-down began, he felt a slight jolt when the access arm of the umbilical tower detached. At nine seconds before liftoff, the mighty first stage engines ignited and the Saturn rumbled to life. The command module was shaking now, and at T-zero the hold-down clamps released. Then the beast was loose!

"Noise, yes, lots of it," Collins recalled, "but mostly motion as we are thrown left and right against our straps."

Meanwhile, back on earth a million spectators on the ground and 600 million others watching on TV gasped as smoke and steam billowed from the launch pad and the rocket slowly rose on a pillar of fire. It took the rocket ten full seconds to clear the umbilical tower. Meanwhile the question ran through nearly everyone's mind: Would it explode? Many rockets had. But the Saturn thundered upward, gathering velocity quickly. Within minutes it had vanished into the sky.

During the next four exciting days, Armstrong, Aldrin, and Collins described their lunar journey to fascinated audiences on earth. "The moon I have known all my life . . . has gone away," Collins remembered, "to be replaced by the most awesome sphere I have ever seen." The great disc that filled their window was now three-dimensional, with the belly bulging so Collins felt he could almost touch it. As they approached ever closer, the moon took on a menacing aspect. Collins called it a "withered, sun-seared peach pit." Skimming over the crater-pocked surface, Collins found it "stark," "barren," and downright "scary."

Soon Armstrong and Aldrin left Collins alone in the command capsule and descended to the moon's surface in the lunar module.

Then the big moment came. Armstrong opened the hatch and gingerly stepped down the ladder. His foot touched the surface. "That's one small step for a man, one giant leap for mankind," he told the spellbound audience on earth.

John Kennedy's promise had been kept. How ironic that the young president was dead and that it was Richard Nixon, Kennedy's arch political adversary, who put through the congratulatory phone call to the astronauts from the White House.

### Visiting NASA

The facilities at the cape are divided between NASA and the U.S. Air Force. NASA's Spaceport USA, on the grounds of the Kennedy Space Center, is by far the more imposing. It is visited yearly by around 2.5 million people, making it one of Florida's five most popular attractions. It is especially crowded at launch times, when it affords the public its closest view.

The Rocket Garden is a fascinating collection of seven space missiles dating back to the Mercury/Redstone and the Mercury/Atlas, which launched Alan Shepard in 1961 and John Glenn in 1962. The

*Rocket Garden at the Kennedy Space Center. The small Mercury/Redstone rocket, which carried the first American into space, is in the center.*

Gemini/Titan is also on display. Dwarfing them is the huge Saturn IB, whose 1.6 million pounds of liftoff thrust mocks the Redstone's feeble seventy-eight thousand pounds.

In addition, the Rocket Garden boasts a full-scale model of the lunar module that carried the astronauts on their descent to the moon. It is an ungainly piece of equipment. Small wonder that Michael Collins called it "the weirdest looking contraption ever to invade the sky."

A space shuttle replica, on other Spaceport grounds, is open for inspection. Next to the shuttle are its twin booster rockets and the even larger external fuel tank. When in use, the tank stores liquid hydrogen and liquid oxygen in separate compartments at temperatures far below zero. To maintain the extreme cold, the tank has a coating of insulation. Oddly, local woodpeckers enjoy burrowing into the insulation, and one shuttle launch had to be postponed when startled inspectors found nearly two hundred 'pecker holes!

There is enough glitz and glamour at the Spaceport to make anyone want to speed off to the stars. The IMAX movies are particularly attractive, enabling viewers to enjoy the adventure of space travel on a screen five and a half stories high.

The new Apollo/Saturn V Center is a must-see. The monster Saturn V moon rocket is suspended above the floor. It is longer than a football field. Also within the massive building are two major theaters. One, called the Firing Room, simulates a rocket launch. The other, called the Lunar Surface, focuses on the moon landing.

Almost everyone takes the bus tours to the towering Vehicle Assembly Building and Crawlerway to Complex 39, where the space shuttles continue to be launched. The complex was built in the 1960s for Apollo's Saturn V rockets, and it was from Pad A that *Apollo 11* started on its epic journey to the moon.

The last Apollo moon landing occurred in 1972. Complex 39 was then adapted for the space shuttle, which had its initial blastoff from Pad A in 1981. The shuttle's main mission is to build an earth-orbit space station from which further missions can be launched to Mars and other planets and their moons. The shuttle has been a major success, except for the tragic explosion of *Challenger* in 1986, killing seven astronauts, who are honored in an imposing monument that also includes the other astronauts who died reaching for the stars.

The Kennedy Space Center may be a far different place in the future than it is today. When the shuttles are retired in favor of a spaceship fleet with launch sites around the country, Kennedy will lose its premier status. But there is already a huge investment in visitor facilities, which will assure its attraction for years into the future. For the cape will forever be remembered as the world's first gateway to the stars.

### Visiting the Air Force Station

Displays at the Cape Canaveral Air Force Station pale in comparison to NASA's Space Center. Although the station is still used for launches of space satellites as well as the Mars probes, it is otherwise a quiet place. Aside from a small and slightly musty museum, there is not much to see. But what is there rings with history. Even the mustiness adds to the authenticity.

The museum grounds make up Complexes 5, 6, and 26—all National Historic Landmarks. It was from Complex 26 that the very first U.S. satellite, *Explorer I*, was launched in 1958. The Explorer had what was called a "tub" at the top—as can be seen by the rocket currently on Pad 6. This tub revolved five hundred times a minute and was designed to give the Explorer stability when the eleven second-stage rockets within it boosted the satellite toward orbit.

*From this cramped firing room some of the earliest rocket launches were conducted. It is now part of the Air Force museum.*

Though largely forgotten today, the launch of *Explorer I* was a major event. A reporter watching the successful liftoff was so excited that he didn't know what to compare it to. At last he gasped, "It even topped Ted Williams's ninth inning homer in the 1941 All Star Game!"

On Pad 5 is a Redstone rocket with a Mercury capsule on top. A similar space vehicle was on the same pad in May 1961 when it launched Alan Shepard on the first American manned flight. Shepard, huddled in the cramped capsule, waited so long for liftoff that he wet his pants. Thereafter, body waste systems became standard equipment. On Pad 26 is an Atlas rocket surrounded by the oldest gantry scaffolding on the cape.

Launches were controlled from blockhouses close to the pads. Blockhouse 26 is part of the Air Force museum. The computers are still there as they were in the early 1960s. From narrow windows, composed of three panes, each four inches thick, visitors can look out on the Atlas rocket the way scientists did when the space program was new and there was a deadly competitor called the Soviet Union.

The Air Force Station is included in a special bus tour from Spaceport USA at the Kennedy Space Center. Or you can drive to it from I-95 via exit 528.

## Port Canaveral

Port Canaveral is home to cruise lines that handle over a million passengers a year. When the ships are in port, it is worth the drive to see them. But even without the ships, the new art deco terminal of the Disney Cruise Line deserves a visit. The Army Corps of Engineers dug the port channel in the early 1950s for the delivery of heavy rocket cargoes to Cape Canaveral.

**I-95**

# Kennedy Space Center—Fort Pierce
**77 miles**

*The Indian River*

From Port Canaveral it is a quick trip on Florida 528 back to I-95. Or you can take scenic A1A along the Indian River. Although the Indian

River has given its name to Florida's best-known grapefruit, it is not actually a river but a wide saltwater lagoon that extends south for around 130 miles, or a little beyond Palm Beach.

Highway A1A follows the barrier beaches between the river and the Atlantic Ocean. For travelers with ample time, this is the way to go, although one may wish there were not so many motels and strip-malls. But there are breaks where the natural vegetation takes over. The road is regularly diverted by such inlets as those off Sebastian and Jupiter, then it continues on the other side.

The Indian River is alive with pleasure craft as well as larger ships using the Intracoastal Waterway. At rare intervals a barge appears from Louisiana carrying a huge external fuel tank for the space shuttle.

## Cocoa

Cocoa, four miles east of I-95 on Florida 520, had its beginning with citrus growers who migrated to the area along the Indian River after the Civil War. Life was difficult at first, for the mosquitoes were so thick that each home had a bug brush beside the door. But eventually some of these planter families became wealthy. One such

*In 1916 Edward and Byrnina Porcher built this mansion in Cocoa to celebrate the success of their orange plantation on the Indian River. Byrnina kept birds and tropical plants in the rear sunroom.*

husband-and-wife team was Edward and Byrnina Porcher, who celebrated their success by constructing a two-and-a-half-story Greek Revival mansion beside the Indian River in 1916. This home, at 434 Delannoy Avenue, is open to the public.

Byrnina Porcher was talented as well as lovely (her portrait, done during a trip to Italy, hangs in the house). She kept a collection of tropical birds on the porch and loved to play the grand piano and to paint flowers. Some of her oils still grace the mansion. She died there of cancer in 1937.

While you're in Cocoa, why not stroll around old Cocoa Village? It is filled with vintage buildings, including the handsome Aladdin Theater, at 300 Brevard Avenue. Opened in 1924 and now on the National Historic Register, it once showed silent films with such stars as Rudolph Valentino and Laurel and Hardy. Black patrons were restricted to the balcony and had to enter by way of the fire escape.

The Merritt Island Causeway (Florida 520) leads across the Indian River to Merritt Island, probably named for Pedro Marratt, a surveyor for the Spanish government. It is believed Florida's citrus industry got its start on Merritt Island as a result of orange seeds washed ashore from Spanish ships, which carried the fruit to prevent scurvy.

Continuing east, Florida 520 crosses the Banana River to the white sands of Cocoa Beach, where the city pier extends eight hundred feet into the ocean. On it are several restaurants with wonderful views of water, waves, and surfers.

# Sebastian

From Cocoa, I-95 continues to skirt the St. Johns wetlands, which extend westward as far as the eye can see. The river has its source just south of Melbourne.

Sebastian is eight miles east of I-95 on County Road 512. The site was well-known to the Spanish, who named it in honor of St. Sebastian, clubbed to death by the Romans. The holy name did nothing to prevent the wrecking of an eleven-ship treasure fleet just south of the Sebastian Inlet in 1715. Nearly three hundred years later, an optometrist during a lunch break found the remains of one ship in just eight feet of water. In it was gold and jewelry estimated at upwards of $1 million!

That such a ship was located was not a surprise, for Sebastian Inlet had already proved to be a treasury of Spanish ships. An even greater cache had been found a few years earlier, when the fabulous *Atocha*, which went down in 1622, was discovered by Mel Fisher. Within its crusty hull was the greatest monetary yield in salvaging history. Mel Fisher has put many Spanish coins and artifacts on display in his museum at 1322 US 1 in Sebastian.

# Vero Beach

Vero Beach is eight miles east of I-95 on Florida 60. In 1891, postmaster John Gifford was searching for something to call the little village. When nothing else seemed right, he chose Vero, which happened to be his wife's first name. The postal authorities approved, and Vero it was. "Beach" was added later.

## The Ordeal of the Dickinsons

Three hundred years ago, the area around Vero Beach was the domain of the fierce Ais tribe, whose main village was probably on North Hutchinson Island, across the Indian River (in those days called the River of the Ais) from the modern city. One cold, bleak day late in 1696, two dozen half-frozen English shipwreck victims stumbled into Ais territory. Among them was Mary Dickinson, still nursing her six-month-old baby boy, and her husband, Jonathan, whose journal of their nightmare in Florida would become a classic story of hardship and fortitude. They had already made their way sixty weary miles up the beach from Jupiter, the site of their wreck, but they still had nearly five hundred more to go before reaching the English colony at Charleston.

The Ais did not kill the Englishmen, which they were tempted to do. Instead they permitted them to scavenge the "gills and guts of fish picked off a dung-hill," as Jonathan put it. No wonder the survivors were glad to be soon on their way. The Ais probably gave the incident no more thought, yet, ironically, the account of the Dickinsons' brief sojourn among them provides about the only written memory of these now-vanished people.

## Vero Beach and Baseball

Since 1948, Vero Beach has been the home of the Los Angeles Dodgers' spring training camp. Exhibition games are played from March to early April. The Vero Beach minor league team's season lasts from mid-April to early September. Later, professional football outfits sometimes use the facilities for warm-weather conditioning.

The site had been a naval air base before Bud Holman, a Vero Beach businessman, built the stadium that bears his name at 4101 Twenty-sixth Street. Many baseball experts believe the facilities at Holman Stadium are the finest in Florida.

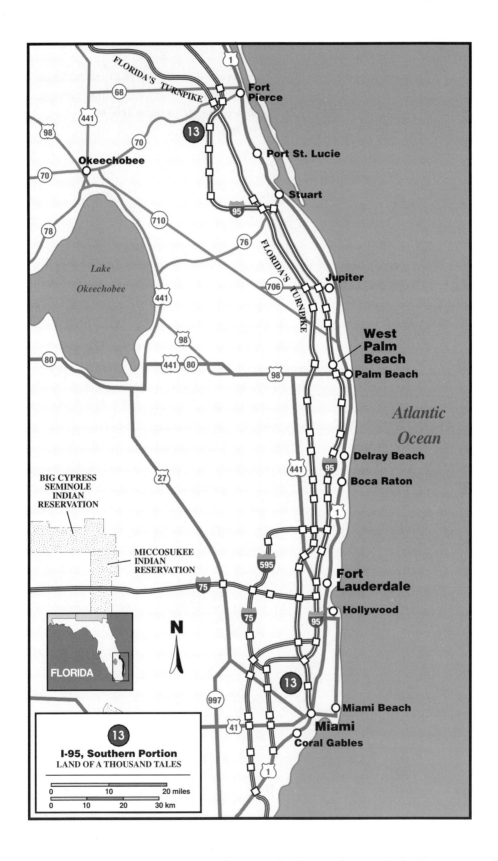

FLORIDA'S TURNPIKE

68

441

98

70

70

**Okeechobee**

78

710

76

FLORIDA'S TURNPIKE

706

441

98

80

441 80

98

27

**BIG CYPRESS
SEMINOLE
INDIAN
RESERVATION**

**MICCOSUKEE
INDIAN
RESERVATION**

75

75

595

75

997

41

1

**N**

**FLORIDA**

1

**Fort
Pierce**

13

Port St. Lucie

Stuart

95

**Jupiter**

**West
Palm
Beach**

Palm Beach

*Atlantic*

*Ocean*

Delray Beach

441 95

Boca Raton

1

**Fort
Lauderdale**

95 Hollywood

13

Miami Beach

**Miami**

Coral Gables

1

*Lake*

*Okeechobee*

1

13

**I-95, Southern Portion**
LAND OF A THOUSAND TALES

0       10        20 miles
0    10    20    30 km

# ☞ 13 ☜

# *I-95, Southern Portion*

## LAND OF A THOUSAND TALES

# Fort Pierce—Palm Beach
**54 miles**

## Choosing Among I-95, Florida's Turnpike, and US 1

When I-95 reaches Fort Pierce, it meets Florida's Turnpike coming in from the Kissimmee Valley. Here both expressways lose their country aspect and become, in effect, a series of city bypasses as they parallel each other to Miami.

Which should you take? I-95 is toll-free, but it is rather crowded during weekdays, especially at rush hour. The turnpike has a toll, but it is a more relaxing drive. So the choice is yours.

A few miles east, US 1 parallels I-95 and Florida's Turnpike. US 1 is the old Dixie Highway, built in the 1920s as the major road from the Midwest to Miami. T. H. Weigall has left us a marvelous description of the Dixie Highway as he saw it from a train in 1925:

> The main road, the great Dixie Highway, was running nearer to the line now, and I was able to make out in more detail the incredible assortment of humanity that, in Ford and Rolls-Royce, on bicycle and on foot, was pouring down towards Miami. . . . Most of these equipages had the family goods roped on to the rear; camp beds, washing-stands, even the conventional parrot of caricature.

## Fort Pierce

Fort Pierce is five miles east of I-95 (six miles east of Florida's Turnpike) on Florida 70. The fort was built during the Second Seminole War when, as headquarters of the army of the South, it was the anchor of a line of army posts reaching across the peninsula to Tampa.

In 1841 young Lieutenant William Tecumseh Sherman entered the fort with the fierce Seminole chief Coacoochee as his prisoner. Coacoochee demonstrated his defiance by donning the vest of a soldier he had shot, the blood and bullet hole prominently displayed. But ultimately the proud man was shackled and shipped off beyond the Mississippi with the majority of his defeated tribe. The site of the fort is now occupied by a small park, in the 900 block of South Indian River Drive.

# Jupiter

Jupiter was the site of a vivid episode of hardship and fortitude. It started on August 23, 1696, when Englishman Jonathan Dickinson, his young wife, Mary, and their six-month-old baby boy (whom she was still nursing) boarded a small sailing vessel in Jamaica bound for Philadelphia. With them were two other white passengers, the Dickinsons' ten slaves, both men and women, as well as one Indian girl and a crew of nine.

A storm struck off the Florida coast, and their ship was wrecked just north of the inlet that appeared on English maps as Hobe (on later maps as Jove) and would eventually be transformed into Jupiter. Before long, a mass of Hobe braves brandishing Spanish knives came running down the beach toward them. The Hobes, after scavenging everything from the ship that was of use to them, led their captives down the beach to the inlet, then ferried them across to their village, which consisted of crude wigwams made of saplings bent into an arches and covered with palmetto fronds.

Most of the Indians wanted to kill and eat their prisoners on the spot, believing they were English, the hated enemies of their friends, the Spanish. But the chief was not sure, since one of the sailors spoke Spanish and the rest insisted they were Spaniards. A disgruntled brave muttered, "English son of a bitch," the only words he knew.

The Indians at Jupiter were vassals of those to the north at Vero Beach, so when Jonathan and the others insisted that they travel north, the chief let them go—though with great reluctance.

Their goal was the English outpost at Charleston, almost six hundred miles away. To get there, they would have to hike past many hostile tribes as well as brave the Spanish at St. Augustine. Nonetheless, they set out. It would take them four hellish months to reach Charleston. On their way the weather would turn icy, and Indians would strip them of all their clothing. Their feet would become bloody, and walking would become agonizingly painful. They would go for days without food. Mosquitoes and flies would be a constant torment. Before it was over, five of them would be dead. But the Dickinsons survived. That was fortunate for us as well as for them—Jonathan's journal has become a Florida classic.

## Touring Jupiter

Modern Jupiter is vibrant with Dickinson history. Jonathan Dickinson State Park is off US 1 west of town. From there an excursion boat goes up the Loxahatchee River on a 4.5-mile narrated tour through the moss-draped wilderness. Canoes can also be rented.

Blowing Rocks Preserve is located on Jupiter Island's beach, only a few miles from where the Dickinsons' ship was wrecked. It can be reached by a short, pleasant ride on A1A north of town. Administered by the Nature Conservancy, the park presents much the same seascape as it did three hundred years ago. At high tide, wave spray shoots through holes in the rocks, giving the formation its name.

*Water still pops through holes at Blowing Rocks near where the Dickinson party suffered shipwreck in 1696. Jonathan Dickinson's tale of suffering and fortitude has become a Florida classic.*

*Burt Reynolds and the Citrus Queen at Florida State University in 1963.*
—Florida State Archives

The exact location of the Indian village of Hobe has been established from its old garbage heap, which, after the centuries covered with sand and vegetation, turned into a mound called a "midden." In later years, settlers named DuBois built a home on the mound, and eventually a public park was established between the house and the inlet. Here you can watch boats sailing to and from the Atlantic, just as long-vanished Hobe fishermen once did. The site can be reached on A1A, south a short distance from the inlet bridge. Turn left when you reach Jupiter Beach Road, then left again on DuBois.

The place from where the shipwrecked victims were ferried to Hobe has, since 1860, been occupied by a picturesque lighthouse. It was built, ironically, by George Meade, who just three years later would be the federal commander who defeated Robert E. Lee at Gettysburg.

For people to whom the past is measured in years, not centuries, Jupiter is famous as the stomping grounds of Burt Reynolds, Hollywood's number-one box-office draw from 1978 through 1982. Among his most popular movies were *Deliverance, Smokey and the Bandit,* and *The Longest Yard.* When Reynolds turned to television, he scored his greatest success with *Evening Shade*, for which he won the best actor Emmy in 1990.

Reynolds was a Florida lad who made it big. His father was the police chief of Riviera Beach, just down the coast from Jupiter, and Burt attended Florida State University in Tallahassee, where he was a football star. And although the roguishly handsome actor was completely at ease amid the glamorous hoopla of California, he kept his Florida roots, maintaining a residence both on the west coast and at Jupiter—commuting between the two in his private jet.

Reynolds bought a home on Hobe Sound, not too far from where the Dickinsons had spent their time in abject misery. But there was no misery at Valhalla, as Reynolds called his pleasure palace—not while some of Hollywood's most glittering stars played there. Sally Field strayed with Reynolds as they were filming *Smokey and the Bandit II* in 1976. Six years later Dolly Parton, Jim Nabors, and others larked about after filming *The Best Little Whorehouse in Texas*. Dinah Shore was a regular at the 160-acre ranch Reynolds purchased just west of town. They rode horses together along the romantic, wooded trails. Tammy Wynette bought a large house at Jupiter Inlet so she could be close to Burt and the action.

Burt was so enraptured by the little town that he built one of Florida's handsomest small theaters on A1A, not far from the ocean. Opening in 1979, it provided a first-rate stage where young actors could hone their talents. Of course, the performances were consid-

*The picturesque lighthouse at Jupiter rises across the inlet from the ancient Hobe village where Jonathan Dickinson, his young wife, and twenty-four companions were held captive in 1696.*

erably enhanced by the addition of glitzy outsiders, such as Carol Burnett, who starred in *Same Time Next Year*. Burt and his friends enjoyed the performances from an upstairs private box with a secluded dining room. One of his guests was Elizabeth Taylor, who spilled a drink in her lap.

Burt Reynolds was Jupiter's Great Celebrity. Even the little people loved him. One of them, known simply as the Fountain Lady, would sit regularly beside the entry fountain for a quarter of an hour before curtain time waiting to get a glimpse of Burt, then she would vanish before the play started.

Reynolds spent wildly. He put a lot of money into his theater, which boasted lavish Moorish arches and his name on the two-story, illuminated logo. He installed a racetrack on his ranch and raised expensive thoroughbred horses. He invested $20 million in the Po' Folks restaurant franchise. On a whim he would think nothing of renting a huge yacht and taking his friends on a cruise along the Intracoastal Waterway to Fort Lauderdale. He bought $1,500 hairpieces, wore each for a week then discarded it for another.

By the time Reynolds married Loni Anderson, he was beginning to feel in a financial pinch. His theater was unable to turn a profit. His horses were not winning races. His restaurant venture was turning disastrous. One day Loni came to him crying that the local grocer had even cut off their credit!

When Burt and Loni divorced in 1994, it was clear that Burt had serious money problems. Although he sold his theater and took other measures to regain solvency, it was impossible. In addition to the loss of $20 million on his restaurant venture, he owed $44,000 on just his credit cards, to say nothing of the $122,000 due his hairpiece supplier. Then, too, there was the undisclosed hefty settlement with Loni, which included $15,000 per month for support of their adopted son. When CBS sued him for $3.7 million plus interest on a loan he hadn't fully repaid, Reynolds knew he had no choice except to declare bankruptcy. "I have a lot of pride," he lamented, "and filing Chapter Eleven tears me apart."

Today the former Burt Reynolds Theater is presenting shows as the Jupiter Theater at the corner of A1A and Indiantown Road. The Moorish arches are filled in, and the dazzling fountain has become just a circular planter. Reynolds's ranch, long a tourist attraction, is five miles from the I-95 and turnpike exits, going west on Indiantown Road (Florida 706), then south on Jupiter Farms Road.

# Palm Beach

## *The Successes and Failures of Henry Flagler*

Palm Beach was just another desolate barrier island until a storm hit in 1878 and kindly deposited a Spanish ship loaded with twenty thousand coconuts. The Spanish abandoned the wreck, and local inhabitants began planting the coconuts. Soon the growth was luxuriant, giving Palm Beach its name and making the island unique along the coast. Thus, when Henry Flagler was looking for a place to build a couple of luxury hotels, Palm Beach was a logical choice.

By 1894 Flagler's railroad had reached Lake Worth, opposite the island of Palm Beach. Here he constructed a town for the railroad workers, appropriately called West Palm Beach. Then he turned to the island itself. On the east side he built the cavernous Royal Poinciana, the largest wooden hotel in the world. Meanwhile, on the Atlantic shore he purchased a small hotel called the Palm Beach Inn. Soon he greatly enlarged the hotel and renamed it the Breakers.

Even as his business enterprises were flourishing, Flagler's personal life was taking some distressing turns. His wife, Alice, began acting strangely. She claimed the czar of Russia was in love with her (though she had never met him) and that they would be married after she killed Henry. Flagler, justifiably concerned, had no choice

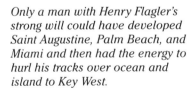

*Only a man with Henry Flagler's strong will could have developed Saint Augustine, Palm Beach, and Miami and then had the energy to hurl his tracks over ocean and island to Key West.*

but to commit Alice to an asylum, which she entered in 1897 and where she spent the remaining three decades of her life, pining for the czar.

Though Flagler was now in his late sixties, he was still a virile man and had taken a mistress while Alice careened into her fantasy world. Now he became attracted to Mary Lily Kenan, nearly thirty-eight years younger than he. In order to divorce Alice, he bribed Florida's governor and much of the legislature to pass a bill permitting him to shed his insane wife (after he voluntarily provided an estate of $2.3 million for her maintenance and comfort). He and Mary Lily were wed in 1901.

### The Wonders of Whitehall

Flagler wanted to present his bride with a new house on Palm Beach. He had something modest in mind, for they would be there only during Januarys and Februarys. But she insisted on a mansion, which Flagler obligingly built. With its glistening marble walls, Mary Lily named it Whitehall.

Whitehall was a thing to behold. The front doors opened into the great marble hall, over one hundred feet long and forty feet wide, featuring a ceiling inset with gold and ivory designs and a large oval painting in delicate pastels.

On the left of the marble hall was the Italian Renaissance library, decorated in rich reds. On the right end of the hall was the Louis XVI salon, done in soft grays and silvers, with cupids gamboling on the ceiling. It was here that the ladies retired while the men smoked their cigars after a sumptuous meal in the Francis I dining room, which was immediately west.

Directly across from the entry, the marble hall opened onto a courtyard, with a sparkling fountain and a statue of Venus. The courtyard led to the spacious Louis XV ballroom.

Despite all its splendor, it is not clear that the Flaglers got an extraordinary amount of pleasure from Whitehall. Although in 1903 they had a gala party in the ballroom, Henry was getting too old to enjoy such festivities—he was seventy-three by then. So the ballroom was seldom used thereafter.

Neither did Henry frequent the library, for he was not much of a reader and collected books mainly for the quality of their leather bindings. The Flaglers and their guests (who were often Mary Lily's family from North Carolina) found the Louis XIV music room a good place for concerts by the accomplished musicians they hired. But Henry was growing deaf and could appreciate only throbbing marches and other loud pieces, such as the "Anvil Chorus."

Henry spent most of his time in the offices he and his staff occupied on the first floor's southwest wing, for now he was engaged in his greatest undertaking—construction of the Overseas Railroad to Key West. As a result, Mary Lily was forced to spend a great deal of time alone. But the huge house was meant for laughing groups, not for a solitary woman. The marble hall was actually foreboding as the shadows gathered during the long winter nights. So Mary Lily took refuge in the morning room on the southwest corner of the second floor.

What does one of the richest young women in the world do as her husband becomes ever more remote? Mary Lily turned to alcohol and drugs. Her physical condition may also have been undermined by syphilis, which it is believed she contacted from Henry.

In 1913 Henry took a nasty fall in the bathroom and complications set in. After a short illness, he died and was buried at the Presbyterian Church in St. Augustine beside his first wife and his

*Henry and Mary Flagler's once-proud Whitehall mansion at Palm Beach had been demoted to a mere hotel lobby when this picture was taken—probably in the 1940s.* —P. H. Yonge Library of Florida History, University of Florida

daughter, Jennie. After Henry's death, Mary Lily spent a few winters at Whitehall before marrying a former beau, Robert Worth Bingham, in 1916. She lived only eight months with Bingham, dying of a heart attack according to some, of syphilis according to others, and of murder according to a somber legend that will not be stilled. Bingham used the money he inherited from Mary Lily to purchase the *Louisville Courier-Journal,* and from there his life became a tale of intrigue that has attracted its own coterie of storytellers.

However, most of Mary Lily's fortune went to her cousin, Louise Clisby Wise. Louise was not interested in Whitehall, and the mansion remained vacant until she sold it. The new owners converted it into a luxury hotel in 1926, adding an incongruous ten-story tower in the rear. The marble hall was demoted to the hotel lobby, and the library, music room, and salon became cocktail lounges and recreation areas. As the hotel clientele changed, plans were made to carve the marble hall into dressing room cubicles for a spa. But in 1959 Henry's granddaughter, Jean Flagler Matthews, bought the mansion at the eleventh hour. She ripped down the inappropriate tower and converted Whitehall into the fine museum that is so attractive today.

### The Fabulous Breakers Hotel

During Flagler's era, his Florida East Coast Railroad crossed Lake Worth, where autos now speed over the Flagler Bridge. Royal Poinciana Way was originally an extension of the railroad, which accounts for its unusual width. The railroad curved south from Royal Poinciana Way to deliver Flagler's guests to the door of the Breakers, and from there to the Royal Poinciana Hotel. Over the years, the Royal Poinciana aged badly, and it was finally torn down in 1936.

The Breakers had a more dramatic history. In 1925, twelve years after Flagler's death, a spectacular fire burned it to the ground. However, Flagler's heirs reconstructed it into the splendid edifice that became a monument to the opulent twenties. Its lobby has architecture befitting a medieval cathedral. Its Alcazar lounge would grace any European palace. Its Florentine dining room has an aura of luxury rarely seen in America.

Today, the Breakers is trying to attract a younger set—and its summer rates may do just that. Even if you do not reside at the hotel, you should visit it. You'll never see such magnificence for just the price of parking.

*Addison Mizner, architect
and former boxer, virtually
created Palm Beach's
highbrow Worth Avenue
shopping district.*
—Florida State Archives

## Flamboyant Architect: Addison Mizner

Half a mile south of the Breakers is Worth Avenue, one of America's most exclusive shopping areas. Worth Avenue did not exist in Flagler's day. Then, the area was known for Alligator Joe's Reptile Farm. But when Addison Mizner built the Everglades Club in 1918 at the western bend of the avenue, it became the "in" place for the upper crust.

Mizner quickly became the darling architect for Palm Beach society. Yet, strangely, he did not have formal training as an architect. His preparation consisted mostly of poking around Spanish buildings in Guatemala City when his father was a U.S. envoy extraordinaire. Later this burly, three-hundred-pound giant spent time as a gold prospector in Alaska and a boxer in Australia.

After completing the Everglades Club, Mizner designed two more major buildings on the west end of Worth Avenue. Even today Via Mizner, completed in 1924, and Via Parigi, completed a year later, are jewels, with enticing alleyways and appealing little courtyards, surrounded by Spanish-style structures with rust red–tiled roofs built in staggered levels.

The architect made his home in Via Mizner's five-story tower. Here he kept his pet monkey, Johnny Brown. When Johnny Brown

*Addison Mizner, always egotistical, built Via Mizner in 1924. He had his office and home in the tower, where he also kept his pet monkey, Johnny Brown.*

died in 1927, Mizner buried him in the courtyard, where his small tombstone can be found to this day.

Mizner did not do well after the Florida real estate bust of 1926. Much too heavily involved in a venture at nearby Boca Raton, he had to rely on handouts from friends to keep him going. In 1933 he became seriously ill, but he maintained his joie de vivre to the end. When his brother, Wilson, who was a character in his own right, sent him a wire: "Stop dying. Am trying to write a comedy," Mizner wired back: "Am going to get well. The comedy goes on." But only hours later he was dead of a heart attack.

Mizner's architecture provided Palm Beach with a style typically its own. Many of his homes can be seen during a drive or stroll along ritzy South Ocean Boulevard (A1A). Watch for house numbers 720, 780, 1200, 1550, 1560, 1800 (once Mizner's residence), and 1820.

The most famous house on South Ocean Boulevard, Mar-a-Lago, is not a Mizner creation, though it was done in his style. Located where South Ocean curves sharply west to meet the Southern Boulevard (US 98) Bridge, it was built in 1927 for breakfast-food heiress Marjorie Post. Although its 115 rooms make it the largest home on South Ocean, from the roadside you can see only the ornate gate and the top of the seventy-five-foot-high tower where Marjorie once installed an azure-colored electric beacon to provide her guests with a magical blue moon.

The house remained mostly hidden from public view when Donald Trump turned it into a private club, whose gala opening in 1995 featured flapper dancers as a salute to the memory of Marjorie Post.

### The Kennedys

These days, Palm Beach is better known to many people for Kennedy family escapades than for the more lasting accomplishments of Flagler or Mizner. The former Kennedy house, at 1095 North Ocean Boulevard, was sold to a private party in 1995. If the home were not obscured by a thick hedge, you would see a large structure with the typical Mizner staggered facade and roof lines of various heights. There is a wide veranda with tennis courts and a swimming pool. The beach is beyond.

Although a young John F. Kennedy spent many happy days at the home, as president he stayed at a more secure residence when visiting Palm Beach.

The most publicized Kennedy episode began on the night of March 30, 1991, when Senator Ted Kennedy, Patrick Kennedy, and William Kennedy Smith decided to go to the Au Bar, at 336 Royal Poinciana Way, for drinks and fun. Amid festivities, William met Patty

*The Au Bar in Palm Beach was a Kennedy family haunt. It was here that young William Kennedy Smith had a highly publicized late night misadventure in 1991.*

Bowman, a pretty young woman who had driven down from Jupiter. By the time the bar was closing, Ted and Patrick had left, and William talked Patty into driving him home.

After they arrived at the Kennedy mansion, they went walking on the beach, at which time, Patty alleged, William forced her to have sex. Patty called the police, and a highly visible trial took place at the county courthouse in West Palm Beach. After ten circuslike days, with TV cameras recording every spicy detail, the jury found William not guilty.

## Delray Beach

Delray Beach's history is not unusual for the Atlantic side of Florida. The settlement began with the advent of Henry Flagler's East Coast Railroad in 1896. The boom of the 1920s resulted in a flurry of Mediterranean-style buildings along Atlantic Avenue, the town's main street, which led toward the beaches. Delray Beach survived the Depression, yet almost went under with the advent of outlying shopping malls in the 1970s and 1980s. This was when things got interesting.

Not until it became obvious that the center of the fifty-thousand-inhabitant city was close to extinction did officials commission a task force to examine the problem. This group was composed of local businesspeople, minority leaders, and civic-minded citizens. It came up with a recommendation for reviving Atlantic Avenue. But it was not a plan that called for large government loans and substantial changes to the neighborhoods involved. Instead, it suggested that the city go ahead mostly on its own by widening the sidewalks, installing paving stones, erecting ornate streetlights, burying the utility lines, and planting trees and flowers. The city hoped that this modest beginning would spur private groups to become involved.

And so it happened. Through conferences, get-togethers, and a three-day retreat by 125 local activists in 1988, grassroots momentum grew. The talent came from within the community. When citizens complained of problems, the city was disinclined to solve them with money and so-called experts from the outside. The complainers were told to organize and come up with their own solutions. The city was a facilitator only.

Suddenly there was a new spirit in Delray Beach. Creative individuals, often aided by loans from the city, began turning dilapidated buildings along Atlantic Avenue into trendy sidewalk cafes and boutiques. Young couples began fixing up scores of old homes nearby. The Colony Hotel, a once-gorgeous but now run-down relic from the 1920s, was refurbished and quickly became a proud land-mark once more.

Meanwhile, the city was doing its share. No private business wanted to tackle downtown's chief eyesore, a grimy elementary school, mostly abandoned, with a menacing chain-link fence sur-rounding it. So the city restyled it and reopened it in 1990 as the Cornell Museum of Art and History. Almost instantly, artists appeared in Delray, and soon their galleries began further enhancing Atlantic Avenue. Another city project was a new world-class tennis center in the mainly black-populated portion of Atlantic Avenue.

The spectacular success of Delray Beach's "from the bottom up" technique became the talk of city planners everywhere. In 1993 the National Civic League designated Delray Beach as an All-American City for its success in restoring the downtown as well as in reducing crime and preserving historic sites. *Florida Trend,* the state's highly respected business magazine, ran a major article in 1995 on Delray Beach entitled "The Best-Run Town in Florida."

*The old Colony Hotel has been refurbished and stands proudly on Delray's revitalized Atlantic Avenue.*

## The Morikami Museum

In addition to its remarkable downtown revival, Delray is known for the lovely Morikami Museum. The extensive grounds upon which the museum and the surrounding Japanese garden and nature walk are located were donated by George Morikami, in memory of the vanished Yamato colony.

The Yamato colony was one of the more unusual experiments in Florida's many colonization schemes. In 1903 the Henry Flagler Model Land Company urged Jo Sakai, who had just graduated from the New York University of Commerce, to encourage his compatriots in Japan to come to Florida, where the land along the East Coast Railroad would supposedly support a cornucopia of vegetables and pineapples never imagined by those used to the tired soil of Japan. Sakai induced a group of around thirty young men and women to form a cooperative and migrate to Florida.

The colony led a struggling existence for two decades. When the boom of the early 1920s sent land prices soaring, most of the farmers sold out and migrated to other locations. The only remaining member was George Sukeji Morikami.

Morikami preferred the solitary life, living as a virtual hermit in a mobile home almost lost amid his beloved pineapples. Although he began turning considerable profits on land investments, raising pineapples was his consuming interest, and eventually he had up to ten thousand under cultivation—his main outlet being the Publix supermarkets.

As Morikami grew older, his thoughts returned to the days when he was a young man and his friends and neighbors were with him. They were gone now—most dead, the others scattered like rice chaff in a typhoon. But the colony must not be forgotten!

So, as he entered his eighties, he decided to donate two hundred acres of his large land holdings to Palm Beach County and the state of Florida for the erection of a museum. It was to be called the Yamato-kan and would be patterned after a Japanese villa, with an interior pebble garden and an exhibition of farming tools similar to those used by the Yamato farmers in the early 1900s. It would be on a tiny island upon which there would be typical bonsai plantings.

But Morikami was never to see his Yamato-kan, for he died suddenly in 1976, at the age of eighty-nine. However, his cherished museum opened the following year.

As time passed, many people grew to enjoy the Morikami setting, with its Japanese ideals of tranquility and respect for nature. Such was the interest that in 1993 a new thirty-two-thousand-square-foot museum was opened across Morikami Pond from the original Yamato-kan. The modern museum has kept the Japanese architectural style but, in addition, has large exhibition galleries, a permanent collection of Japanese artifacts, and an authentic Japanese tea house, where visitors can observe the traditional tea ceremony. For those who want to enjoy a quiet light repast, there is an oriental sandwich shop overlooking the placid pond.

The attractive museum is at 4000 Morikami Park Road, between the turnpike and I-95 via the Atlantic Avenue turnoff and Carter Road.

## I-95 AND FLORIDA'S TURNPIKE
# Palm Beach — Miami
### 64 miles

## Boca Raton

*The Fantasy World of Addison Mizner*

In 1925 Addison Mizner, the wealthy and eccentric architect who put Palm Beach on the map, decided to do the same, only more so, for the area along the inlet that looked like a "rat's mouth" to the early Spanish. He and his associates secretly bought two choice miles of beach property at Boca Raton and announced plans for what Mizner proclaimed would be "the world's most architecturally beautiful playground." Mizner's fame, enhanced by the name of T. Coleman du Pont as backer, ensured great ballyhoo in the press.

Mizner's dreams knew no bounds. He platted an entire city with grand hotels and a splendid golf course. He drew up a magnificent main street called El Camino Real, with a canal down the middle along which Italian gondolas would glide. He himself would live in a castle in the middle of Lake Boca Raton. The central attraction would be his glorious hotel, the Cloister Inn, completed in February 1926. Opening-day guests were the cream of the social register. The air was festive, and there was a giddy feeling that the days of opulence would go on forever.

But even then the Florida land boom was collapsing. There had been too much speculation, too many purchases of bad land, too many promises never kept. After du Pont pulled out, Mizner could not sell his holdings and went bankrupt. The hotel closed and fell into disrepair. Mizner went back to Palm Beach, where he managed to exist only with the help of friends, until he died in 1933.

Modern Boca Raton has many vestiges of Mizner and the Roaring Twenties. The Cloister Inn has been modernized and greatly enlarged with a 250-room tower. It is now the sumptuous Boca Raton Resort and Club, open only to hotel guests.

The Camino Real continues to be an important thoroughfare, though the canal has been filled in. Many of the middle-class homes Mizner built in Old Floresta are lived in today. The old town hall still stands. So, too, does Mizner's administration building at the corner of the Dixie Highway (US 1) and Camino Real.

## Fort Lauderdale

Going beyond Boca Raton, I-95 and the turnpike lead to Fort Lauderdale, Florida's fifth largest city, famous worldwide for its beaches and for its upscale shopping district along Las Olas Boulevard.

Yet for all its current glitter, Fort Lauderdale began with a few grubby shacks along the New River. One of the earliest settlers, William Cooley, had a house and a small mill where he made something called coontie root starch, which he exported to northern markets. The homestead was dangerously exposed on the frontier, and one day in 1836, when William was away, a band of howling Seminoles descended on the home and massacred his wife and his three children and their tutor.

Two years later, Major William Lauderdale built a log fort just upriver from the massacre site as part of the U.S. Army's successful strategy of hunting down the Seminoles and shipping the majority off to the Western plains.

The New River was quiet for many years thereafter, until Frank Stranahan arrived in 1893, at which time he began operating a ferry on the old Cooley site. Soon he moved his ferry station a short distance east, where he also opened a trading post at the point where the river met the sand road that ran along the coast and would one day become the Dixie Highway and eventually US 1.

Many of Stranahan's customers were Seminoles, peaceful now, who canoed down the New River from their hidden retreats in the Everglades, whose marshy vastness began just a few miles to the west. They came 150 at a time, their boats laden with otter skins, egret plumes, and alligator hides. Men, women, and chattering children—

*The 1901 Stranahan House has been beautifully restored. Seminoles trading with Frank Stranahan often slept on the porch.* —Stranahan House

the Seminoles always made a colorful and noisy entry. Stranahan, a quiet, fair-dealing man, had their respect and complete trust.

Flagler's Florida East Coast Railroad, which arrived in 1896, opened the sleepy little village to the outside world. Although the population was only fifty-two mosquito-slapping inhabitants, a station was built, and soon a dock was extended into the New River. Rail connections enabled farmers to carry in their harvests of tomatoes and other produce on sputtering, two-cylinder, gasoline-burning scows called "pop boats."

Stranahan continued to prosper, and his reputation undoubtedly helped him when it came to courting Miss Ivy Cromartie, the pretty teenage lass who taught in the one-room schoolhouse that was built in 1899. When they were married one year later, they formed a partnership that was to provide the developing town with its most active civic-minded couple. Frank became a leader in banking and real estate, and Ivy developed into an activist with the Audubon Society, the movement for women's vote, and for Seminole education.

By 1910 nearly 150 persons lived in the vicinity, and soon Stranahan's store was joined by other riverfront establishments, including a bank, a hotel, and a lumber mill. Although a downtown fire, so frequent in the era of wooden structures, wiped out most of these buildings in 1912, within a few years the river was again humming, now with a fleet of steamboats that chugged through the long canal to Lake Okeechobee and from there all the way to Fort Myers on the Gulf of Mexico.

Smaller boats took daytime picnickers on the two-mile trip downstream to the Atlantic beaches, though the beaches were mostly dense tangles of mangroves and not especially appealing. Access to the beaches became a great deal easier when a road and bridge across the swamps was completed in 1917—with the financial aid of Frank Stranahan. Then the mangroves were gradually removed and beachfront facilities were constructed.

### Riverwalk and Other Renovations

With the opening of the Dixie Highway in 1915, the arrival of trucks and land transportation brought the decline of the New River and the gradual emergence Las Olas Boulevard as the city's downtown. The buildings along the river decayed and were almost forgotten until work began on an imaginative project called Riverwalk in 1989—a project partially financed by the sale of over fifteen thousand paving bricks, into which patrons engraved two-line messages to posterity for sixty dollars apiece.

Riverwalk is now a one-and-a-half-mile landscaped pathway along the north side of the waterway. The walk passes restaurants and parks, and water taxis are available for river transportation. Also on the Riverwalk is the New River Inn, now a museum of south Florida history.

Riverwalk is anchored on the east by the Stranahan House at Las Olas Boulevard and US 1. The 1901 residence has been painstakingly restored and is open for tours. Inside, the Stranahans' possessions are on display, including the chocolate set Ivy used to serve her numerous friends in the Women's Suffrage Society. Frank's office has many photos of early scenes along the New River.

The years were not kind to the Stranahans. When the Fort Lauderdale Bank, of which Frank was president, collapsed during the Great Depression, Frank, despondent over his financial ruin as well as that of many of his friends, took his life in the New River. Ivy had little choice but to turn her home into a restaurant. In addition, she often rented out rooms on the second floor, herself sleeping in the attic when necessary. She lived a long life, dying at the age of ninety in the back room that is now the administrative office.

Riverwalk parking is sometimes difficult, but the garage at the Museum of Discovery and Science is available. The museum, at 401 Southwest Second Street, is an architectural masterpiece and is well worth a visit. The river bend here is near the site of the Cooley massacre. A park at the Fourth Avenue Bridge commemorates the bloody event.

Renovation activity has not neglected Fort Lauderdale's famed beaches. Here a recent $26-million project has created a twenty-foot-wide, pink-paved promenade edged by a gracefully modernistic low wall. Gone are the days of the wild college spring breaks, portrayed with so much gusto in the 1960 movie *Where the Boys Are*. The long, luscious beach is now much more sedate, and a bevy of sidewalk cafes have even nudged aside the seedy beer joints that once rock-and-rolled on the other side of A1A.

Fort Lauderdale is actually on an ambitious and well-financed course to replace Miami as south Florida's premier tourist destination. Within the next few years, $1.5 billion will be invested in tourism-related facilities. More than half will go into the regional airport, which, when added to the already bustling Port Everglades cruise-liner headquarters, will enable tourists to arrive in safety and luxury. Other funds will go into Brickell Station, an entertainment and retail complex where the railroad, which dates back to Henry Flagler, crosses Riverwalk.

Most observers feel that Fort Lauderdale is well on its way—a fact recognized by the readers of *Money* magazine when in 1996 they voted Fort Lauderdale the best large city to live in.

The city of Hollywood is a few miles south of Fort Lauderdale. Rather than returning to the expressway, you may take A1A; however, after leaving Fort Lauderdale, the road is slow and not particularly scenic.

# Hollywood

Hollywood has had a colorful past. In 1921, Indianapolis developer Joseph W. Young, padding through a mangrove swamp, decided that this undeveloped area would be just right for what he called his "dream city." Perhaps influenced by his earlier successes in California, he named the mosquito-infested wilderness Hollywood-by-the-Sea. After he laid out Hollywood Boulevard, an impressively broad thoroughfare intersected by a trio of huge traffic circles, he began the ballyhoo that many believe initiated Florida's most delirious and disastrous decade.

Young's sales organization was reputed to be Florida's largest, topping even those of such heavy hitters as George Merrick in Coral Gables and Carl Fisher in Miami Beach. Effort was concentrated in the northern states, where Young's flamboyant marimba band would play at fairs, summer concerts, and about any gathering where potential buyers stopped to breathe. He also had a troupe of Florida ladies in gaudy plumes and long split skirts prance their horses in the Fourth of July and other parades—carefully outfitting them so no one would guess they were really men. Hollywood—the name became ever more alluring to winter-weary Midwesterners. Obligingly, Young had a fleet of sixty gleaming white buses that carried beguiled multitudes to his burgeoning Sunshine City. To handle even more curiosity seekers, he chartered Pullman cars for monthly excursions. Steamboats, too, were jammed with Young's bookings.

The influx of buyers was so great that Young had to house them in tents until completion of his hotels, the largest and most grandiose being the Hollywood Beach, which he boasted was the finest anywhere, including Paradise itself. Young built the hotel on a "hurry-up" schedule, with construction continuing both day and night, when batteries of floodlights burned so brightly that the hotel could be seen for half a mile inland. When the railroad embargo of Florida took place in 1925, Young calmly bought two large freighters to carry cement from Belgium.

These were good days for Joe Young, still in his forties. "He sang, hummed, or whistled most of the time," recalled his secretary. He was devoted to his wife, for whom he named his private yacht, and to his three young sons. He was a jovial, likable, and very confident person. He was also very rich.

Yet Young was as vulnerable as his friend Addison Mizner and the other promoters when Florida's bubble burst in 1926. Vastly overextended, he could not meet his mortgage payments, and within a few years he had lost everything except his home on Hollywood Boulevard. From here he watched helplessly as his cherished town struggled through the soul-wrenching years of the Great Depression. The carefree crowds were gone. His magnificent hotel was almost deserted. Weeds and sand covered the streets he had laid out during the exuberant times. Certainly the low point occurred when Al Capone and the Chicago mob moved in with their gambling operations. With his dreams in ruins, Joseph Young died suddenly in his home of an apparent heart attack in 1935.

But now the good times are returning. Visitors can again enjoy the Hollywood Beach Hotel, which has been artfully restored. It is directly on the Atlantic, along which the highly active oceanfront boardwalk, first built in the Young era, extends for a dozen or so miles.

The city itself has streetscaped its downtown, centered along Young's broad Hollywood Boulevard. The area called Young Circle anchors the downtown on the east with park greenery and an outdoor concert theater. Young's former home at 1053 Hollywood Boulevard can be viewed from the street, which itself is something of a master-piece, with its majestic royal palms leading toward the pink palace that is the Hollywood Beach Hotel.

For folks not in a hurry, the trip to Miami can be continued down A1A, which runs along the ocean—not that you can see much water for all the high-rise hotels and condos, which have long provided Bal Harbor and other communities with a reputation for glitz. The hotels are still there: the Fontainbleau, the Doral, et al., though nowadays the glitz has grown a bit dusty. Then comes Miami Beach, which is a quirky world all to itself (see chapter 2).

For those wanting to use an expressway system, take I-95 from Hollywood if you are heading directly into Miami. It will pass by the Liberty City section, site of serious riots in the 1980s. Upon reaching downtown Miami, I-95 offers easy access to the attractive and historic Bayfront Park entertainment area.

If, on the other hand, you want to skirt Miami, take the turnpike, which loops out to the west, where it offers connections with I-75 across the Everglades or with US 1 heading to Key West.

*The 1920s Hollywood Beach Hotel again glitters like new.*

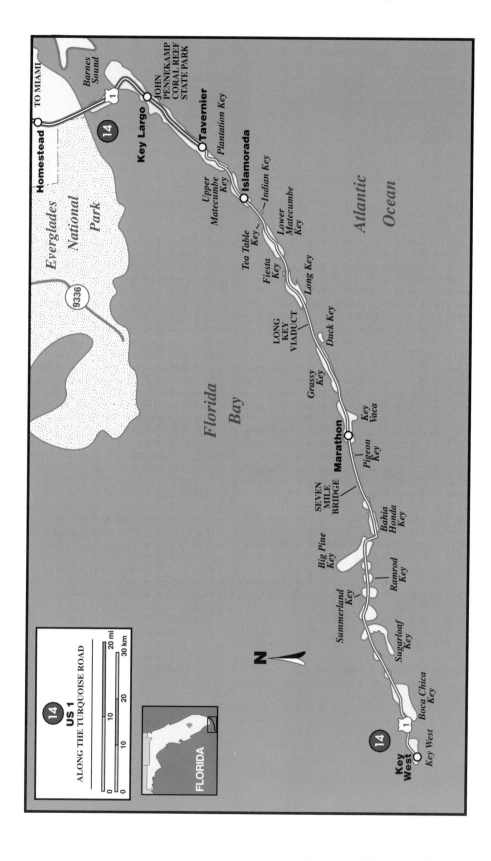

≈ 14 ≈

# *US 1*

## ALONG THE TURQUOISE ROAD

US 1

# Miami—Marathon

**107 miles**

*Origin of the Keys*

The Keys are a thin line of islands beginning at Key Largo and continuing more than one hundred miles mainly west along US 1 to Key West. They comprise two distinct groups of islands. The Upper Keys extend from Key Largo to Bahia Honda. A hundred thousand years ago they were part of a reef, born when the ocean was higher and tropical currents brought nutrients to the tiny coral polyps, building one shell on top of the other.

The same reef continued into the Lower Keys, but there was a subsidence of the land beneath it, allowing a thick layer of a granular limestone sand called *oolite* to form over the coral. When the ocean fell during the buildup of polar ice during the Glacial Age, the exposed oolite hardened into a low mound some forty miles long and up to fifteen miles wide. This mound was cut by tides running between the Atlantic Ocean and the Gulf of Mexico. After the northern glaciers melted and the ocean rose to the present level, the channels were flooded, and the mounds became the islands that run from Big Pine Key to Key West. These keys have thick growths of mangroves, many bays, and in other ways are quite different from the Upper Keys.

*The Spanish in the Keys*

The Spanish, based in nearby Havana, were familiar with the Keys. They called them *cayos,* meaning "low islands." Juan Ponce de León sailed through the cayos in 1513, when he named them the Martyrs. Later, many received individual names. The biggest island was called Key Largo. Nearby were the Matecumbe Keys (Upper and Lower),

*273*

from *matar hombre,* or "to kill a man," undoubtedly relating to some bloody incident now long forgotten. Less threatening was the island where the manatees, or sea cows, played. It was called Key Vaca, or Cow Key. The "deep bay," valued as a refuge during storms, became Bahia Honda, famous today for its beautiful beach.

### John James Audubon

When Audubon appeared in the Keys in 1832, he was already a well-known artist. He had gone to England six years earlier, where a prominent engraver had begun publishing the first of four volumes of Audubon's beautiful bird drawings. After the king himself had ordered a book, Audubon's success was assured, though it had been a struggle to reach this point.

Audubon had been born out of wedlock after a casual liaison between a rough sea captain and a humble French servant girl on the island Haiti. His mother died while he was an infant, and his father did not adopt him until he was fifteen.

Audubon spent a short time in France, but his father, fearing the boy would be drafted into Napoléon's army, sent him to America. There he lived near Valley Forge, where he met his future wife, Lucy, in 1807. The couple migrated to frontier Louisville, Kentucky, in 1807,

*Some of John James Audubon's best paintings are of the birds he discovered during a trip from Saint Augustine to Key West in 1832.*
—Historical Museum of South Florida

where twenty-two-year-old Audubon opened a trading post. But he was not a shopkeeper, and the enterprise failed miserably. Later, when he tried to run a lumber mill, he not only failed but landed in jail for debt.

Through it all, Lucy was a pillar of strength. Indeed it was she, with her job as a teacher, who supported her husband and their two sons. After all else failed, Audubon turned to painting. Even then, it was in England, not the United States, that he had achieved his first real success.

The Florida Keys offered Audubon an exceptional opportunity to paint exotic birds that had never been captured on paper, certainly not with the hand-colored beauty that would emerge in Audubon's marvelous engravings.

He was fortunate to obtain passage aboard a U.S. warship, the *Marion,* a sixty-foot schooner patrolling for smugglers. It had a shallow draft, ideal for penetration of the shoals and shallows that abounded along the Keys. The ship left Charleston April 19, 1832.

The *Marion* coasted Florida for six days before arriving at Indian Key, where Jacob Housman made a comfortable living salvaging goods from wrecked ships. Housman and his wife, Elizabeth Ann, welcomed Audubon with enthusiasm. Housman even lent him one of his most knowledgeable employees, whom we know only as Mr. Egan. Egan knew every cove and mudflat in the innumerable keys, having accessed them in search of loot from wrecked vessels.

With Indian Key as their base, Audubon and Egan roamed far out in the turquoise waters. Birds were everywhere. While on one key Audubon wrote,

> I felt for a moment as if the birds would raise me from the ground so thick were they all round, and so quick the motion of their wings. Their cries were indeed deafening. . . .We ran across the naked beach, and as we entered the thick cover before us . . . we might at every step have caught a sitting bird.

He had beautiful weather, and he described how late one afternoon he was sailing through placid water with the sun tinting the fleecy clouds. It was then that he had one of his greatest thrills:

> Far away to seaward we spied a flock of Flamingoes advancing in "Indian line," with well-spread wings, outstretched necks, and long legs directed backwards. Ah! Reader, could you but know the emotions that then agitated my breast! I thought I had now reached

the height of all my expectations, for my voyage to the Floridas was undertaken in a great measure for the purpose of studying these lovely birds in their own beautiful islands.

As he sailed through the keys, Audubon felt in awe:

My sensations were joyous in the highest degree. . . . It is on such occasions that the traveller feels most convinced that, the farther he proceeds, the better will be his opportunities of observing the results of the Divine conception.

It was well that he felt such exhilaration, for he needed it to balance the travails. Voracious mosquitoes attacked any exposed body part. Even the netting used to cover the men before they slept did not give total protection. And there was the heat: Audubon's clothes were always wet with perspiration. Thorns were everywhere. Along the beaches were jagged rocks made slippery by the decaying seaweed that coated them.

The sailors aboard the cutter thought Audubon was a madman. Perhaps his most insane venture, as far as they were concerned, was the time he and Egan, hunting birds in the Lower Keys, pushed their boats nine miles through stinking mudflats until they reached the haunt of an exotic species of heron.

After five days, the cutter left Indian Key and headed leisurely toward Key West. They camped one night on Key Vaca, not far from the current Marathon airstrip. The next night they were at Bahia Honda, and on the evening of May 4 they glided into the harbor at Key West.

## The Overseas Railroad

After Audubon's departure, the Keys remained relatively quiet—except for the usual shipwrecks and hurricanes. That is, until Henry Flagler, not content with having opened Florida's entire east coast with his railroad, turned his attention on the Keys after Congress passed the Panama Canal Act in 1903. With that, he pictured Key West developing into a major Caribbean port. So in January of 1905, Flagler made a personal inspection of the Keys, at the end of which he announced that work on the rail extension would begin that April. His experts predicted it would be completed in three years.

Right from the beginning, more problems were encountered than expected. The way from Homestead to Key Largo was through saw grass swamplands. Though dredges sucked up the muck and built

*Building the Long Key Bridge. Concrete soon will be poured into the wooden forms. After the concrete dries, the forms will be removed and the bridge arches will remain.* —Historical Museum of South Florida

an embankment, the bedrock was so close to the surface in places that the dredges could not float, so dikes and locks had to be constructed. And Barnes Sound had to be bridged in order to reach Key Largo.

Across Key Largo, the roadbed had to be raised by means of rocks blasted from the native coral. Partway through the island, a body of water not on the surveys appeared. They called it Lake Surprise, and fifteen months were spent forming the causeway across it. More embankments had to be constructed across Tavernier and Plantation Keys.

The first real open water was encountered at the Matecumbe Keys. But it was at Long Key that the masterpiece bridge of the early years was constructed. It had 186 graceful arches extending over two miles of water. The bridge so impressed Flagler that he made it the railroad's logo, appearing on all company letterheads and ads.

Up to five thousand construction men were employed. At first they lived on houseboats, but after a hurricane swept many boats out to sea in 1906, killing 135 men, land barracks were provided. One of the largest labor camps was on Key Vaca, near the modern town of Marathon.

*A train traverses the Seven-Mile Bridge in 1926. Gauges set "stop" signals when the wind exceeded fifty miles an hour.* —Historical Museum of South Florida

For a while, officials considered ending the railroad at Marathon, since ahead lay a large expanse of water that challenged Flagler's most experienced engineers. Thus a large terminal was built that included a train turnaround, repair facilities, and executive quarters. There were also docks for the steamships that began regular runs to Havana.

But Flagler was determined to reach Key West, and in 1908 work was begun on the structure that was called The Great One, which we know today as the Seven-Mile Bridge. The first segment was relatively easy, for it went only to Pigeon Key. But then the Moser Channel had to be crossed, calling for installation of a swing bridge to accommodate ships. Finally came the main section: 210 arches across open water.

The Seven-Mile Bridge ended at Bahia Honda, where another bridge, the loftiest in the entire system, led to Big Pine Key. At Big Pine the most difficult portion of the enterprise was over. Though Key West was still thirty-one miles distant and bridges had to be constructed across the channels dividing Summerland, Sugarloaf, Boca Chica, and several other keys, none were particularly long nor difficult. On January 21, 1912, four years behind schedule, the entire line from Miami to Key West was completed.

The very next day, Flagler entered Key West in his private railroad car. There was a huge celebration, with Flagler the guest of honor. But he was eighty-two years old and nearly blind. As youngsters sang welcoming songs, Flagler told an aide, "I can hear the children but I cannot see them." Nonetheless, it was a joyous occasion, for his dream was completed. "Now I can die in peace," he said. Sixteen months later he did.

## The Overseas Railroad and the Hurricane of 1935

Overseas Railroad officials were constantly worried about hurricanes. Although weather forecasting was primitive, they were able to keep track of barometric air pressure, and on the evening of September 1, 1935, they watched as it began to lower precipitously—indicative of an approaching storm. Ships coming into Miami warned that something fierce was brewing in the Atlantic.

During the next morning, pressure continued to drop, and the skies over the Upper Keys became threatening. Winds increased. Foremen at the large labor camp at Islamorada on Matecumbe Key became concerned. The island was only seven feet above sea level, and already waves were breaking far up on the beach. At 2:35 P.M. a foreman telephoned Miami and urgently requested that a train be dispatched to extricate his people. The strain in his voice, when combined with other reports of the storm's high winds, convinced his superiors of the danger.

But it was Labor Day, and a special train crew had to be rounded up. Additionally, a locomotive and six coaches had to be assembled, which took two precious hours. Then, although the train started at 4:35, it was delayed ten minutes at the Miami River drawbridge, open for holiday boaters.

At last the train roared down the track for Islamorada. However, at Homestead the engineer decided to shift the locomotive from the front of the train to the rear so he would not have to return in reverse. This took fifteen vital minutes.

The relief train reached Snake Creek at 6:50. It was getting dark. The wind whistled, and the air smelled of peril. While the engineer stopped to take refugees aboard, a loose cable swinging in the wind caught the engine cab. The crew worked frantically to cut it loose, but it took them an hour and a half. Meanwhile the black core of the hurricane was almost upon them. Barometers stood at the lowest level ever recorded in the Western Hemisphere.

By the time the train reached Islamorada, the key was already partially flooded. Adding to the problem, a driving rain prohibited the engineer from seeing the station. He overshot it and had to stop and restart when he learned where he was. Again, more time lost.

Finally the station was found, and the frightened men, women, and children clambered aboard. Loading took only five minutes. By now the wind had reached 200 mph and was rocking the coaches dangerously. The engineer reached for the throttle, and the train was ready to race for safety.

But time had run out. A mighty tidal wave nearly two stories high rose from the ocean. With a fearsome roar it rumbled toward the train. The passengers shrieked in terror as they heard the thunderous wall of water approaching. Then it crashed into them. Railroad cars were picked up like toys and hurled off the tracks. Ocean water smashed through the windows, drowning many passengers and sweeping others into the powerful surf. Cries for help were lost amid the wild ferocity of the waves and the howling wind.

When rescue crews arrived the next day, 570 bodies were found. Funeral pyres burned for days. Hundreds more people had been swept out to sea, and their bodies were never recovered.

The railroad was in disrepair. Tracks were twisted, and many had simply vanished. Embankments had been washed away; utility piers and sheds were also gone.

Luckily, Key West had barely been touched, and even in the hardest-hit keys the concrete viaducts and bridge supports stood as firm as when they had been built three decades earlier. However, the railroad officials had had enough of "Flagler's Folly," as some called it, for the Overseas Extension had never paid its way. They sold the line—once valued at more than $27 million—to the federal government for a mere $640,000. The government converted the old railroad bed into a highway, which opened in 1938. President Franklin Roosevelt led a motorcade down it the following year, ending the trip with a glittering reception at the Casa Marina Hotel in Key West.

### Driving the Keys

The drive from Miami on US 1 is mostly suburban as far as Homestead, twenty-five miles south. The rich earth around the town, once part of the Everglades, provides many of the winter vegetables, particularly tomatoes, for the eastern markets.

*The fiercest hurricane could not destroy Henry Flagler's railroad bridges across the keys. But obsolescence did.*

The remains of Hurricane Andrew, which devastated the area in August 1992, are still visible in the form of concrete slabs where blown-away buildings once stood. Andrew left 38 persons dead and 175,000 homeless as it made its violent and erratic course across the southern United States.

South of Homestead, US 1 follows the route of Flagler's Overseas Railroad. The road runs through vast stands of low-growing mangroves trees, which thrive in the shallow, brackish water. They are protected by law, for their extensive prop roots are ideal breeding places for young fish, shrimp, and crabs, while their branches provide nesting sites for ospreys, herons, egrets, pelicans, and many other birds. The ditch from which dredges obtained material for the rail embankment still borders the road.

At Key Largo, watch for the Cross Key Canal, along the banks of which you can see the ancient coral reef that forms the key's bedrock. For a close view of a living reef, take the glass-bottom boat at Key Largo's John Pennekamp State Park.

At Islamorada on Upper Matecumbe, there is a roadside monument to the victims of the 1935 hurricane. Nearby is the Theater of the Sea, which presents excellent shows in a water-filled quarry dug by Flagler's workers.

Tea Table Key has a turnout where plaques present a history of the surrounding islands, including Audubon's Indian Key, visible on the Atlantic side.

The Long Key Bridge, which provided the railroad with its logo, is now a quiet fishermen's haunt beside the modern auto bridge.

Marathon was once the terminus for the Overseas Railroad. Extensive train yards and docks for ships communicating with Havana were just south of the Seven-Mile Bridge.

US 1

# Marathon—Key West

**48 miles**

The Seven-Mile Bridge begins at Marathon. In railroad days, trains were allowed to travel only fifteen miles an hour over it, so the trip took half an hour. From the windows, passengers could see only island dots on the water, beautiful with its changing tapestry of blues and greens, and the tropical birds that so delighted Audubon.

Bahia Honda is now a state park, with camping and some of the most pleasing vistas in Florida—particularly along the Atlantic shore. Before the modern auto bridge was built, US 1 soared over the old railroad bridge's uppermost superstructure. "The view from the top," wrote one concerned highway department official, "is so beautiful that it is most difficult to keep tourists from stopping . . . even though the roadway now, in the 1960s, is very sub-standard in its width."

Big Pine Key is home to about three hundred rare Key deer: little animals barely two feet high. One of their greatest dangers is from autos, so drive with care. Perhaps even more deadly in the long run is the development of the Keys, which deprives the deer of their natural habitat. Indeed, overdevelopment in general is a concern, whether it involves destruction of the natural vegetation, pollution of the water, or difficulty of hurricane evacuation. For this reason the county has placed severe restrictions on future building.

Although the Lower Keys, which begin at Big Pine, are not as spectacular as the Upper Keys, they have a charm all their own. Here, land, sky, bays, and trees blend in soft pastel grandeur. These were some of Audubon's choice hunting grounds.

Sugarloaf is one of the more interesting of the Lower Keys. A loaf-shaped tower was built here in 1929 as a home for bats, which in turn, would feast on the mosquitoes that kept vacationers from enjoying this subtropical fishing retreat. The bats would supposedly be attracted to the tower by the delectable mixture of bat dung and ground-up sex organs of female bats with which the tower had been laced. But the bats were apparently as repelled by the horrible stink as were vacationers, and none took up residence. Today the tower has been reconstructed (minus the bat perfume) and is on the National Register of Historic Places.

There are twenty-one bridges between Big Pine and Key West. Flagler's structures are now used by fishermen, not trains. Many have guardrails that were once the very rails over which steam locomotives chugged.

# Key West

The Spanish knew and feared Key West. They called it *Cayo Hueso,* meaning "island of bones," which may have related to the remains of Spanish sailors drowned from the ferocious storms that often hit the galleons heading home from Cuba and Mexico. In 1821 Spain ceded Florida to the United States, and around this time John Simonton purchased the island from the Spanish for two thousand dollars. It was then that the place became known as Key West.

Gradually the little town grew wealthy, its inhabitants scavenging from the ships that were constantly being wrecked off the coast. In many homes the most prized possessions were pieces plucked from the sea. The population was around two thousand when James Audubon visited it in 1832.

### Audubon at Key West

Audubon stayed on Key West only seventeen days, but he made good use of his time. From his base at the home of master wreck-scavenger John Geiger, he probed into the key's most inaccessible crannies. A record of Audubon's visit was kept by Benjamin Strobel, who found him to be "amiable in his disposition" as well as "the most enthusiastic and indefatigable man I ever knew."

Indefatigable he surely was. At three o'clock one morning, Audubon met Strobel, along with two boatloads of other locals, and set out on a circuit of the island. While the boats followed with supplies, Audubon, Strobel, and a few others poked along the shore:

> Not a pond, lake or bog, did we leave unexplored [Strobel recalled].
> Often did we wade through mud up to our knees, and as often were
> we obliged to scramble over the roots of the Mangrove trees which
> happened in our course. About 8 o'clock, the sun came out intensely
> hot; we occasionally penetrated the woods to escape its scorching
> beams, and as often were driven from the woods by myriads of
> Musquetoes and Sandflies. One of our party gave out about this
> time and took to a boat. Most gladly would I have followed his lead,
> but was deterred by pride.

The party moved on, swatting and sweating. Not only were they
more uncomfortable than they had even been, but the trip was
apparently useless, for not a single unusual bird was found. Nonetheless, Strobel continued, "Audubon went on neither dispirited by
heat, fatigue, nor bad luck." Toward midmorning, when they reached
the lighthouse on Whitehead Street, they were "tolerably well broken
down," as Strobel so quaintly put it. Strobel was not inclined to
accompany Audubon again, though he admitted that for the artist
"this was an every day affair."

Strobel and the others must have breathed a little easier when
Audubon left. Yet they had never known anyone like him. "Not soon,"
Strobel wrote with admiration, "will the recollection of this surpris-
ing man pass from my memory."

After Audubon's departure, Key West's prosperity continued.
The city's influence was felt statewide when Key Wester Stephen
Mallory became a U.S. senator and later served as secretary of
the navy in the Confederacy. The cigar and sponge industries made
Key West their home, and the navy opened a base. Then Flagler's
railroad spanned the ocean and provided the city with fast communication to the mainland. By this time Key West, with thirty
thousand inhabitants, had become Florida's largest and wealthiest-
per-capita city.

### Key West During the Depression

But the 1920s found Key West in horrible shape. The salvaging
opportunities had ended. The naval base had virtually shut down.
The sponge trade had headed to Tarpon Springs, and the cigar
industry had moved to Tampa. Furthermore, the railroad had not
brought the bonanza it had promised, and the real estate bust of
1926 had virtually ended tourism. The final blow came with the Great
Depression, beginning with the stock market crash of 1929.

By this time most citizens had lost faith in their town, and more than half had fled to the mainland—leaving those remaining to rattle past decaying buildings and down deserted streets. And fully 80 percent of those were living off government handouts!

With its tax base utterly devastated, Key West could no longer meet its financial obligations and declared bankruptcy. The state of Florida, itself in a fiscal mess, was unable to come to Key West's aid. In an action of questionable legality, rule was turned over to the federal government. Thus, during many of the mid-Depression years, administration of local governmental affairs was conducted by Julius Stone, autocratic head of the Federal Emergency Relief Administration (FERA).

### Ernest Hemingway in Key West

Key West in the 1930s has been vividly portrayed by Ernest Hemingway in his novel *To Have and Have Not.* He conveys the feeling of hopelessness through his main character, Harry Morgan, who is reduced to smuggling goods and aliens from Cuba to make a living. The center of Harry's world is the bar run by Sloppy Joe Russell, whom Hemingway calls Freddy Wallace. Into the bar come the "have-not" locals and as well as wealthy tourists—the "haves." There, too, are a bunch of quarrelsome army vets, who, though Hemingway did not know it at the time, were destined to die in the horrible hurricane of 1935. Even Julius Stone makes a brief appearance in the form of Frederick Harrison. When a local boat captain grumbles that he never heard of him, Harrison retorts, "You will . . . and so will every one in this stinking jerkwater little town if I have to grub it out by the roots."

Ernest Hemingway had always been something of a maverick. Born in 1899 to a prosperous doctor and his iron-willed wife, as a teenager he held rowdy boxing matches in his basement. Graduating from Oak Park High School in Illinois, he refused to go to college. Eager to get away from his family, particularly his mother, Ernest went to Kansas City, where he worked as a cub reporter for the *Star.* Hardly was he there than the advent of the First World War sent his adventurous spirit tingling, and off he went as a Red Cross volunteer to the battlefront in Italy. There, he behaved heroically, rescuing a man under fire and receiving shrapnel in his leg, sending him to a hospital.

In 1921 he married Hadley Richardson. Two years later, he got his first literary pieces published. His strong language caused his father to send his complimentary copies back to the publisher, refusing to have such "filth" in his house.

Rejection by his parents helped Ernest choose Europe over the United States as the setting for most of his novels. There, the disillusioned expatriates of America's "lost generation" provided the characters for his first major novel, *The Sun Also Rises,* published in 1926. It was an instant success and established the twenty-six-year-old as an up-and-coming young writer.

While in Europe, Hemingway became enamored with Pauline Pfeiffer, a talented American journalist. In 1927 he divorced Hadley—who had used her trust fund so they could travel through Europe and had recently given him a son—and then he married Pauline. The next year, the newlyweds returned to the United States so their expected child would be born an American.

Pauline had a rich uncle who in 1931 gave them the money to purchase a home, at 907 Whitehead Street in Key West. Pauline lovingly decorated it with antiques she had collected from Europe. As the home began to ring with the voices of their two growing boys, Hemingway fixed up a writing room on the second level of the guest house in the rear. It had floor-to-ceiling doors that overlooked the shrubs below, many of which he himself had planted. Here Hemingway wrote the novel *A Farewell to Arms,* based on his war experiences in Italy. It was published in 1930. With good sales and wonderful reviews, Hemingway's fame grew to the extent that the couple had to build a wall around their grounds to discourage sight-seers.

Almost immediately, Hemingway began work on *Death in the Afternoon,* describing the high drama of Spanish bullfighting. Published in 1932, the novel also revealed Hemingway's obsession with death, which had developed since his father's suicide by pistol several years earlier.

Hemingway wrote furiously during the mornings and caroused in Key West during the afternoons and evenings. One of his favorite drinking buddies was Sloppy Joe Russell, who owned a dive on Greene Street. Hemingway would go to the bar nearly every day, and immortalized it in his novel about Key West, *To Have and Have Not,* which came out in the Hearst magazines in 1934. It was at Joe's saloon that he met an attractive young woman named Martha Gellhorn. The next time he went to Europe, it was with Martha rather than Pauline.

As Pauline saw Ernest slipping away, she became almost neurotic about her appearance, for she was four years older than her husband. She began coloring her hair in order to look younger. She promised to give Ernest all the money in the savings account her father had set up for her if he would just not get involved with another woman. Desperate to keep Ernest at home, she put in a swimming pool—Key West's first. But Ernest complained that it cost too much and angrily hurled a penny onto the deck, claiming Pauline had taken his last cent for its construction.

At this time, Ernest was working on a monumental novel about the Spanish Civil War, *For Whom the Bell Tolls.* Yet writing was difficult, for sounds from the pool below distracted him. Soon he grew to dislike Key West, too, complaining about "this F.E.R.A. Jew administered phony of a town." He began spending much time aboard his fishing boat with Sloppy Joe and other cronies. He became vain, cruel, and slovenly. Finally, in 1939 he told a sobbing Pauline that he was leaving her. The following year he married the vivacious Martha and lived most of his remaining twenty-two years in Cuba.

Though Ernest left, Pauline and her sons continued to reside in the house on Whitehead. After she died in 1951, the home remained in the family for another ten years. When it was finally sold, the new

*Ernest Hemingway owned a house in Key West during the 1930s. He had many drinking buddies, including "Sloppy Joe" Russell, on the left. Hemingway was not so amiable toward the women he married.* —Historical Museum of South Florida

owners bowed to the demand that it be made a national shrine, and eventually it was placed on the Register of Historic Landmarks.

As for Hemingway, his later years were not happy. He divorced Martha in 1946 and wed Mary Welsh. Although he won the Nobel Prize for Literature in 1954, he worried that his writing skills were deteriorating. In addition, he had tax problems and fell under FBI surveillance for what the agency thought were possible communist connections. His lifelong bouts with depression increased, and he went to the Mayo Clinic for treatment. But in 1961 his suicidal tendencies won out. At around seven on a Sunday morning, Mary heard a shotgun roar and found him in the upstairs foyer of their Idaho home with the entire top of his skull blown off.

### Modern Key West

The revival of Key West started with the efforts of FERA administrator Julius Stone to spruce up the city and make it appeal to tourists. The renewal of the naval base during World War II also aided Key West. At this time, a pipeline was run out from the mainland, giving Key West its first dependable drinking water. With the navy

*President Harry S. Truman (with cane) and top administration officials at the Little White House on the Key West naval base in 1947. By night guests would play poker at a table that is still on display.* —Historical Museum of South Florida

also came President Harry Truman, who used the converted commandant's quarters as his vacation White House between 1946 and 1952.

A tour of Harry Truman's Little White House should be on the list of any history buff. The feisty man comes alive as one sees such personal items as the table where he played poker and sipped whiskey with his guests, who ranged from top generals and admirals to the chief justice of the United States.

During the infamous Mariel boat lift of 1980, the base was the landing site for Castro's rejects from Cuban jails and institutions. American authorities had been forewarned of the exodus and had made plans for resettling around three thousand people. Instead, up to twenty thousand people arrived in just the first few days. They were jammed into one navy hangar for almost a week in one-hundred-degree heat. Food ran out, water was short, and tempers flared. Clubs and knives were made from government cots, and only President Carter's hurried dispatch of a Marine battalion saved a full-scale riot from devastating Key West. Eventually most of the Cubans were resettled in Miami.

Today many navy ships moor at the old Trumbo docks, which can be seen at the northwest tip of the island. Originally the docks were the terminal for Flagler's Overseas Railroad. The story goes that when Flagler was told there was insufficient land at Key West for a terminal, his response was: "Then make some." His chief engineer, Howard Trumbo, did just that.

Key West's renovation gained momentum when the Audubon House, at 205 Whitehead Street, was restored in 1960 and opened to the public. Although Audubon spent only a short time here, the home has been refurbished in a style that evokes his memory. So, too, do some of his most beautiful engravings.

Hemingway's residence, at 907 Whitehead, is the island's most popular attraction. His writing room is much the same as when he was there composing many of his immortal novels. The controversial swimming pool remains, as does the penny he slammed on the deck: Pauline, with a surprising sense of humor, encased it there.

Other Hemingway haunts abound. Joe Russell's original bar, the Blind Pig, at 428 Greene Street, is still there, although under a different name. In 1937 Joe's landlord raised the rent from three dollars per week to four dollars, so he stomped half a block down Greene to the corner of Duval. There he opened a new bar, named Sloppy

Joe's at Hemingway's suggestion. It sells T-shirts as well as burgers and a more-than-goodly supply of suds. Joe Russell died in 1941 following a heart attack in Havana.

Another historical highlight is Marriott's Casa Marina Hotel. Built between 1918 and 1921 as a major destination for travelers on Flagler's Overseas Railroad, it had a checkered career after the hurricane of 1935 closed the line. First the navy, then the army, and then the Peace Corps occupied the building. Thereafter it was closed for a number of years, until Marriott did a superlative rehab job in 1979. Now it is again a major vacation destination. The lavishly landscaped grounds offer spectacular views of the ocean. Off the lobby are many vintage photographs of Key West during the years from Flagler to Truman.

*Joe Russell named his Key West bar "Sloppy Joe's" at Hemingway's suggestion. Ernest hung out here to absorb the local atmosphere.*

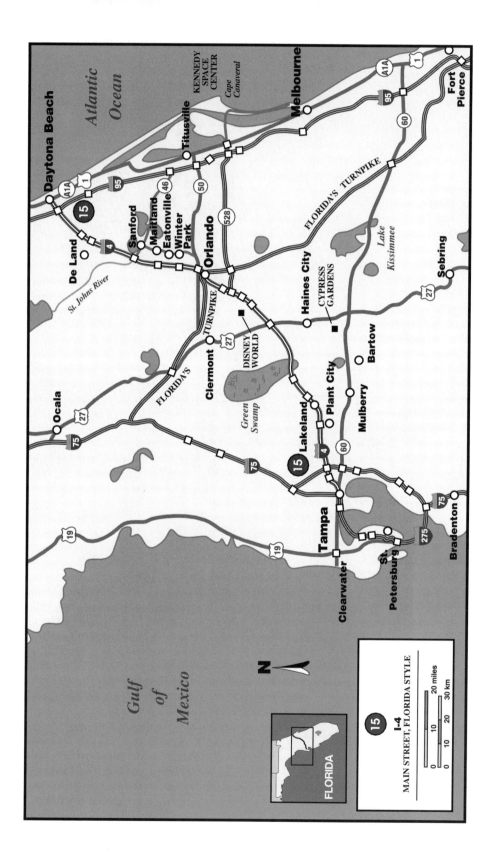

# ∽ 15 ∽

# *Interstate 4*

## MAIN STREET, FLORIDA STYLE

# Daytona Beach—Orlando

**47 miles**

Although I-4 is only 134 miles long, it has had repercussions for Florida far greater than its size. Running between Daytona Beach and Tampa, it crosses Florida's Turnpike just west of Orlando. In 1964 this intersection occurred in the midst of a large, virtually uninhabited swampy area. Walt Disney, flying over the still-uncompleted I-4, turned to his associates and declared, "This is it!" The rest, as they say, is history.

The advent of the Disney organization resulted in a whole chain reaction whereby there was a tremendous influx of middle-class Northerners, who in turn caused the central part of the state to lose its distinctive Southern orientation. The expressway became a sort of demarcation line between the old-time Democratic population above it and the newer, more Republican population along it.

Driving west on I-4 from the I-95 turnoff at Port Orange, you pass through a series of old beaches, now covered by sand-loving plants such as pines and saw palmetto. In a few miles you come to a barely distinguishable elevation where hardwood trees become mixed with the pines. This is the DeLand Rise, which forms the divide between the Atlantic plain and the St. Johns River basin.

The forest is the home of black bears, a threatened species. Part of the threat comes from motorists, who have difficulty seeing the bears at night. More than fifty bears are run down and killed each year in central Florida alone.

# DeLand

The city of DeLand was founded by Henry A. DeLand, an upstate New York manufacturer who accumulated a modest fortune in baking soda. His sister, Martha, convinced him to make the difficult trip to Florida to see the acreage she and her husband, O. P. Terry, had just purchased. Thus, in 1876 DeLand, accompanied by his wife, Sarah, and their teenage son and daughter, took the train from New York to Jacksonville.

At Jacksonville they embarked on the Brock Line's steamboat, *Hattie*, and chugged up the St. Johns River, probably spending the night at Palatka. Then they continued to Enterprise, seat of the virtual wilderness called Volusia County. In Enterprise, the DeLands stayed at Jake Brock's rambling hotel overlooking Lake Monroe. The historical society in DeLand has the original hotel registration signed by Henry himself.

O. P. Terry had driven down in a horse and buggy to meet Henry at the Brock House, and the next morning the two started out for Terry's place. There was no good road, and the way led through palmettos and slash pine. The sand was deep, and several times the wagon became stuck, which necessitated digging and a lot of hard work. DeLand wanted to turn back, but Terry urged him on. Eventually they reached the log cabin of John and Clara Rich, about twenty miles from Enterprise, where they spent the night.

Henry admired the country around the Riches' and bought 160 acres as a speculative venture. Soon thereafter, he formed a real estate company to sell land plots and, to help sales, founded a private college, called the DeLand Academy. It had all of eighty-eight students when the first building, DeLand Hall, opened in 1884.

Two years later, the college got a financial boost from John B. Stetson, the wealthy hat manufacturer from Philadelphia. In return Stetson demanded that the institution be renamed after him. Henry DeLand must have thought that a mere name change was a cheap price to keep the college, which was one of the most attractive selling points of his growing town. So Stetson University was born. Not surprisingly, it had a Stetson Hall, which was larger than DeLand Hall. Stetson became head of the board of trustees and lived in the mansion that still stands at 1031 Camphor, just off Florida 15A.

Henry was very active during the town's early period. Perhaps his most lasting monuments are the trees that shade Woodland Avenue, DeLand's main street. Henry and his daughter, Helen, who

*DeLand Hall at Stetson University was built in 1884. The university was named for hatmaker John Stetson.*

was also greatly involved in town affairs, induced the settlers to plant these trees by offering them fifty cents off their tax bills for several years.

Henry never built a home in DeLand—perhaps the fact that his wife went insane had something to do with this. Instead, he spend most of his time at the Harland Hotel, which he built at nearby Lake Helen, named for his daughter (who later published her reminiscences in a delightful book entitled *The Story of Lake Helen and Deland*, which is for sale at the historical society). Meanwhile, Henry had sold many acres to citrus growers on a money-back guarantee, and when the big freeze of 1895 killed their trees, the buyers demanded the return of their money. Henry went bankrupt, and Stetson took over his holdings. DeLand then returned north.

Today, both the city of DeLand and Stetson University are thriving. Henry DeLand has been honored by the West Volusia Historical Society, which has taken over an old house at 137 West Michigan they call the DeLand home, although Henry did not reside there. However, John Stetson owned the home, built in 1886, using it as rental property for university faculty. Now it is a free museum.

As for the university, both DeLand and Stetson Halls are still in use. So, too, is Flagler Hall, donated by the East Coast railroad tycoon

Henry Flager. Indeed, Stetson University eventually became such a collection of vintage buildings that much of the campus has been designated a National Historic District, as has DeLand's revitalized downtown. A self-guided walking-tour leaflet is available at the public relations office (once an undertaker's parlor!), at 516 North Woodland Boulevard.

## Cassadaga

At exit 54 on I-4 is the road to the tiny community of Cassadaga (population under four hundred). The spiritualists from New York who founded it in 1894 chose the location because they felt that special psychic powers emanated here. The name came from that of their original settlement, which itself was derived from an Indian word meaning "place beneath the rock" (not "house of the devil," as many Floridians of the disapproving sort prefer to believe).

At first, the settlement was simply called The Camp, for it consisted merely of tents. Nowadays the spiritualists live in wooden homes scattered among the trees. Name your reading—it's there: astrology, palmistry, numerology, tarot cards. You can even experience past-life regressions. If you are too busy to spend time in Cassadaga, phone the Cassadaga Hotel and you can get a long-distance reading.

Cassadaga has achieved a national following. Many major newspapers and such TV programs as *20/20* and *A Current Affair* have aired stories on the hamlet.

The modest hotel fits right into the otherworldly atmosphere. The units have no radios or TVs. Nor are children under eighteen allowed, since this is a place for serious forays into the Great Mysteries, not for idle amusement. But if you just want a few moments in Cassadaga without the mysteries, you can stop at the hotel for pastries and coffee in the morning or soup and a sandwich later in the day.

## Orange City and Blue Spring State Park

Orange City is a city in name only, for its population is less than six thousand. But it has an incomparable asset in Blue Spring State Park. Blue Spring was an attraction from the days when Florida was still a British province. Naturalist William Bartram visited the spring with his father, John, in 1765, and nine years later was back—this time alone.

Bartram docked his little sailboat, battered and thoroughly soaked from a hurricane, at a nearby British indigo plantation. Eager to see Blue Spring once more, he induced the plantation owner to leave his sixty slaves under the supervision of an overseer and to accompany him on horseback four miles to the spring. Here is the account he wrote in *Travels of William Bartram:*

> [We found] a vast fountain of warm, or rather hot mineral water, which issues from a high ridge. . . . A pale bluish or pearl coloured coagulum covers every inanimate substance that lies in the water. . . . The creek, which is formed instantly by this admirable fountain, is wide and deep enough for a sloop to sail up. . . . The water is perfectly diaphanous, and here are continually a prodigious number and variety of fish; they appear as plain as though lying on a table before your eyes.

Blue Spring is now a very popular state park. In the winter, manatees often lumber up the St. Johns to Blue Spring, where they enjoy the warm water. Only about two thousand manatees remain in existence, and scientists are uncertain whether the species can survive the propeller blades and other hazards that are reducing their population by up to 10 percent yearly.

Part of the creek has been roped off for swimmers and snorkelers to loll around in the seventy-two-degree, still-diaphanous water. The park provides changing rooms.

*Blue Spring State Park near Orange City. Botanist-explorer William Bartram was fascinated with the "vast fountain" when he visited it in 1774.*

*An early steamboat on a small river. Florida teemed with such vessels until the railroads sunk them.* —P. H. Yonge Library of Florida History, University of Florida

Along the bluff beside Blue Spring Creek is a wooden walkway that passes through a leafy archway of huge hardwoods, presenting much the same vista as greeted Bartram more than two hundred years ago. Before culminating at the St. Johns River, the walkway passes the old Thursby House, built on an ancient Indian shell mound dating back to 2000 B.C.

Narrated boat rides are available along the historic St. Johns.

# DeBary

### *A Steamboater's Mansion*

At 210 East Sunrise Boulevard is the renovated mansion of Count Frederick DeBary, St. Johns River steamboat mogul. The mansion, built in 1871, was the height of backwoods elegance. Presidents Grant and Cleveland, General Sherman, and the Prince of Wales (who later became the King of England) were among those who enjoyed the feasts and fellowship at DeBary Hall, where chilled champagne freighted from New England was a staple. So much bubbly was consumed that DeBary lined his garden with empty bottles. Guests frolicked in the count's swimming pool, said to be the first in Florida with cemented walls. Other times they galloped through the woods on hunting steeds, each of whom had its name on a plaque, some of which can still be seen in the barn.

Though the count died in 1898, the home remained in the family until his last heir, the pert and impulsive Leonie, crashed in her private plane in 1941.

# Enterprise

Half a mile east of DeBary Hall on DeBary Road is Enterprise. Insignificant today, it once was the county seat as well as the location of the Brock House, one of Florida's most famous hotels, owned by the crusty steamboat captain Jacob Brock, whose story is told in chapter 4.

The Brock House was built in 1856 and endured until 1937. It sat at the intersection of Main Street, Lakeshore Drive, and DeBary Road, a site now occupied by the United Methodist Children's Home. A few pilings from Brock's old steamboat wharf can be seen from the foot of Clark Street.

# Sanford

Beyond DeBary, I-4 crosses the St. Johns River at the point where the river widens to form Lake Monroe, named in honor of the fifth U.S. president, James Monroe, in whose term Florida was acquired from Spain. The city of Sanford is on the lake's southern shore.

Sanford has had a curious past. It could have been, and perhaps should have been, central Florida's major city, rather than Orlando. As early as the 1830s, the army recognized the importance of Sanford's location on the St. Johns for steamboat navigation. Thus it established Fort Mellon as its main supply point for the interior, with nine steamboats servicing it. From here, several roads radiated out, the main one running through Fort Maitland and Fort Gatlin (Orlando) to Fort Brooke on Tampa Bay, a route now approximately followed by I-4.

Fort Mellon became a gathering place for the Indians when twenty-five hundred of them camped here in 1837, during an interlude in the Second Seminole War. At this time, Osceola reestablished his friendship with Lieutenant John Graham, who had a fondness for one of Osceola's daughters. Eyewitnesses reported that during the Battle of the Withlacoochee two years earlier, Osceola had ordered his braves not to shoot at Graham, who was a large man and an easy target. After the war the fort was abandoned, and Enterprise, across Lake Monroe, became the center of activity.

Things changed with the arrival of Henry Sanford in 1871. Sanford was a wealthy and important man. His father had been a rich Northern manufacturer who had sent him to Europe for his education. Henry proved to be a brilliant student, graduating cum laude from Heidelberg University, and had no trouble obtaining a position in the American diplomatic corps.

Although Sanford was an austere person, whose somber dress earned him the nickname "Black Crow," he apparently was a capable diplomat, for in 1861 President Abraham Lincoln appointed him minister to Belgium. In that new position, Sanford decided he needed to brighten his appearance along with his title. With the Civil War now raging, he decided to become a noncombatant officer. For that purpose, he donated three cannons to the Minnesota militia in return for a general's commission. Thereupon he designed his own uniform, complete with shining epaulets and a crimson sash.

At the same time, he added to his luster by marrying Gertrude DuPuy, a pretty and vivacious woman of twenty-three, about half his age. She was from an aristocratic Philadelphia family but, having lived in Europe for years, spoke with a French accent. With a beautiful wife, a good job, a prestigious title, and ample investment income, Sanford was now at the pinnacle of his career. But he wanted more.

Possibly through information from Count DeBary, Sanford learned of land for sale around Lake Monroe. Ah, to build a city and have it named after him—now, that would be success! So Sanford bought twenty-three square miles of choice property along Lake Monroe and dragged an unwilling Gertrude along to see it.

When they arrived by steamboat, they found very little except the ruins of Fort Mellon. But it was just what General Sanford had hoped for—a fresh new world awaiting the hand of the master builder. However, to Gertrude, accustomed to the perfumed luxury of Europe, it was horrible.

Henry became obsessed with his town and invested large sums of money in it. He imported 30,000 trees, including 140 different types of citrus, to determine which grew best—and in effect became the father of the orange industry. He also built a six-hundred-foot steamboat pier, as well as the magnificent two-hundred-room Sanford Hotel. And he was able to lure the railroad of Henry Plant into his town.

Despite Sanford's efforts, the town was never profitable. Gertrude began to despair. She called Florida "a vampire that sucked the repose and beauty and dignity and cheerfulness out of our lives."

During his last ten years, Sanford was constantly harassed by creditors. He aged severely. He became fat and walked with a stoop. Possibly suffering from liver disease, he died in Florida in 1891, at the age of sixty-eight. Gertrude spent the next decade trying to extricate herself from his debts.

## Modern Sanford

During the years that followed, the town continued to struggle. The citizens felt held down by the pushy politicians of Orlando, their aversion dating back to the days when the uncouth cattleman Jake Summerlin prevented General Sanford from transferring the county seat from Orlando to Sanford. The resentment did not abate when the town of Sanford broke off from Orlando in 1913 and formed its own rump county, called Seminole, the smallest in the state.

Today, Sanford is moving along. It attracted a major mall beside I-4, and its downtown has been beautifully restored as part of Florida's Main Street program. It has a fine historical museum, where Henry Sanford's black crow suit and his general's uniform are on display. A short distance east of the museum, a marker at Mellonville Avenue and East Second Street indicates the approximate location where Fort Mellon once stood.

*Sanford's depot in 1906. The town once dreamed of outstripping Orlando. The Pico Building in the background still stands.* —Florida State Archives

Henry Plant's 1887 railroad hotel, shaped like a Turkish mosque, still exists at Commercial and Oak. Sometimes as many as four locomotives stood smoking and snorting on the tracks at the depot in front of the hotel. The local railroad headquarters was across Commercial Street in the Welaka Building. The railroad superintendent lived in the house at 420 Oak. Both the hotel and the railroad headquarters are on the National Register of Historic Places.

Among the most appealing aspects of Sanford are the cruise boats that leave from the site of Henry Sanford's wharf for short but scenic excursions through Lake Monroe and along the St. Johns River.

## Maitland and Eatonville

Beyond Sanford, I-4 parallels the former military road over which foot soldiers and mule wagons made their way between the string of forts that connected Fort Mellon with Tampa Bay during the Second Seminole War.

Fort Maitland was an important post, more so than nearby Fort Gatlin in Orlando. As it was the custom to name forts after men who had died during conflicts, Fort Maitland honored Captain William S. Maitland, who had received serious battle wounds and later, in South Carolina, drowned himself to end the pain. A typical fort, Maitland was surrounded by a wall of sharpened pine logs eighteen feet high, with blockhouses at diagonal corners.

The coming of Plant's railroad in 1880 was a godsend to the struggling community, since it was now on the main line through Sanford, Orlando, and Tampa. The settlers decided to incorporate, but they found they did not have the required thirty voters. So they induced some black citrus-farm workers to become residents, and together they voted the town into existence.

But to the whites' consternation, the blacks elected one of their own as mayor. To remedy this situation, Joshua Eaton and two other whites agreed to donate some land west of town and to construct a church and an assembly hall if the blacks would move. Black leaders, apparently overjoyed at the opportunity to begin American's first all-black town, incorporated Eatonville in 1888.

Today, Maitland is a prosperous suburban town. The site of the fort is now a small city park beside US 17/92, which is the old military road. Across the highway Lake Lily, with its distinctive water jet, has become the community showplace, on whose shores is the reno-

*Zora Neale Hurston was a pioneer black writer in the 1930s and 1940s. Her last years were spent as a housemaid. She died poor and virtually forgotten.* —Orange County Historical Museum

vated Waterhouse Residence, built by a city founder in 1884. Nearby is the historic railroad dating back to Henry Plant, now the route of Amtrak. The Maitland Historical Museum is nearby, at 221 West Packwood Avenue.

As for Eatonville, it led a quiet existence, and to this day its population is under three thousand. It would be virtually unknown if it weren't for writer Zora Neale Hurston.

## Zora Neale Hurston and the Black Experience

Born in Eatonville around 1891 (she kept the exact date secret), Zora Neale Hurston achieved recognition in the 1930s, when her vivid portrayals of African American life were published in national magazines and she was featured on the cover of the *Saturday Review of Literature.* The *New York Times,* reviewing one of her novels, called it a "well nigh perfect story."

Yet fame was fleeting. Hurston's writing could not earn her a living, and one of her last jobs was as a housemaid for a wealthy white family in Miami. By the time Hurston died in 1960, she did not even have the funds for her burial. She lies in a segregated cemetery in Fort Pierce.

But Hurston's final years should not obscure her achievements. In 1935 she published *Mules and Men,* based on her exhaustive collections of black folklore, many of the selections dating back to slave remembrances. In *Jonah's Gourd Vine* she gave unforgettable glimpses of her parents' life. Then in 1937 she published *Their Eyes Were Watching God,* which many regard as her best work. Here she used Eatonville for the setting. Along the way she also wrote short pieces, such as "How It Feels to Be Colored Me" and "My Most Humiliating Jim Crow Experience"—pieces that were among the first to penetrate into the white press.

Hurston published her autobiography, *Dust Tracks on a Road,* in 1942. In it she introduces her grandmother, a former slave, who with good reason did not have a friendly feeling toward whites. When John Hurston came courting her daughter, Lucy, Grandmother looked at his light skin and called him "dat yaller bastard"—an opinion she maintained for the rest of her life.

Despite Grandma's derision, John Hurston became a successful man. He was Eatonville's mayor for three terms and also a prominent preacher. Zora's family lived in a large house, although it barely had space for Mom, Pop, eight rambunctious kids, and feisty old Grandma. Mom ruled the roost. Every evening the kids would come to her room and she would review their schoolwork. No loafing was allowed.

Zora was mostly a good student, if you discounted her multiplication tables. She loved games, and all the neighborhood children came to her yard for hide-and-seek in the moonlight. In the daytime she'd play baseball with the boys; first base was her favorite position. She always wanted to be right in the middle of things.

Zora was an independent sort of girl, sassy sometimes. Her father did not like her spirit, for he had learned to bend in the white man's world and believed that she should, too. "It did not do for Negroes to have too much spirit," she remembered her father telling her. "He predicted dire things for me. The white folks were not going to stand for it. I was going to be hung before I got grown."

But Zora's early experiences with whites did not seem to bear out her father's predictions. The whites in Maitland and the blacks in Eatonville knew and respected one another. When Lucy Hurston gave birth unexpectedly to little Zora, she was alone and might have died had not a white man from Maitland happened to have come calling with a gift of sweet potatoes and half a hog. It was he who cut the umbilical cord and tended to Lucy until a midwife came an hour later. Little Zora and the white man became fast friends.

Growing up in Eatonville, Hurston met other whites, though not many in the all-black town. Occasionally ladies from Maitland visited her school. What she remembered most about them were their hands. "They were long and thin, and very white, except near the tips. There they were baby pink. I had never seen such hands. . . . I wondered how they felt."

Hurston's childhood world fell apart when her mother died. Then her father drove her in the buckboard to the Maitland station, where she took the train to Jacksonville to live with a brother while she went to high school. Later she went to Barnard College in New York City, where, because she was black, she was not allowed to attend the graduation prom.

Today, Eatonville honors Zora Neale Hurston, and all black artists, at the museum named in her honor, at 227 East Kennedy Boulevard. As for the Hurston home, it has been torn down, though its site was on the south side of Kennedy Boulevard, just west of West Street. Gone, too, is the building across the road, at 501 East Kennedy, that housed Joe Clarke's general store—the center of the community. However, the old Macedonia Baptist Church, where Hurston's mother was buried, still stands.

And there is Lake Bell on the town's southern flank, home of Mr. Pindir, the alligator king, who a little girl's imagination saw paddling down the water in the flaming red of a rising moon, "with thousands on thousands of his subject 'gators moving silently along beside him and behind him in an awesome and mighty convoy."

## Winter Park

Past Maitland on I-4 is the turnoff to Winter Park, which locals consider the cream of suburban Orlando. Thus the citizens became quite disturbed in 1954 when the planned route of I-4 would have run through a choice site now occupied by the civic center. After considerable agitation, I-4 was rerouted to its current location several miles west.

Winter Park was originally just another railroad town, and the depot of 1882 was the first building erected. However, Winter Park soon boasted the largest hotel in the entire state: Henry Plant's Seminole— until it went up in a swirl of smoke, cinders, and broken dreams in 1902.

Built on the shores of several lakes, Winter Park once echoed with the whistles of steamboats hauling timber to nearby mills. Now,

*Boats take visitors through Winter Park's picturesque lakes and canals.*

excursion boats at the foot of Morse Boulevard take visitors on hour-long scenic tours, which visitors have been enjoying since 1938.

If you go to Winter Park, use the Fairbanks exit. Be sure to drive through Rollins College, one of the top small schools in the Southeast. The campus features a pleasant melange of Spanish architecture, capped by a replica of Seville's famed Giralda Tower. On the grounds is the Cornell Fine Arts Museum, which a national magazine has called the best free museum in the nation.

Next, why not visit the vintage shops of Park Avenue, Winter Park's answer to Palm Beach's Worth Avenue? You may want to eat at one of the restaurants at the upscale Park Plaza Hotel, built in 1921. And you should visit the Morse Museum, at Park and Canton, with its beautiful and extensive display of Tiffany glass.

### A Drive Past Orlando and the Theme Parks

Beyond Winter Park, I-4 enters the Orlando metropolitan area.

To the west is the Marriott Hotel, highlighted by a pair of red accent lines running around the upper portion. Immediately north is the Orlando Arena, where the Magic basketball team plays its home games. You might be able to spot its low, rounded outline.

Now watch on the east for the golden dome of the three-story Exchange, a key building in the rollicking entertainment attraction known as Church Street Station.

As you are about to leave downtown Orlando, to the east is the city hall, with its white facade and dark dome. Typical of Orlando's playful spirit, when the city hosted the international soccer championships a few years ago, the dome was painted to resemble a soccer ball.

A few miles south of downtown, you can make out the Citrus Bowl in the western distance. Several miles later, you will spy a tower that looks like it is sporting a derby hat. This is a motel that marks the exit to International Drive to the east. I-Drive is studded with motels and chain restaurants. However, there are some impressive high-rises farther down the road, such as the brand-new Omni Rosen that some say looks like a great pipe organ, and the Peabody Hotel, famous for its decades-old duck pageantry, which is presented each day in the lobby. There is, too, the Orange County Convention Center, a long, low fortress of a structure that has become one of the major such facilities in the nation.

To the west is Universal Studios, the entrance of which is marked by a hotel with twin towers. In times past, the hotel hosted Ronald Reagan and many other dignitaries.

Soon you will come to the Sea World exit, marked by the Renaissance Hotel, boasting the world's largest resort atrium lobby. In a moment, to the west you will pass the high-rise hotels of Disney's Lake Buena Vista—including the Hyatt Regency Grand Cypress, whose interior is certainly one of the most opulent you will ever encounter. At about the same time, to the east you will see the Marriott World Center, with its castlelike spire in which glass elevators run.

Now come the entrances to Disney territory. There is nothing to see from the highway, for the parks are far back in Disney's extensive grounds. But if you would like a rather quick tour via the monorail, turn to the Disney section in chapter 1.

## Celebration

South of the US 192 exit is the town of Celebration. This is not a theme park, but it could almost be one. Celebration is a town being built by Disney over a period of roughly fifteen years that will eventually house around twenty thousand people. It is intended to be a nostalgic re-creation of the days when life was supposedly simple and wholesome. The town stresses neighborliness; to help facilitate this, the lots are narrow and front porches abound. Garages are in the rear, for cars are relegated to a minor role that involves slinking down alleys. Streets are meant primarily for people, bicycles, and dogs.

For visitors, Celebration boasts restaurants and a lakeside park in the quaint downtown that somewhat resembles the Magic Kingdom's Main Street.

Although Celebration is not the experimental prototype city of the future that Walt Disney dreamed of, it is an interesting attempt to resurrect traditional values of strong family and community ties.

I-4

# Orlando—Tampa
87 miles

Beyond Celebration, I-4 makes a slight ascent onto the narrow Citrus Ridge. The ridge extends from Clermont on the north along US 27 to Lake Placid on the south—a hundred miles through some of the most lush orange-growing country in the world. However, you won't be very impressed with the oranges along I-4; the groves here were destroyed by a frost in December 1989, and all that remain are either stumps or trees planted since that time. Most of these hills will probably never be replanted, for long-range plans call for metropolitan Orlando to expand in this direction.

I-4 crosses the ridge's rounded crest at the turnoff to Haines City, named for Henry Plant's strong-arm superintendent, Colonel Henry Haines, who refused to stop his trains there until the settlers named their town after him. Haines City likes to be known as the Gateway to the Scenic Highlands, which are described in chapter 16.

At the Haines crossroad is Baseball City. This stadium rocks with enthusiasts when big-league teams meet here during spring training each March.

## The Green Swamp

Once past the US 27/Haines City turnoff, I-4 begins a gentle descent from the Citrus Ridge. Before you know it, the landscape is filled with large trees, mostly cypress. Don't be alarmed if the cypress have lost their needles and appear lifeless. They will become full again in the spring. Wherever there are cypress, you can expect the ground to be very damp. And that is the case here, for this is the Green Swamp, a massive and vital aquifer for all of central Florida.

The Green Swamp is named after its matting of water-loving trees and is not the sheet of stagnant water its name implies. It is a swamp nonetheless, and in many places the ground will tremble if you stomp on it. The swamp extends westward nearly to US 301, where it caused Hernando de Soto and his army untold difficulties in their futile search for El Dorado. Later, the Green Swamp became the lair of Osceola and his warriors during the Second Seminole War.

# Lakeland

Although not exactly on the Citrus Ridge, the city of Lakeland is a kind of unofficial capital of the orange-producing area, for it is the headquarters of the Florida Department of Citrus, as well as of Citrus Mutual, the state's largest growers' organization, with over twelve thousand members.

Historically, Lakeland is famous as the location of the world's largest collection of Frank Lloyd Wright buildings. They are on the campus of Florida Southern College, where, beginning in 1938, twelve structures were built—with six more on Wright's drawing board when he died in 1959, at age ninety-one. Wright called Florida Southern the "only truly American campus."

### The Tumultuous World of Frank Lloyd Wright

In many ways, it was strange that Florida Southern should chose Wright as its architect, for his personal life was hardly an example to young collegians. Morals were never a strong point with Wright. He felt he was above common morality. Marriage, he wrote to a friend, "is a barnyard institution. I am a wild bird—and must stay free."

In 1909, leaving his wife and family in the United States, Wright went to Europe, where he became intimate with the spouse of a former client. Returning to America, he built a home in Wisconsin into which his mistress moved. Although he called the beautiful place Taliesin, after an ancient Welch poet, newspapers blared that it was nothing more than a glorified "love nest." The headlines became even more lurid when a psychotic servant took an ax and murdered the mistress, her two children, and four guests. Fortunately for Wright, he was not there at the time.

Although he was pugnacious and caustic, Wright had an irresistible appeal to women, and soon a second mistress, Miriam, was ensconced in Taliesin. Wright eventually married Miriam, but the relationship did not last. After he took a third mistress, Miriam began legal actions that forced Wright and his new lover to hide out like common criminals. In 1926 they were actually arrested and spent the night in a Minnesota jail.

Meanwhile, through all the unrelenting turmoil of his personal life, Wright was achieving international stature as one of the world's most innovative and creative architects. He had a fierce devotion to his own brand of architecture—one that swept away the frivolous decorations of the current styles to reveal the basic sleek lines of what Wright called prairie architecture. He designed his buildings to be part of, and an enhancement of, the environment.

His brilliance burned away old ideas. "What we did yesterday we won't do today," he told one of his staff. "And what we do tomorrow will not be what we'll be doing the day after."

The stock market crash of 1929 made things difficult for Wright, for many fewer commissions came in. However, one was for the Johnson Wax Headquarters. This emerged as a major work in graceful modernity that embellished his reputation. Thus, two years later, when the officials at Florida Southern went hunting for someone to design their campus, they were influenced toward Wright by an article in a Chicago architectural magazine.

Florida Southern's offer came when Wright and his staff at Taliesin were almost desperate for work. Although the college president, Ludd Spivey, was so brazen as to contact Wright even though the college happened to have no funds at the moment, Spivey's golden tongue worked and the deal was struck.

Wright took the train down to Lakeland. His entry was not auspicious, for the locomotive broke down and the architect, now seventy-one years old, had to walk along the rails the last mile to town. Neither was the campus much—just a trio of tired redbrick buildings interspersed among orange trees. But it had potential.

Wright began his first building, the Anne Pfeiffer Chapel, in 1938. Then in 1941, the Carter, Walbridge, Hawkins Seminar Building went up. To save money, the construction of both buildings was done mostly by the students themselves.

*Caustic architect Frank Lloyd Wright makes notes during construction at Florida Southern College in Lakeland.*
—Florida Southern College

*Frank Lloyd Wright designed the futuristic Anne Pfeiffer Chapel at Florida Southern College in 1938. The neat precision of the building lines does not reflect Wright's tumultuous private life.* —Florida State Archives

By the time work started on the Thad Buckner Building, World War II had made materials difficult to come by. To make matters worse, Wright was under investigation by the FBI for possible antiwar activities. It was true that he did not think America should be fighting on the side of England, for his Welch heritage gave him an almost inborn hatred of the English, who had conquered his country so many ages ago. But the FBI concluded that Wright was not dangerous, and the investigation was called off.

In 1948 the Emile E. Watson–Benjamin Fine Administration Building was completed, as was the fountain plaza—and both are among the first structures visitors see when entering the campus.

The Lucius Pond Ordway Building was Wright's favorite. Built in 1952, it retained its originality to such an extent that half a century later it provided the futuristic setting for an episode on TV's *SeaQuest* series.

Although by now Wright was in his early eighties, he was still actively interested in the college that he called his "child of the sun." Students occasionally found him stomping around the campus—an arresting figure in his wide-brimmed hat, coat worn over his shoulders like a cape, and cane that he could wave menacingly.

Nor had age diminished his irascibility. When college officials complained that his buildings were leaking and suggested he be more practical with his designs, he brushed off their objections and went his own stubborn way—and to this day many of his buildings still leak. When contractors installed yellow stained-glass in the Danforth Chapel, he called it the color of liver bile and demanded that it be replaced (but the college did not have the money, so it stayed).

Perhaps most typical of Wright was the time he was the featured speaker at an important fund-raising banquet. When the local politicians who preceded him became too windy, he abruptly rose from his seat at the head table, gave a "grumpf," and belligerently stalked out of the auditorium.

Florida Southern is handling the twenty thousand annual visitors as best it can (the private college has less than nineteen hundred students) by providing self-guided tour literature. Formal tours are given for groups of ten or more if they call in advance.

# Mulberry

### The Weirdest Drive in Florida

Eleven miles south of Lakeland on Florida 37 is the crossroads of Mulberry. Tiny though it may be, it is the nexus of a mighty mining

*In the 1890s phosphate fever hit Florida, causing an influx of miners similar to the western gold rush. The hamlet of Mulberry was the center of activity. The area is still the world's major supplier.* —P. H. Yonge Library of Florida History, University of Florida

industry that supplies a staggering 30 percent of the world's phosphorus, a fertilizer ingredient vital for crop growth.

Despite its importance, the viewing of phosphate mining is not high on tourists' must-see lists. Thus the museum at Mulberry is small, occupying a couple of old boxcars and an abandoned wooden train-depot behind the village hall, at the corner of Florida 37 and Florida 60. Yet there are some excellent exhibits concerning the origin of the phosphate deposits from the bones of uncountable animals that lived and died here 10 million to 15 million years ago. These beasts included mastodons, saber-toothed tigers, and even whales, who cruised the region during high-water periods. Indeed, so plentiful are the animal remains that geologists refer to them as the Bone Valley Formation.

The phosphate was discovered in 1889, and the ensuing miners' rush was akin to that involving western gold. At one time, nearly two hundred companies were frantically scratching and squabbling over the rich boneyards. Now the field has narrowed to a dozen large, sedate corporations.

Modern mining operations begin with huge cranes, some six stories high, stripping away about twenty-five feet of overburdened soil, which they deposit nearby in mountainous ridges. Once the phosphate layer is exposed, draglines dig up the phosphate, which is mixed with water and sent through pipes to the processing plant, where it is converted into phosphorus.

Although the operating companies do not encourage on-site tours, you can drive through the mining area by taking Florida 37 from Mulberry three miles south to County Road 640, then you turn east and continue seven miles to County Road 555. You will find yourself amid a barren world of rock pilings and phosphate dust. Processing plants rise in the distance like ancient monoliths. You would almost expect a prehistoric saber-tooth to come crashing toward you.

But the days when strip miners could walk away from such devastation ended with a Florida law in 1975. Now each digging has to be reclaimed within two years. The overburden must be put back and, where it is not enough to refill the excavation, a lake or wetland must be created. Thus you will often see beautiful grasslands, often with cattle grazing, and little lakes where wild birds swarm.

County Road 555 leads to Bartow, with its colorful county courthouse. From there, US 98 will take you back to Lakeland and I-4.

## Steamers and Seminoles

As I-4 continues westward from Lakeland, it closely parallels Henry Plant's railroad. In the early 1880s, Plant City was the rip-roaring railhead as Henry raced to complete the line before his franchise expired. The rails from Sanford met those from Tampa near Lakeland just three days before the deadline.

Fourteen miles west of Plant City, you will see a tall water tower with what looks like an Indian arrow shot through it. If you wonder how the Seminole tribe is doing, turn off on exit 6 and follow the signs to the Seminole Gaming Palace. The big items in the palace are bingo and poker, which churn out tribal tribute twenty-four hours a day, seven days a week. The tribe bought nine acres of land here in 1982, turned it into a reservation, and hired an outside management company to run both the palace and the neighboring Sheraton Hotel.

I-4 ends near downtown Tampa, six miles from the Seminole Gaming Palace.

*From Plant City a main line extended south through the pine lands to Arcadia and beyond.* —Florida State Archives

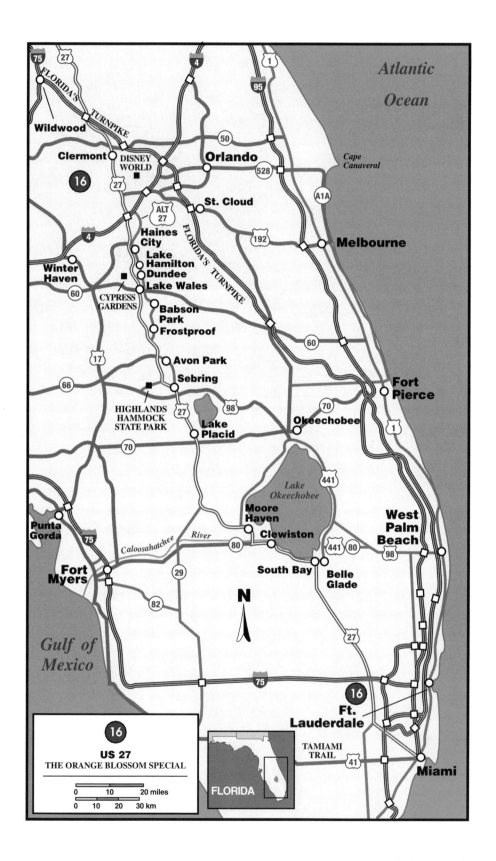

**Atlantic Ocean**

**Gulf of Mexico**

Wildwood

Clermont
DISNEY WORLD
**16**

**Orlando**
Cape Canaveral

St. Cloud

ALT 27
Haines City
Lake Hamilton
Dundee
Lake Wales
CYPRESS GARDENS

**Melbourne**

Winter Haven

Babson Park
Frostproof

Avon Park
Sebring
HIGHLANDS HAMMOCK STATE PARK
Lake Placid

Okeechobee

**Fort Pierce**

*Lake Okeechobee*

Moore Haven
Clewiston

**West Palm Beach**

Punta Gorda

*Caloosahatchee River*

South Bay
Belle Glade

**Fort Myers**

**N**

**16**

**Ft. Lauderdale**

TAMIAMI TRAIL

FLORIDA

**Miami**

**16**
**US 27**
THE ORANGE BLOSSOM SPECIAL

0   10   20 miles
0   10   20   30 km

# ☞ 16 ☜

## US 27

### THE ORANGE BLOSSOM SPECIAL

# Clermont—Haines City
**32 miles**

## Citrus Ridge

During much of the distance between Clermont and Miami, US 27 travels along Florida's Central Ridge. This ridge formed during an interval in the Ice Age when the glaciers melted, causing the oceans to rise more than two hundred feet above the present level and flooding most of peninsular Florida, except for the central spine. Here, huge quantities of sand were thrown up by the waves to become high dunes. At the foot of the dunes, wide beaches formed.

When ice returned and the sea level fell, the highest dunes remained as Iron Mountain, site of both the Bok Tower and the hill near Clermont topped by the Citrus Tower. The former beach also remained as the Coharie Terrace, eroded into the graceful hills that make up most of the ridge.

Could the ocean again cover the Florida peninsula and lap at the foot of the Bok Tower? It is possible, but certainly not in our time. Nonetheless, some scientists worry about the melting of the Antarctic ice cap and warn of the catastrophic effect of higher ocean levels if the ice should slip off that continent.

The ridge's original vegetation—pines—have since been chopped down and their place taken by boundless orange trees. The ridge is ideal for the orange trees, which are finicky plants that insist on ample water as well as rapid drainage.

But the northern portion of the ridge is susceptible to frosts, and if the temperature drops below twenty-five degrees—even for a short period—the orange trees die. During December 1989, a freeze utterly devastated the groves north of Haines City. This brought financial disaster and caused many growers to relocate farther south, to nonridge counties where the harvest per acre was far less but the danger of killing freezes was eliminated.

## Clermont

The town was founded in 1884 by a development company , one of whose managers had been born in Clermont, France. Perhaps the town is most well-known to travelers for the twenty-two-story Citrus Tower, built in 1956 to offer visitors a windy vista of the hills covered with 17 million orange trees. The great tower still stands, but tourists must be content with the hills alone, for the freeze of 1989 wiped out the citrus trees one and all. However, some new trees have been planted, and the tower grounds now offer an educational opportunity to inspect many different citrus varieties.

### Horizon West: The Long Shadow of Metropolitan Orlando

Going south from Clermont, US 27 continues through former citrus lands. In many places, all that remain of the groves are tall irrigation pipes. Often the fields are reverting to pines. In any event, most of them will never be replanted with citrus because the area falls within the extension of metropolitan Orlando called Horizon West. This long-range plan calls for orderly development, with small towns containing village greens and with the controlled placement of malls, shopping strips, and other commercial developments.

## Haines City

US 27 crosses I-4 at the Haines City interchange. On the northeast side of the intersection is Baseball City. A few years back it was called Boardwalk and Baseball, and it had a large amusement park attached to it. The amusement park was part of Circus World, which went belly-up in 1986. Boardwalk soon followed, and now Baseball City is largely deserted, except when it becomes the spring training grounds for the Kansas City Royals.

Haines City is several miles south of the baseball stadium. Being on Henry Plant's railroad (and named for his superintendent), Haines City had dreams of becoming a vacation headquarters. In 1925 promoters built a massive hotel tower, nine stories high with super-lative views of the ridge. The tower was completed just in time for the great bust of 1926 and today stands in bleak decay.

# Haines City—Lake Placid

**65 miles**

## US 27 or the Scenic Highway?

Two highways run south from Haines City. The main route is the fine multilane road that was built in 1956 and bypasses the dozen small towns that are strung like beads along the ridge. The other is the original route, now known as Alternate US 27 and, farther south, as County Road 17. Together they form the Scenic Highway, a name that dates back to the 1920s, when the federal highway system did not exist and important roads had names, not numbers.

Which should you take? If you are time-bound, US 27 should be your choice. But if you have more leisure, you will enjoy the alternate route as it wends fifty-five miles through the heart of orange-grove country. Or you can travel partway on one road and part on the other; the two are only several miles apart, and there are periodic connecting links. The trip on US 27 is outlined here, and a description of the alternative, Scenic Highway route follows.

## Cypress Gardens

### The Swami of the Swamp

The turnoff to Cypress Gardens is six miles south of Haines City. Cypress Gardens is Florida's oldest theme park. That the beauty of Cypress Gardens exists today is largely through the efforts of Dick and Julie Pope. As a pair, they were perfect for each other. "Dad was outgoing," recalled Dick Jr. "He was a born salesman. Always figuring out a way to promote what he was doing. Mother was the business end. She helped him keep what he made."

Dick Sr. was born in 1900 and during the 1920s was a public relations man in New York City. But the Depression hit him hard, so when he and Julie read about a man down South who was making money showing his garden to tourists, they headed for Florida.

In Winter Haven, they learned that a defunct yacht club on Lake Eloise was for sale. The club included a small building, a run-down pier, and, oh, yes, many pretty cypress trees along the lake's swampy edges. Dick and Julie bought the club, the pier, and sixteen acres of mostly swamp.

By now they had consumed nearly all their funds, but when Dick tried to attract investors, they laughed and called him the Swami of the Swamp. Nonetheless, Dick and Julie were determined to create a tourist attraction, and they somehow managed to borrow enough azaleas from their neighbors to call the place a garden. They paid some locals a dollar a day to dig narrow canals through some of the property. They also scrounged up a boat to take visitors on rides along the canals. Then in 1936 they opened the park.

In the early years, visitors were few, for during the Depression not many people were squandering their meager funds on frivolities such as boat rides. Even the little show that Dick put on by towing a surfboard behind a motorboat failed to increase attendance much. After water skis were invented in the late 1930s, Dick began trying them out. But when World War II began, he went into the service. Julie was left to run the park and raise their two children, Dick Jr. and Adrian. With almost no one coming to the park, Julie volunteered to teach the soldiers from a nearby base to water-ski free of charge. In return, the government allowed her fifteen gallons of tightly rationed gasoline a week.

Somehow word got around that instead of lessons, Cypress Gardens was putting on water-ski shows. One morning, a bunch of soldiers arrived on a military bus to see such a show. Julie, quick on her feet, told them it would begin shortly and to stroll the gardens in the meantime. Then she hustled off to the elementary school, rounded up half a dozen boys and girls, led by Dick Jr., age twelve, and had them put on an improvised show.

After the war, the park became a major attraction, due largely to Dick Sr., whose experience at public relations enabled him to get photos of pretty water-skiers to appear in magazines and newspapers across the nation. And he himself was a show as he soared over the water in the glider wing that he attached to an aquaplane.

Cypress Gardens had many good years, the climax coming in 1972 when attendance reached 1.7 million, at which time Dick turned management of the park over to his son. But by 1982 it had become clear that Disney World, Sea World, and Busch Gardens were eating

*Dick and Julie Pope, founders of Cypress Gardens in 1936, photograph their son, Dick Jr., and daughter, Adrian.* —Florida Cypress Gardens, Inc.

*Cypress Gardens water-skiers perform before casual onlookers in the 1940s. The central building still stands, but the lakefront now contains a pair of spectators' stadiums.* —Florida Cypress Gardens, Inc.

away at Cypress Gardens's visitor base. New capital and fresh ideas were needed. So in 1985 Dick Jr. sold out to the publishing giant Harcourt Brace Jovanovich. Yet Harcourt was soon to have its own troubles. Four years later it sold out to Anheuser-Busch, which in 1995 sold the park back to its own management group.

Today, Cypress Gardens is reinvigorated. The flower festivals and a unique butterfly house have combined with the water-ski shows to help lure tourists back. And while the water shows are still spectacular, the park's primary goal is to become one of the world's premier botanical gardens. If its gorgeous floral displays are any indication, it is well on its way.

So what remains of the Pope era? There is a small museum called Cypress Roots, with vintage photos and poignant displays of such memorabilia as the gaudy jackets Dick loved to wear. The 1940s Magnolia Mansion serves light refreshments. Many of the canals Dick dug still provide waterways for the electric boats. Southern belles still wear costumes started by Julie. And the office in which they spent so many years planning and achieving still stands as part of the administration building.

Dick Jr. lives in Winter Haven. "I seldom go back," he said. "When I sold out, I was ready to leave. It had gotten to be a grind. We were up against companies with huge financial power. In many ways I was sad when I left, but I was glad to close the door."

And what did his father think? "Dad never knew," Dick Jr. added. "He had Alzheimer's disease the last four years of his life."

Continuing south, US 27 passes the turnoffs to Lake Wales, Babson Park, Frostproof, Avon Park, and Sebring—towns described further on in this chapter, in the Scenic Highway section. After skirting Lake Jackson, US 27 comes to County Road 634, the route to Highlands Hammock State Park.

## Highlands Hammock State Park

Highlands Hammock is about three miles west of US 27, not far from the town of Sebring. The hammock is a large group of towering oaks, hickories, and sweet gums rising in the midst of the surrounding pine lands. A slight depression in the underlying limestone allows moisture and humus to collect here, making it ideal for such deciduous trees.

Having very rich soil, the hammock was a prime candidate for farmland. The hammock's natural vegetation certainly would have disappeared had not George Sebring Jr. sold an airplane to Donald Roebling from Clearwater; and had not Donald taken his rather daring mother, Margaret, for a ride; and had not Margaret been entranced by the beauty of this shimmering green island standing out from the drab pines. Had not these events occurred, then Margaret would not have contributed the thousands of dollars toward the hammock's purchase around 1930, which saved it for posterity.

The value of this unique ecosystem caused Franklin Roosevelt to send the Civilian Conservation Corps here in 1933. The first CCC headquarters was in an abandoned nightclub in nearby Sebring. But soon buildings were constructed on-site for the two hundred young men who built access roads and nature trails into the tangle of hardwood trees and saw palmetto.

The Sebring CCC unit was part of a massive national anti-Depression program that ultimately gave temporary employment to 2.25 million needy men between the ages of eighteen and twenty-five. From their monthly wages of thirty dollars, the young men were required to send at least twenty-two dollars back to their families. There were fifteen hundred camps throughout the United States, of which Florida, as an underpopulated region, had only thirty-three.

Sebring citizens looked on the CCC with mixed feelings. Tensions developed when three CCC youths robbed a lunch stand near Sebring in 1936. Nonetheless, by the time the CCC ended in 1942, the pro-

*Highlands Hammock State Park has buildings dating back to the Civilian Conservation Corps (CCC) of the 1930s.*

gram had converted the Highlands Hammock into an attraction that has made valuable contributions to Sebring's economy.

Today a paved three-mile roadway curves through the central part of the hammock, providing access by autos, or by bicycles that can be rented in the park. The road is, in effect, an eerie pathway through tall trees whose massive limbs draped with Spanish moss reach across the pavement like great hairy arms. The air vibrates with the calls of birds and other animals mostly unseen. You are in another world.

From the roadway, eight separate hiking trails lead into the leafy depths. One of them, the Cypress Swamp Trail, has an elevated walkway rebuilt along the one constructed by the CCC back in the 1930s. For people who want leafy depths with less effort, there are tram tours, which depart from the interpretive center. The guide will point out various birds as well as any sightings of alligators, deer, and perhaps the elusive, highly endangered Florida panther.

Two of the wooden CCC buildings still stand. One has been converted into a store and sandwich shop, and the other into the interpretive center. During CCC days, the young men could purchase at the store whatever sundries they could afford on the meager five to seven dollars that remained from their monthly wages. The interpretive center was the CCC meeting hall.

When visiting Highlands Hammock, heed a word of caution: Bring your mosquito repellent!

# Haines City—Lake Placid
### 55 miles

The stretch of Alternate US 27 and County Road 17 known as the old Scenic Highway was first paved in 1918. It was all of nine feet wide, built by convicts in leg chains.

## Lake Hamilton

During the winter and spring, the parking areas of Lake Hamilton's Lykes Pasco Packing Company are filled with open citrus trucks heaped with fruit.

As the Scenic Highway heads toward Dundee, another citrus hamlet, it passes deserted gas stations with squat overhanging roofs.

Patrons stopping for gas here in the 1920s and 1930s used hand levers to force the fuel to the ten-gallon glass cylinders atop the pump, from where it could be drained into their cars' tanks.

# Dundee

At Dundee, the highway makes a sharp turn to pass through the downtown, as main roads typically did during the first few decades of the twentieth century. Development of Dundee began in 1911, when the railroad was built to this point. The town was probably named after Dundee, Scotland, to show that it was in the highlands.

Out of Dundee the road is just two lanes. It winds around picturesque lakes and characteristic ridge hills, bright green with bushy orange trees. The perspectives are long, and the air is often fragrant with blossoms. The road sometimes passes ancient motels where the units are formed around a U, and Ma and Pa greet tourists in the front office.

Soon, Iron Mountain appears in the hazy blue distance, capped by the tall shaft of the Bok Tower.

### The Bok Tower Gardens

Edward Bok, builder of the tower, was a man of immense energy, of lofty idealism, of supreme confidence in his abilities, and of a titanic ego. Thus, when he retired from the editorship of the *Ladies Home Journal* at the relatively young age of fifty-six, he was not content until he had left the world a personal monument that satisfied all the components of his many-faceted personality.

A singing tower on peninsular Florida's loftiest prominence fulfilled all his requirements. By dominating the area with sight and sound, it proclaimed the presence of Edward Bok. But despite Bok's underlying motivations, the tower chimes are beautiful, and the tower itself is a twenty-story masterpiece of Gothic grace. Enhancing the tower is its setting of flowers, lily ponds, and arching shade trees that soothes the soul.

Edward Bok knew he had two personalities. One was the blunt, hard-driving, no-nonsense editor. The other was a gentler sort who loved beauty and had a sincere desire to make the world a better place. For nearly all his life, his gentle part lived in a bottle, as Bok himself put it. But his workaday persona was charged with energy. Even in childhood Bok was aggressive. In 1870 he came to America as a boy of six with his Dutch parents. Before long he was helping the family survive by selling ice water on horse-cars in Brooklyn.

But journalism was in his blood, and when he was only twelve he began writing a column for the *Brooklyn Eagle,* using his school chums as reporters. By the age of twenty-one he had started his own magazine. Soon Bok caught the attention of bigwigs at Scribner's, for whom he began writing a column. The column, in turn, attracted Cyrus Curtis, owner of the *Ladies Home Journal,* and Bok took over as the magazine's editor in 1889.

Bok instantly realized that American women craved more than the bland fare that the magazine was presenting. Thus he revised the fiction department and published stories by the top writers of the era, including Mark Twain and Rudyard Kipling. Nonfiction also improved as he hired quality columnists, such as Teddy Roosevelt, who wrote incognito while he was president. Later, Teddy's distant cousin Franklin also contributed articles for Bok.

More than that, Bok did something new in magazine publishing— he printed information on ladies' fashions, interior decorating, the latest dance steps. He actually had women writing on women's affairs—which was a switch. Under Bok, the *Ladies Home Journal* became the premier women's magazine and an important force in American culture.

But behind it all, Bok maintained a paternalistic attitude toward women. As he admitted, he had not "the slightest desire, even as an editor, to know them better, or to seek to understand them." When the suffragettes began agitating for women's right to vote, he was solidly against it. "American women," he wrote, "were not ready to exercise the privilege intelligently and . . . their mental attitude was against it."

In 1896, Bok married Mary Louise Curtis, daughter of the owner of the *Ladies Home Journal.* Was this merely a way to gain favor with her father and further his career? There is no way of knowing, yet it is curious that he mentions her only once in his autobiography of more than three hundred pages.

Bok retired in 1919, and three years later he established a nature sanctuary at Iron Mountain, Florida—a place for meditation as birds sang and the fragrance of flowers wafted by on tepid breezes.

Iron Mountain was only 298 feet high, but it was the loftiest point in peninsular Florida. It was mainly sand, but it had some low-grade ore deposits that gave it both its name and the distinctively ruddy

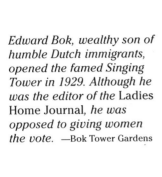

*Edward Bok, wealthy son of humble Dutch immigrants, opened the famed Singing Tower in 1929. Although he was the editor of the* Ladies Home Journal, *he was opposed to giving women the vote.* —Bok Tower Gardens

color of its soil. There was only scrubby vegetation, mostly pines and underbrush. Bok shaved the "mountain," laid a piping system for water, and brought in tons of black dirt, out of which he created ponds and gardens. At the same time, he planted broadleaf trees that have since grown into a canopy of cool greenery.

A tower, similar to ones in his native Netherlands, was designed to be the park's centerpiece. It was a massive column twenty stories high, sheathed in pink Georgia marble and coquina from St. Augustine. A crown of heron statues ringed its pinnacle. Entrance to the tower was gained through a large door with a series of thirty brass panels depicting scenes from the creation in Genesis.

Inside the tower were fifty-seven bronze bells imported from England, the largest of which weighed almost twenty-five thousand pounds and the smallest just seventeen. These bells did not move but were rung by clappers connected by steel wires to a keyboard, which was located in a soundproof room directly beneath them. Here, a carillonneur rung the bells by hitting the keyboard with his fists (for the high notes) and his feet (for the low notes).

In 1929 the Bok Tower Gardens opened, the ceremony being conducted by Bok's friend President Calvin Coolidge. Bok intended that the public could use the elevator to enjoy the majestic view from the top. But he soon found that the constant influx of persons,

*Bok Tower under construction 1927. The tower was designed so visitors could take an elevator to the top. But Bok, who had a study on the ground floor, found the visitors too disturbing, so he closed public access.* —Bok Tower Gardens

most of whom were noisy and some downright boisterous, was so disruptive that he closed the interior to the public—and it remains so today.

Bok had an office/study on the tower's ground floor, in a large room containing a fireplace. But he lived at the nearby village of Mountain View, an ultra-exclusive community so upper-crust that its hundred-odd showplace homes were built without kitchens—the residents preferring to dress formally for meals at the posh Colony House on the community's grounds. Bok died in the mansion's second-floor bedroom in 1930, with his eyes on the Singing Tower, which rose gracefully in the distance. His grave is at the foot of the tower beside the brass door.

Today, the carillon bells still ring out over the countryside. Visitors flock to hear the concerts, view the majestic tower, stroll the extensive gardens, and partake of the tranquillity and beauty that Bok bequeathed us. The tower, long a National Historic Monu-

*Lake Wales's 1928 railroad station is now a historical museum.*

ment, was elevated to a Historic Landmark in 1994—an honor only 4 percent of monuments achieve.

## Lake Wales

In 1911, Lake Wales was just a turpentine-and-lumber camp when the arrival of the Atlantic Coast Line opened the region to permanent settlement. At this time, four gentlemen formed the Lake Wales Land Company, and during the early and mid-1920s the town became part of the feverish land speculation rampant throughout Florida.

Much of Lake Wales's downtown reflects the Roaring Twenties, especially along Park Avenue, the town's prim main street, which is on the National Register of Historic Places. The town is dominated by the eleven-story Hotel Grand—a defunct memento to the dream Lake Wales had of becoming the great metropolis of central Florida. The historical museum is in the restored 1928 Atlantic Coast Line depot, on Alternate 27. For a special culinary treat, visit Chalet Suzanne, begun in 1931 during the depths of the Depression. The soups are so good that some of them accompanied the *Apollo 15* and *16* moon missions.

The ubiquitous groves begin again outside Lake Wales. Open-trailer wagons are often parked along the roadside: some are heaped with oranges, others are empty and waiting to be filled. From late winter to late spring—harvest time—the two-lane road is heavily traveled by citrus trucks, so going may be slow.

# Babson Park

*The Strange Prophet*

Eight miles south of Lake Wales, the road turns into the village of Babson Park, a collection of homes strung out along Crooked Lake. The community was begun in 1923 by Roger Babson, one of the more unusual gentlemen to travel down life's Scenic Highway.

Babson was born in 1875, grew up in New England, and graduated from the prestigious Massachusetts Institute of Technology. A brilliant intellect, he and his wife, Grace, started an investment-counseling business that brought him to the attention of Woodrow Wilson, who appointed him assistant secretary of labor during World War I. In the 1920s, Babson became well known for his business reports. When he accurately forecast the stock market crash of 1929, his fame was assured.

Babson became interested in Florida when, during a bout with tuberculosis, doctors had advised him of the state's healthful climate. In 1923 he bought land along Crooked Lake, both as an investment and as a winter location for his business. There he erected a bank building, apartments, and stores. But because he could not get other businesses to come to this isolated place, he donated the buildings to the college he founded in 1927 and named after his granddaughter, Camilla Webber.

With Webber College, the village began to flourish. Roger Babson enjoyed his role as patriarch, but he also began to display certain unusual characteristics. When he dined out, he counted the peas on his plate to be sure he was not getting short-changed. He also tried to market chocolate-covered fish, certainly the oddest food ever presented to the American public. And he established the Gravity Research Foundation, which he ardently believed would discover how to provide everyone with free power by tapping into the rotating earth.

He became egotistic and rude. Once while strolling, he encountered the Webber College president, who greeted him with a friendly "Good morning." Babson glared at him and snapped, "When a 'good morning' is to be said, I'll say it."

Even Franklin Roosevelt felt Babson's barbs—as when the president asked him to name a job he wanted, and Babson replied that he'd like to be advisor to the most powerful man in the world. Before Roosevelt could react to the apparent flattery, Babson added that that man was Joseph Stalin. Babson did not become part of FDR's administration.

Both Babson and his wife were very religious, and when Grace died in 1960, her will set aside one hundred thousand dollars for one hundred years as reward money for children under sixteen who could recite a certain number of Bible verses. Roger died a very wealthy man seven years later, at the age of ninety-two.

Today Webber College is a respected institution, though it has less than five hundred students. It is partially financed by the generous endowment that Roger Babson left it. The building Babson constructed to house his business during the winter is now Old Main, a single-story stucco building with a red-tile roof, facing Alternate 27.

On the campus is a curious six-foot-high cemetery marker erected by Roger Babson to remind everyone that he is the proud descendant of a radical sixteenth-century London preacher who was burned at the stake. The two would probably have been soul mates.

From Babson Park, the Scenic Highway makes a long descent to the Coharie Terrace, a wide beach during the Glacial Age. There are almost no commercial buildings along the road, just the endless orange groves and a turquoise lake in the distance.

# Frostproof

Frostproof was the location of a military post when the area was a sandy pine barren and Seminoles lurked in the shadows. The Indians believed that a huge serpent lived in Clinch Lake, and in 1907 certain white residents claimed to have seen the beast—which was thirty feet long!

Things have changed since then. As the location of the huge Cargill Juice plant, the little town is one of the busiest places on the ridge during harvest time, November through March. The plant's demands for oranges causes an influx of trucks and trailers that jams the parking lot, which spans two entire city blocks.

South of Frostproof, the ridge gives way, momentarily, to cattle flatlands. Here, Alternate 27 crosses the railroad tracks and merges

*Harvesting oranges. The sandy, well-drained soil of Florida's central ridge makes it ideal for citrus growing.* —Florida Department of Citrus

with US 27. They continue together for seven miles until the Scenic Highway branches off and becomes County Road 17 to Avon Park.

## Avon Park

Avon Park was named by homesick English settlers for Stratford-on-Avon, birthplace of their beloved William Shakespeare. Here the Jacaranda Hotel offers a glimpse of the 1920s and 1930s, when the rowdy St. Louis Cardinals baseball team made it their headquarters for spring training.

Beyond Avon Park, County Road 17 passes through more orange groves, now interspersed with homes, until it reaches Sebring, nine miles farther on.

## Sebring

In 1911, George Sebring laid out the town in anticipation of the coming of the Atlantic Coast Line, which reached it the following year. The founder's family had a tradition of town-building, coming from their namesake—Sebring, Ohio—site of their pottery factory.

George saw the location as a good real estate investment, and in order to emphasize its appealing climate he formed the main street

On the Circle, Sebring, Fla.

*Sebring's circle was designed to resemble the sun of ancient Greek legend when it was planned in 1911.* —Sebring Historical Society, Inc.

into a circle, after the mythical Grecian Heliopolis (City of the Sun). Then he built himself a mansion on the shore of Lake Jackson, a block or so from the circle.

His enterprise prospered, and by 1920 the town had nine major resort hotels served by trains such as the Orange Blossom Special. A good-time committee was formed to jazz up the town's social life. The population shot up from just seven hundred in 1920 to more than seven thousand in 1926. So great was the influx that many persons had to live temporarily in tents. Sixty-three real estate agents could not keep pace with the demand for land.

But in 1926 the balloon burst, as it did all over the state, and within a few years half of Sebring's citizens had shuffled off, many broke, most fed up with Florida.

During the early 1940s, about all that kept the village alive was the establishment of Hendricks Field as a bomber training center. Things got even worse when US 27 was built in the 1960s, effectively bypassing the City of the Sun with its circle that had become a traffic obstruction.

## The Sebring Racetrack

When Alec Ulmann first visited Sebring, shortly after World War II, he was searching out unused hangar and aircraft facilities for the conversion of military planes to civilian use. At Hendricks Field he found what he needed—and much more, for he saw that the airfield could easily be utilized as an auto raceway, approximating, on a smaller scale, that of France's famed Le Mans.

For this purpose, Ulmann would make use of the airport's still-active runways, which became straightaways where cars could accelerate to their maximum. But Ulmann felt that endurance, even more than speed, would prove the value of a car. Thus, the ultimate shape of the course would not be oval but would contain S-bends and a hairpin turn. Some said the strange layout took on the ungainly appearance of a humped-back, legless alligator with a broken tailbone.

In many other ways Sebring would be different from the oval tracks, such as at Indianapolis, which Ulmann in his book *The Sebring Story* called a "disappointment." Sebring would be an endurance test for sports cars that anyone could own, not for expensive, souped-up racers. In Ulmann's attempt to simulate actual road conditions, he included the problems that any driver could experience. For example, if a contestant had engine trouble on the track, he either had to make the repairs himself on the roadside or push his vehicle to his mechanic's pit, which could be several miles! The twelve-hour race would continue into the night, when only the cars' headlights would show the way.

The first race was held March 15, 1952. There was just a smattering of spectators and only thirty-two contestants. It was an ordeal. Generators burned out, crankshafts broke, and differentials were lost. Only thirteen cars finished. The winner was presented a trophy from the back of a pickup truck.

Despite the lack of attendance, the event began to attract media attention when it was sponsored by Shell Oil the following year. Auto manufacturers saw Sebring as a place where they could test their cars and, if they won, gain priceless material for advertising. But the track was not laid out to accommodate manufacturers. It was tough, as indicated by Ulmann's quotation from an *Esquire* magazine article describing the experience of participant John Fitch in 1953:

> Fitch and his co-driver, Phil Walters, alternated three hour stints during the twelve hour race. The track was marked by hay bales and steel oil drums filled with sand. Hardly had Fitch taken over

*An early contestant warms up at Sebring. The track opened in 1952. Today more than 90,000 persons, most in campers and RVs, watch the wild March races.* —Sebring International Raceway

than he saw Phil Hill's Ferrari, forced to turn off the track by a bad brake lining, disemboweled by a house foundation unseen in the unmowed grass. Later Tony Cummings's engine caught fire and, when he turned into the field, he set the grass to flame and burned his car almost beyond recognition.

The race continued. Dick Irish's motor quit and he had to push his Excalibur two miles in torrid heat to the pits. Soon Fitch passed Pearsall's Jaguar upside where it spun out of control when a brake locked.

Night came. The road was getting slippery with hay thrown out when the cars hit the bales along the roadside. Now each slow car became an obstruction as its rear end loomed up suddenly in the blackness. Worse were the oil drum markers. Upset by cars making tight turns, the drums rolled onto the race track, where they crashed into cars and caused untold damage, but fortunately no wrecks.

It was with great relief that Fitch saw the bright rocket announcing the end of the race. He and Walters had won!

## Sebring Today

The racetrack is most active in mid-March, when more than ninety thousand spectators gather, most in campers that park on the grounds. The spirit is festive, as many have attended for years and meet old friends here. Sebring has no stands; instead, viewing mounds give fans a close-up of the action. There are three days of trials, then the main event, which runs from 10 A.M. to 10 P.M.

The track is also in use throughout the year, what with the shooting of commercials and with endurance testing, so visitors will usually find something to watch.

As for Sebring itself, it is a Main Street town, and its downtown business district is worth a visit. The circle is still there, with its quaint 1926 streetlights, rescued at the eleventh hour from the city dump. West Center Street runs from the circle down to Lake Jackson, where the public library now occupies George Sebring's home site. Beside it are the civic center, the Highlands Museum of the Arts, and the Highlands Little Theater.

The Kenilworth Lodge, built in 1916, was the town's showplace. It has been refurbished and is open to the public. Smaller is the Santa Rosa Inn of 1924, offering twenty-one rooms with claw-feet bathtubs and other vintage furnishings.

From Sebring, County Road 17 continues through more groves until it ends at US 27 a short distance from Lake Placid.

US 27

# Lake Placid—Miami
150 miles

## Lake Placid

Lake Placid has one of the tall shafts so popular in an earlier era. Built as the Happiness Tower in the 1960s, it gave spectacular views of the surrounding orange groves. The town was another of those communities strung out along the citrus ridge and brought to life by the railroad. The old depot at 19 Park Drive is now occupied by a historical museum. Lake Placid is famous among gardeners as a center for caladium farms.

Beyond Lake Placid, citrus groves close in around the highway. These are mostly new fields, planted when the industry moved south after the great freeze of 1989. The trees reach out to the very horizon and bathe the air with a sweet heavy fragrance when they bloom in the winter.

### The Sugar Empire

The orange groves end rather abruptly as the ridge begins to break up, beyond the hamlet of Venus. Soon the land becomes scrubby and wild. Just past Palmdale, which is more a name than a settlement, US 27 descends gently into the Lake Okeechobee basin. Although the lake is unseen fifteen miles east, the soil turns from the clean, well-drained sand of the ridge into the wet black dirt of a former swamp.

These flatlands were actually part of Lake Okeechobee when it was much larger. As the lake shrunk, the former bottom began to support a rich growth of plants. Over the centuries, the remains of these plants became the humus that has made the soil so rich. This fertility, combined with the region's subtropical climate and a considerable amount of fertilizer, has proved ideal for sugarcane.

However, problems have arisen. Some of the fertilizer eventually drained south into the Everglades, where it proved detrimental to the native plants and animals. In 1987 the federal government, claiming that the state had failed to protect the Everglades, actually sued Florida. The suit was dropped, though, when Florida passed the Everglades Forever Act in 1994. With this, a twenty-year program was initiated to control the pollutants by means of filtering marshes. The cost will be close to a billion dollars, to be borne by the sugar companies and the public in a 1:3 ratio. However, the agreement antagonized both the companies and the environmentalists, leaving a bitterness that is sure to grow over the years.

## Moore Haven

US 27 passes over the Caloosahatchee River at the hamlet of Moore Haven. The Calusa Indians dug a canoe-size canal here long before the arrival of the white men. Hamilton Disston built a larger canal in 1883, with the intent of providing a steamboat link with his plantation up the Kissimmee River. When the current canal was opened in 1937, the momentous event was celebrated by a watercade of forty yachts traveling from Stuart, on the Atlantic, to Fort Myers, on the Gulf of Mexico. The water flow is controlled by three sets of dams and locks, one set being just upriver from the US 27 bridge.

## Clewiston

Clewiston did not exist until the Atlantic Coast Line reached here in 1922. It was named for A. C. Clewis, a Tampa banker who provided the funds for the railroad's extension. Nonetheless, it was not until the United States Sugar Corporation arrived six years later that Clewiston's survival was ensured.

Sugar is Clewiston's lifeblood. Here, US 27 is called the Sugarland Highway, and Clewiston proclaims itself "America's Sweetest Town." Although the U.S. Sugar mill is several miles south of town, the presence of the giant is felt everywhere. Even the air has a sweet, almost cloying, scent—for the plant burns sugarcane refuse to run its machinery.

Within the plant, huge rollers crush the cane and extract the juice. The juice is then transferred to evaporators, where the water is removed. The result is raw sugar, which is shipped to out-of-state plants where it is refined into the white substance with which we are familiar. (You can drive by the mill via W. C. Owen Avenue, but no tours are given.)

U.S. Sugar's plant is the oldest of the seven mills operating in the area. The company was founded in 1931, when C. S. Mott, who made a fortune as a founder of General Motors, bought out the failed Southern Sugar Company. Currently the corporation is privately held by the Mott Foundation and the employees. In 1938 U.S. Sugar built a spacious guest house. Today this guest house, still owned by U.S. Sugar, is on the National Register of Historic Places as the Clewiston Inn. It accommodates overnight guests and serves fine meals in its spacious dining room, which has the original 1930s tables and chairs. Among the many celebrities who stayed here was Herbert Hoover, both when he was president and when he came to dedicate the levee bearing his name that surrounds Lake Okeechobee.

Speaking of Herbert Hoover, Lake Okeechobee Boulevard leads from US 27 in the center of town north a short distance to the Hoover Dike Road, which runs directly on top of the 1930 earthen rampart that encircles the lake. At the foot of the dike is a picnic area bordered

*The Clewiston Inn was built as a guest house by the U.S. Sugar Corporation in 1938. It is now on the National Register of Historic Places.*

*The Rim Canal borders Lake Okeechobee, which lies just beyond the Australian pines.*

by the Rim Canal, formed when the dike material was dredged from the lake. Beyond is the former lakeshore (lined by tall Australian pines) and finally the lake itself, barely discernible in the distance.

During high water levels in 1995, there was concern for the aging dike. Seepages were noticed along its length, and at one place water actually bubbled through a four-inch hole. Although the "boil" was sandbagged and the leak stopped, safety concerns remain.

### The Dike around Lake Okeechobee

In the early days, the shores of Okeechobee, which meant "big water" to the Indians, were not well defined, and water often sloshed out the southern end to fan across a broad area as it made its sluggish way to the Gulf of Mexico. This gave birth to the tremendous grassland that explorers called the Everglades.

Settlers realized that the Everglades's rich soil would be ideal for agriculture, and Napoleon Broward became governor in 1905 on a platform of draining the Everglades. The very year he was elected, two dredges began working up the North New River from Fort Lauderdale. Soon, Broward had another pair operating on the Miami River. The governor's program was so popular that a new county, reaching from Fort Lauderdale far out into the Everglades, was named in his honor.

*A dredge around 1907 has dug this canal to help drain the Everglades.* —P. H. Yonge Library of Florida History, University of Florida

But canals were not enough. Fierce hurricanes in 1926 and 1928 hurled Okeechobee water over its shores. Three hundred persons drowned at Moore Haven in the first storm. The second killed so many around Belle Glade that "bodies were piled up like cordwood"—to quote from Marjory Stoneman Douglas, the preeminent historian of the Everglades. To prevent such a disaster in the future, an extensive dike was built along the lake. Rising two stories, it cut Okeechobee water off from all but controlled drainage.

### One Route through the Sugar Fields: US 441 to West Palm Beach

Continuing southeast from Clewiston on US 27, the dike looms close to the highway. There are access points along the route, particularly at the John Stretch Park, where you can get a close-up view of the Hoover Dam, which controls lake water being diverted into the Miami Canal.

At South Bay many people leave US 27 to proceed east on US 441/Florida 80, a splendid four-lane road that passes through Belle Glade, where there is a modest hurricane monument on the public library grounds. Turning east from Belle Glade on US 441, the journey is through some of the world's lushest sugarcane fields. You will

*Flames leap from sugarcane fields near Clewiston as debris is burned. The flash fire does not injure the cane.*

also pass two active mills. Both were started in the early 1960s, when communist dictator Fidel Castro disrupted, and virtually destroyed, the Cuban sugar industry.

Incidentally, don't be alarmed if you see a field suddenly burst into flame. Just prior to harvest (October through March), the growing cane is burned to remove dead leaves that would interfere with juice extraction. The fires last only a few minutes and do not harm the green stalks.

After US 441 is joined by US 98, you are on the route of the once locally famed Connors Highway, built as a toll road in 1924 by Billy Connors, a rich contractor and sugar grower who paved his road just in time to tap the great tourist influx of 1924–26.

US 98 links up with I-95 at West Palm Beach—from where Miami is an easy drive sixty-six miles south.

### The Second Route: US 27 to Miami

If you decide to stay on US 27, you will pass more rich cane fields as well as two other sugar mills. The Talisman mill was largely the creation of William D. Pawley, founder of the famous Flying Tigers squadron of World War II. Beside the highway is one of the original canals, called the North New River, the dredging of which provided much of the road base.

Twenty-five miles beyond South Bay, US 27 abruptly leaves the sugar area and briefly skirts the Everglades for fifteen miles, until it reaches the environs of Miami. Once there, it becomes a city thoroughfare, and it ends in the heart of town.

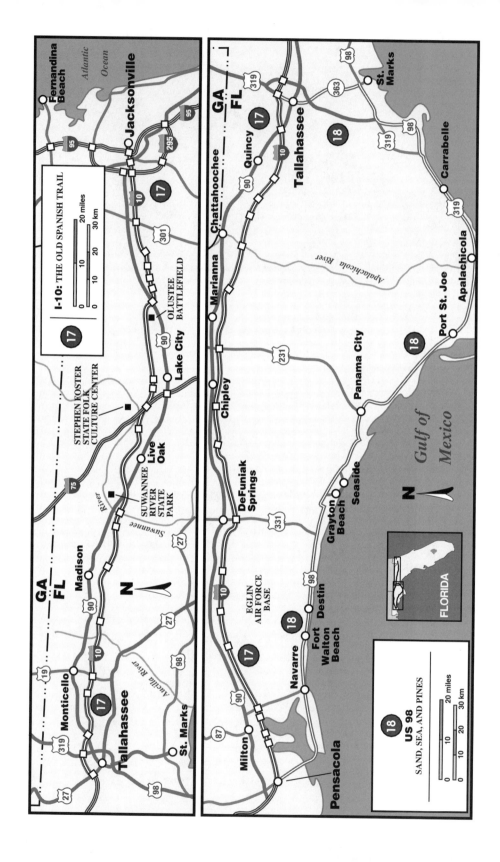

**I-10: THE OLD SPANISH TRAIL**

**17**

0   10   20 miles
0   10   20   30 km

**17** Fernandina Beach

Atlantic Ocean

Jacksonville

95

95

295

10

17

301

OLUSTEE BATTLEFIELD

90

Lake City

STEPHEN FOSTER STATE FOLK CULTURE CENTER

75

Live Oak

River

Suwannee

SUWANNEE RIVER STATE PARK

27

Madison

90

27

N

19

Monticello

10

Aucilla River

98

17

319

Tallahassee

St. Marks

27

98

GA
FL

**17**

319

98

St. Marks

363

319

98

Carrabelle

319

Apalachicola

Tallahassee

**18**

10

90

Quincy

Chattahoochee

Marianna

Apalachicola River

231

Port St. Joe

**18**

Chipley

Panama City

Gulf of Mexico

N

DeFuniak Springs

331

Seaside

Grayton Beach

Fort Walton Beach

Destin

98

EGLIN AIR FORCE BASE

**17**

10

**18**

Navarre

90

87

Milton

Pensacola

FLORIDA

**18**

**US 98**

SAND, SEA, AND PINES

0   10   20 miles
0   10   20   30 km

GA
FL

# ☞ 17 ☜

# *Interstate 10*

## THE OLD SPANISH TRAIL

# Jacksonville—Tallahassee

**163 miles**

I-10 begins in downtown Jacksonville. Heading west, it roughly approximates the old Spanish Trail that ran between the string of missions and ranches once dotting northern Florida. For two hundred years missionaries, soldiers, vaqueros, and Christianized Indians tramped the leafy paths and cattle runs of the Spanish Trail. The way meandered through the rich lands of the Santa Fe River twenty miles south of Lake City before heading north and west to reach the important mission of San Luis on the site of modern Tallahassee. From there it continued westward over the verdant hills to Pensacola.

Many people driving on I-10 for the first time are astonished to discover a gently rolling land with long blue vistas. It is a Florida many never knew existed. Here is what Frank Stockbridge wrote in his 1926 book, *Florida in the Making*:

> The traveler in Florida who will strike westward from Jacksonville either by motor over the Old Spanish Trail, or by railroad, will find himself . . . in a region so different from anything else he has seen in the State, different from everything he is likely to have heard about Florida, that he will be inclined to wonder whether he really is still in the same Commonwealth with Miami, Tampa and St. Augustine.

I-10, after it leaves Jacksonville, passes the exit to Baldwin. The little town was once an important railroad center on Florida's first

343

cross-state line, completed in 1861 between Fernandina, which is just north of Jacksonville, and Cedar Key on the Gulf of Mexico.

# Olustee Battlefield

Twenty miles beyond Baldwin, at exit 45, is the road to the Olustee Battlefield, site of Florida's largest Civil War battle, where ten thousand men fought in February 1864. A Union force had landed at Jacksonville, then marched west toward the Suwannee River, intending to destroy an important Confederate railroad bridge.

Confederates barred their way at Olustee, where the road was bounded by a lake on one side and a nearly impassable swamp on the other. The men battled during the afternoon and on into the twilight. When nearly two thousand Union soldiers had been killed or wounded (to half that number of Confederates), the blue retreated toward Jacksonville.

Today, Olustee is a State Historic Site with an interpretive center and a marked trail through the battlefield.

# Lake City and Vicinity

Lake City was originally called Alligator, after a Seminole chief. The town had a moment of glory during the 1920s, when a brick road connecting it with Jacksonville made this thrilling seventy miles the ninth-longest paved highway in the United States.

## The Memorial to Stephen Foster

At Lake City, the US 41 exit leads north seven miles to the village of White Springs, on the Suwannee River. The town is best known for the impressive Stephen Foster memorial, which consists of a two-hundred-foot-high carillon tower and a Foster museum. Artisans on-site have craft goods for sale. (For a more detailed discussion, see chapter 7).

Beyond Lake City, I-10 follows the route that Hernando de Soto took in 1539 as he pushed his way to Tallahassee, where he made winter camp. You'll pass the town of Live Oak, once famous for tobacco. Although the crop has fallen on hard times, you can still see a few fields from the highway.

## The Suwannee River

Fourteen miles past Live Oak, I-10 crosses the Suwannee River's deep channel. Fifteen thousand years ago, Paleo-Indians hunted mastodons along its shores. Much later, during the debate over statehood, the Suwannee was promoted by St. Augustine and Jacksonville residents as the border between the separate states of East and West Florida.

Before the Civil War, steamboats used the Suwannee River to transport cotton and other products from the many plantations in the vicinity. The end of slavery brought the demise of these plantations.

Suwannee River State Park is located seven miles northwest of the US 90 exit. It is on the site of Columbus, a vanished village of which only the cemetery still exists. Also on the park grounds are the remains of a Confederate earthworks, designed to protect the railroad bridge from Union forces based at Jacksonville—the same troops that were to be defeated at the Battle of Olustee. The park offers picnic tables and some nature trails.

## Middle Florida

During the Spanish and British eras, Florida was divided into two sections, with St. Augustine the administrative center in the east and Pensacola in the west. When Florida became a U.S. territory in 1821, a brand-new capital was established midway between the two older cities. The new town was Tallahassee, and its environs between the Suwannee and Apalachicola Rivers became Middle Florida.

Middle Florida, with its rich hills ideal for growing cotton, quickly became the most prosperous portion of the three sections. Plantations sprung up everywhere. During the antebellum years, Middle Florida produced 80 percent of Florida's cotton crop. To travelers, the countryside was beautiful when the fluffy white fuzz covered the hills. But behind the beauty was the pernicious institution of slavery.

Slavery was everywhere in Middle Florida, from the black men, women, and children laboring in the sweltering fields to the auction houses and slave pens of Tallahassee. Slaves actually made up a slight majority of the region's population.

The fields now have reverted to trees, for cotton fell victim to the deadly boll weevil in the 1910s. At this time, many blacks left for jobs in midwestern cities.

As I-10 approaches the Madison exit, it enters an area where 30 million years ago there existed the Gulf Trough, a northeast-flowing body of water some twenty-five miles wide that connected the Gulf

*Cotton pickers near Tallahassee. During the long slave era overseers often enforced discipline with whips that were especially designed to inflict maximum pain without breaking the skin.*
—Florida State Achives

of Mexico at Apalachee Bay with the Atlantic Ocean in southern Georgia. The trough existed for millions of years before it was filled with sediments from the eroding Appalachian Mountains.

## Madison

Madison was once an important location on the old Spanish Trail, with two missions located nearby. The Santa Elena Mission was the site of a serious revolt against the Spanish governor in 1656. The Indians' grievance centered on being forced to supply the St. Augustine garrison with corn. Spanish soldiers squelched the revolt with such severity that six Franciscan friars left the colony in protest.

Twenty miles west of Madison, I-10 crosses the Aucilla River. Modern road authorities do not think the stream important enough to rate a marker, but in Spanish days it was the border between the Timucua and the Apalachee provinces. Even earlier, it was home to Paleo-Indians who hunted mammoths and other Ice Age animals in the vicinity. One of their spear points was found in a fossilized bison skull taken from the Aucilla River.

## Monticello

Monticello, on the western edge of the former Gulf Trough, is three miles north of I-10. As the seat of Jefferson County, its courthouse is appropriately modeled on Thomas Jefferson's home in Virginia. The town was important during the cotton years, when many planters built homes here. Today, Monticello's historic district still contains over forty buildings of interest.

From Monticello, you can either go back to I-10 or drive on US 90 until it connects with I-10, twenty-four miles to the west. If you take US 90, you will cross Lake Miccosukee. Once, Miccosukee warriors contested Spanish activities and later American activities in north Florida. Had William Bowles been able to establish his Indian state of Muskogee in 1800, his capital would probably have been here. But it was not to be. (Bowles's almost incredible story is described in chapter 18). Now the tribe, reduced to a few hundred members, scrapes out a living in the Everglades.

**I-10**

# Tallahassee —Pensacola

**191 miles**

Going west from Tallahassee, described in chapter 5, I-10 continues through the soft hills. The countryside once supported scores of cotton plantations, where slaves labored in the torrid sun. But Lincoln's Emancipation Proclamation ended both their servitude and the plantation system. Later, tobacco took over and Frank Stockbridge, passing through Quincy in 1925, noted "its sixteen tobacco packing plants and the great warehouses where buyers from all over the country come to purchase the Gadsden County crops." But the tobacco era is also past, and much of the land has reverted to pines. Although with the boll weevil apparently under control cotton is making a comeback, the area is still experiencing economic difficulty.

## Quincy

Quincy is an exception to the area's generally hard-pressed condition. Its downtown sparkles and its mansions sport fresh paint. Why is the town so prosperous? The answer goes back to the early 1920s and is one of Florida's more unusual stories.

At that time, a little company in nearby Atlanta was making their stock public. They were producing a funny new drink, and Mark Monroe, a prominent Quincy banker who liked the taste of the stuff, recommended that his friends buy some stock. After all, it cost only two cents a share! The funny new drink happened to be Coca-Cola, and its stock prices quickly soared into the stratosphere. By World War II, Quincy was the richest town per capita in the entire United States. With a population of just eight thousand, it boasted twenty-five millionaires—and many more near-millionaires. At one time Quincy residents held two-thirds of all Coke stock outstanding. By the 1990s, an original investment of $1,000 was worth $2,500,000!

Small wonder the rosy glow of good times continues to light up the former tobacco town.

# Chattahoochee

Located where the Chattahoochee and Flint Rivers merge to form the Apalachicola, the region was known to Native Americans as "the place of the colored rocks," denoting the brilliant river stones. Because the site was on an important trade route, the Spaniards established a mission here in 1681.

During the long Spanish era, the Apalachicola River separated the provinces of East and West Florida. The Spanish claimed that the later colony extended west to the Mississippi and north to the site of Vicksburg, Tennessee. But after the Pinckney Treaty with the United States, which in 1795 established the boundary at the thirty-first parallel, a team sent to Chattahoochee determined West Florida's upper border to be nineteen miles above the East Florida line—where it remains.

Early on, West Florida was more part of what became Alabama than it was part of the rest of Florida. If Alabama had not become a state while Florida still belonged to Spain, West Florida would probably be included in Alabama today.

# Marianna

## *The Mysterious Marianna Lowlands*

There is a spacious view from the Chattahoochee bluff. West-ward lies the mysterious Marianna Lowlands, extending sixty miles from Chattahoochee to the Choctawhatchee River, "the place of the Choctaw tribe." Whereas the basement rocks bordering the Marianna

Lowlands are oceanic, formed near the dawn of life, the lowland rocks are much younger, formed from volcanoes dating to the age of the dinosaurs. The difference baffles geologists.

US 90, which follows an old stagecoach line, and I-10 both pass through the lowlands, a region with numerous sinkholes and stalactite caves. In 1827 the Reverend Michael Portier explored a cavern three miles north of the modern town of Marianna. Making his way by torchlight, he found himself in a large chamber: "All around thousands of stalactites stretch down from the roof, pointing their hollow spears toward others, of whiter hue, springing upward from the ground." The cave is now part of Florida Caverns State Park.

## *The Saga of Michael Portier*

For centuries Spanish friars had made the arduous journey along the old Spanish Trail between St. Augustine and Pensacola. The experience was not one to be looked forward to, even after the region passed to the Americans, as the Reverend Michael Portier found out. He had set out alone on horseback from Pensacola for St. Augustine on June 12, 1827, and it had taken him ten weary days to get to the Marianna Lowlands. He was thirty-two years old and had been given a Catholic vicariate that stretched from Mobile, his home base, to the Atlantic—almost five hundred miles of muddy trails and trackless forest. Making the bold decision to visit his St. Augustine parish, he kept a journal of his trip. It is a record of hardships almost unbelievable now but commonplace during that era.

East of the Chipola River, Reverend Portier had passed through a seemingly interminable pine forest, "where the air, expanded by the heat and heavy with odor, sickens the traveler at every step, not to mention the suffering caused by the reflected heat of the glowing white sandy soil!" How good it was to reach the river valleys, where the spreading live oaks brought cooling shade. But God only knew why these oases were also home to vast swarms of tormenting flies!

Once in a while Reverend Portier rode past attractive farmhouses where the air was perfumed with magnolia and laurel. He even spent a pleasant night at an inn near Chipley. But that was the exception, and his experience on the banks of the Choctawhatchee was one he would not soon forget.

He approached the river toward evening in the midst of a downpour so sudden that he had no time to don his waterproof cloak, and so was thoroughly drenched by the time he reached the river.

*In the early days most rivers could only be crossed by ferryboat. If the operator was sleeping, drunk, or just obstreperous, travelers had to cool their heels until he was ready.* —P. H. Yonge Library of Florida History, University of Florida

Seeing the ferry on the other shore, he shouted for the boatman, but to no avail. After two hours his voice gave out, and he realized he would have to spend the night in the swamp.

Hovering about him were "all the insects in creation." Even worse, "Ten feet away were alligators sporting in the middle of the channel." They could easily attack him while he was sleeping. "I looked upon myself as lost," he recalled. But, putting his soul in the hands of God, he lay on the sodden ground and somehow managed a fitful slumber.

At dawn he renewed the calling, but with the same lack of success. Now thirst pressed him and he drank the muddy water, mixing in a bit of rum that he had providently brought with him. He was about to turn back when six slaves appeared. They were returning to their plantation on the Chipola River. One of them gave a tremendous bellow that finally roused the ferryman.

Although Portier's mission to St. Augustine was ultimately successful, the trip left him "pale and broken," with an intermittent fever that continued for a month.

## From Chipley to Milton

The way between St. Augustine and Pensacola remained horrible for some time. Actually, the coming of the railroad in the early 1880s made a good wagon way unnecessary. The railroad was so important that such towns as Chipley and De Funiak Springs still bear the names of rail officials.

But it was not until the advent of automobile travel that the need for a respectable highway became apparent. Even with the building of US 90 in the 1920s, the route was mainly sand or gravel except around select towns. One of these was Milton, renown for having three and a half brick-paved miles on its eastern approach. Milton also had one of the largest sawmills in the area. Started before the Civil War, it contained thirty slave-run, steam-powered machines.

The pines through which I-10 passes are second growth, for the original forest was clear-cut between 1880 and 1910. No reforestation was done at this time, which left the barren hills subject to mud slides and ever-deepening gullies. Now, not only has reforestation made the hills green again, but the state has initiated a wildflower program. Thus, for nearly two hundred miles along I-10 between Tallahassee and Pensacola, innumerable crimson clover brighten the landscape.

The hills over which I-10 passes extend only a few miles south before giving way to coastal flatlands, home of Eglin Air Force Base. During World War II Jimmy Doolittle and his men trained here for their much-publicized surprise air raid on Japan in 1942.

## Pensacola

In 1698 the Spanish built a fort on a bluff with a commanding view of the bay, which Native Americans called Panzacola, or "the place of the long-haired people." But the bluff was a perfect target for hurricanes, and after one struck in 1752 most of the garrison moved to what is now Pensacola proper.

When the British took over in 1763, they found the village in disrepair. Nonetheless, they made it the capital of West Florida and laid out the downtown streets that still exist. They also assigned each settler a vegetable plot along the stream that marked the town's northern limit. In later years this became Garden Street.

After twenty years, the British were replaced once more by the Spanish, who promptly renamed the streets. Thus, what was once George Street, probably in honor of the English king, became Palafox, in honor of a Spanish general.

Americans in Alabama and Tennessee believed that Spain encouraged the Indians to attack the pioneers' settlements. Thus Andrew

*Although Andrew Jackson never weighed more than 145 pounds, he had a well-deserved reputation for ferocity when he lead his frontiersmen into Spanish Florida in 1818 during the First Seminole War.*
—Florida State Archives

Jackson, leading an army of angry frontiersmen, invaded Florida in 1818. Although Jackson withdrew after defeating the Indians in what became known as the First Seminole War, the ease with which the Americans took Pensacola convinced Spain of the futility of trying to hold the colony. Thus, three years later General Jackson raised the American flag over Florida during a brief ceremony in Pensacola's Plaza Ferdinand VII. Jackson stayed on as military governor for eleven weeks, hating every moment.

With the advent of energetic American settlers, Pensacola took on new life. Immediately north of Pensacola lay huge tracts of virgin timber, perfect for an expanding nation crying out for cheap lumber. By 1834, twenty-four nearby sawmills were actively grinding up timber. Great quantities of lumber flooded onto Pensacola's wharves, where nearly seventy vessels carried the wood to ports as distant as England and Rio de Janeiro. By this time, Pensacola was Florida's largest town, boasting a population of nearly three thousand.

### The Civil War

The Civil War was a major blow to Pensacola, for Union forces from Fort Pickens, at the harbor mouth, cut off the town's water commerce. Although Confederates at Fort Barrancas, across the harbor, attempted to dislodge them with occasional cannon barrages,

*Federal troops reinforce Fort Pickens during the Civil War. The fort effectively cut off Pensacola's vital shipping.* —P. H. Yonge Library of Florida History, University of Florida

they were unsuccessful. When the Confederates were reassigned to the Tennessee front in May 1862, the Yankees occupied Pensacola itself and remained there for the duration of hostilities.

### The Coming of the Railroad

In 1881, under the leadership of William Chipley and Fred de Funiak, the Pensacola & Atlantic Railroad was incorporated. Spurred by huge state land grants, the P & A built eastward from Pensacola and westward from Chattahoochee, where the railroad from Jacksonville ended. Between Milton and Marianna there were no settlements of any size, and the railroad used old boxcars as stations. Workers hunted wild animals in their spare moments, and fresh meat was common at chow time.

Of course, the railroad builders found the usual Florida hazards, including the dreaded swamp fever. But natural obstacles were even more difficult, the chief being Escambia Bay. When the two-and-a-half-mile bay bridge was opened in 1882, everyone agreed it was an engineering wonder. The inaugural excursion train even stopped in the middle, allowing dignitaries to clamber out, marvel at the sight, and clink champagne glasses to what was called the "greatest event in the history of Pensacola."

*Pensacola was a very active seaport when this photo was taken in 1886. Palafox wharf is on the left and the Baylen Street wharf on the right. The tree in the foreground is in Plaza Ferdinand VII.* —Pensacola Historical Society

The railroad brought an increased wealth of lumber into Pensacola, and the grateful citizens made Chipley mayor.

### Red Lights and Rustling Skirts

By 1900 Pensacola was developing into a port known for rollicking good times. Not only did it attract seamen from the numerous lumber ships that jammed its harbor, it also appealed to sailors from the navy yard (and later the naval air station) and an ample sprinkling of both local and out-of-state businessmen. To accommodate one and all, Pensacola rolled out a petticoat carpet in what became known as the Line—a row of brothels that began at Plaza Ferdinand VII, enlivened Zaragoza Street from Palafox to Baylen, then ran along Baylen between Main and Government Streets. Adding to the festivities were saloons, dance halls, and pool parlors. To have such a district in a town of only twenty-three thousand was quite unusual, and the patrons appreciated it.

The Line did its best to accommodate all levels of customers. The ritzier bordellos were in the 0 to 200 blocks of West Zaragoza. There, only the most genteel callers were accepted by Madam Mollie McCoy. Her girls were outfitted in the best gaudy dresses and were forbidden to drink or smoke or even act indecently in the public areas.

While Miss McCoy charged five dollars in her plush establishment, blokes with less jangle in their pockets could have a fling on Baylen Street for as little as one dollar. However, there they had to be alert not to get robbed in the process. Here the windows often had no shades and, after a shocked naval officer had seen into a bordello where upwards of fifty sailors were cavorting with nude prostitutes, none other than the U.S. secretary of the navy urged the governor of Florida to tone the Line down.

But it wasn't until World War II that the navy had its way—though by then the 1930s Depression had pretty much done the Line in.

### Touring Pensacola

I-10 reaches Pensacola on a long, impressive bridge over Escambia Bay. Once beyond the bridge, the best route to downtown is on I-110. Immediately east of the Gregory Street exit is the modern high-rise Pensacola Grand Hotel, whose lobby is in the 1912 railroad depot. It is a marvelous renovation, and food is served on what was once the train platform.

Palafox Street, across I-110, leads to Plaza Ferdinand VII, which is between East Government and Zaragoza Streets. In the park are memorials both to Andrew Jackson and William Chipley.

*The 1912 railroad depot has become the Pensacola Grand Hotel's impressive lobby.*

*The foundations of the old fort where Spanish soldiers once stood watch are being excavated just east of Pensacola's Plaza Ferdinand VII.*

The surrounding area is nice now, but in the early 1900s it was a tough red-light area. Mollie McCoy's sporting house was at 15 West Zaragoza, and Evelyn's Town Club was at 123 West Zaragoza. Less savory were such gambling dens as the one at Palafox and Pine. Nearby is the wharf area, where in former days you would find rowdy sea ruffians from all over the world shouting and cussing from beneath a forest of ships' masts.

Back in Plaza Ferdinand VII, on the east side is the imposing 1907 city hall, now home of the T. T. Wentworth Jr. Florida State Museum, specializing in the history and natural history of western Florida. Behind the museum are the brick foundations of the ancient Spanish fort. And just beyond is the Historic Pensacola Village complex, among whose buildings is a former warehouse containing a good exhibit on the lumber industry.

The village is bordered by Seville Square, which, together with Plaza Ferdinand VII, marked the perimeter of the fort grounds. Here, the Historical Society Museum occupies the Old Christ Church, which dates back to 1832. During the Civil War, Union soldiers used the building as barracks.

A three-mile drive west on Business 98 (an extension of Garden Street) and Navy Boulevard will take you to Fort Barrancas. Restored in 1980, it is an impressive structure. Since the fort is on the grounds of the Pensacola Naval Air Station, you should also pay a visit to the National Museum of Naval Aviation. This is a huge facility, with planes dating from the navy's first aircraft, a 1911 Curtiss seaplane, and four Blue Angel jets in flight formation suspended from the ceiling.

Fort Pickens, on the other side of the bay, can be reached on US 98 via the Pensacola Bay Bridge and Florida 399 over Santa Rosa Sound. The substantial fort was built mainly by slave labor in 1834. During the Civil War, when it was occupied by Union troops, it engaged in fierce artillery duels with the Confederates at Fort Barrancas.

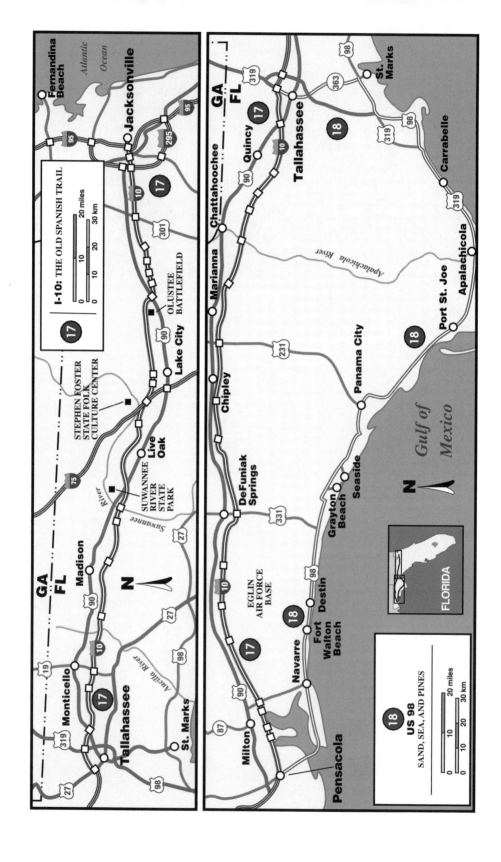

**17** I-10: THE OLD SPANISH TRAIL

0   10   20 miles
0   10   20   30 km

**18** US 98
SAND, SEA, AND PINES

0   10   20 miles
0   10   20   30 km

FLORIDA

GA
FL

**17**

**18**

Gulf of Mexico

Atlantic Ocean

Fernandina Beach

Jacksonville

Tallahassee

St. Marks

Carrabelle

Apalachicola

Port St. Joe

Panama City

Seaside

Grayton Beach

Destin

Fort Walton Beach

Navarre

Milton

Pensacola

DeFuniak Springs

Chipley

Marianna

Chattahoochee

Quincy

EGLIN AIR FORCE BASE

Apalachicola River

Monticello

Madison

Live Oak

Lake City

OLUSTEE BATTLEFIELD

STEPHEN FOSTER STATE FOLK CULTURE CENTER

SUWANNEE RIVER STATE PARK

Suwannee River

Aucilla River

N

# ～ 18 ～

# *US 98*

## SAND, SEA, AND PINES

FLORIDA 363

# Tallahassee—St. Marks

### 20 miles

Drivers wanting a more aesthetic though longer route than I-10 between Tallahassee and Pensacola should consider Florida 363 south to St. Marks, then US 98 west along the Gulf of Mexico. On the way, one can enjoy blue water, white sand, fragrant pines, and quaint towns.

Although Florida 363 is only twenty-seven miles long, it has quite a bit of history for its length. During the antebellum decades, chained slaves made the dreary trip up it from St. Marks—where they had disembarked after a debilitating journey from their African homeland—to the auction blocks at Tallahassee. A railroad began operations along the route in 1837. Initially it consisted of mule-drawn wagons, but in 1839 a steam engine, affectionately called Puffing Billy, was added. The tracks are now gone, and the right-of-way is popular with bikers and hikers.

Around Woodville, Florida 363 descends the low Cody Scarp into the St. Marks Flats. During an interglacial period when the gulf was higher, the shoreline was here. The flats's surface is limestone pocked with numerous sinkholes that often connect to underground rivers. These rivers course through extensive, sinuous caverns—one of which is so long that only fifteen miles have been explored.

At Woodville, a road leads five miles east to the Natural Bridge Battlefield State Historic Site. Here, in the waning months of the Civil War, seven hundred hastily gathered Confederate troops, composed mainly of old men and young boys, turned back a Union force that had landed at Apalachicola Bay and was advancing on Tallahassee.

US 98

# St. Marks—Panama City

**121 miles**

## St. Marks

The village of St. Marks was once one of Middle Florida's more important ports. The Spanish considered it vital and erected Fort San Marcos de Apalache here in 1679. Pirates soon burned the wooden fort, but in 1739 the Spanish began work on a stone stronghold. Although nineteen years later a hurricane, with screaming winds and crashing waves, completely wiped out the forty-man garrison, the Spanish returned.

One of the most colorful episodes involving St. Marks concerned an almost forgotten swashbuckler named William Augustus Bowles, a handsome Britisher, ambitious, daring, and visionary. Sent to America by an English trading company, Bowles soon conceived the

*Despite a hurricane that drowned the entire garrison, Fort San Marcos de Apalache remained an important Spanish post on the upper Gulf of Mexico during the eighteenth century.* —P. H. Yonge Library of Florida History, University of Florida

idea of erecting an independent Indian nation composed of all the tribes who spoke Muskogean—which included the Seminoles, Creeks, and most of the other southeastern natives. In 1790 he took some chiefs to London, where he received support as well as trade concessions. The ship carrying the Indians back actually flew the Muskogean flag.

Bowles made his headquarters at the lake of the Miccosukees, east of Tallahassee. Then he issued a proclamation ordering all foreigners out of Muskogean territory, particularly the Spanish at St. Marks. Because they refused to leave, Bowles declared war and in 1800 descended on the fort with three hundred braves. When he captured a Spanish boat carrying a cannon, the fort commander, aware that his walls could now be breached, angrily surrendered.

But Bowles lacked the strength to maintain his conquest, and the Spanish retook the fort the following month. Four years later, Bowles was captured and imprisoned in Cuba, where he starved himself to death. Dying with him was the dream of a Native American state extending along the gulf and encompassing the site of Tallahassee.

Fort San Marcos is now a State Historic Site, with a small though well-stocked museum. A path leads past a few stone ruins to the location of the Spanish fort, at the confluence of the St. Marks and Wakulla Rivers. The scene is nearly as wild and uninhabited as it was two hundred years ago.

## Carrabelle

The US 98 gulf portion begins at St. Marks. Passing over the impressive Ochlockonee Bay Bridge, the road quickly reaches the hamlet of St. Teresa, named, oddly, not for a saint but for an ordinary lady named Teresa Hopkins. The land from here along the coast for a hundred miles is nearly deserted. But this was not always the case. During World War II, the segment from St. Teresa to Carrabelle was the training ground for upwards of thirty thousand troops.

Army officials believed that Florida's sandy beaches were ideal for perfecting the amphibious landings that were critical in retaking Pacific islands from the Japanese. Though it may have been ideal for the bigwigs, the isolation of Camp Gordon Johnston made some call it the Army Alcatraz. One columnist claimed that duty there was so bad that even the chaplains went AWOL.

*The long row of cotton warehouses contributed to Apalachicola's prosperity in 1857.* —P. H. Yonge Library of Florida History, University of Florida

The army moved out after the war, and today Carrabelle is a pretty little place, with a marina and a lofty bridge that seem to mock the village's scant population. The army experience has been largely forgotten, and now the village's modest claim to fame is the world's smallest police station—which is merely a telephone booth beside US 98, next to the chamber of commerce.

## Apalachicola

The twenty-mile drive between Carrabelle and Apalachicola passes through an almost unpopulated area with pines on one side and the gulf on the other. For many years, travelers rode a one-wagon ferry across Apalachicola Bay. But in 1936 the bay was spanned by the first John Gorrie Bridge, which was replaced by the spectacular modern structure in the 1980s.

The Apalachicola River with its two branches, the Chattahoochee and the Flint, reaches far into Alabama and Georgia, where antebellum plantations produced large harvests of cotton. To take advantage of this, in 1835 the Apalachicola Land Company bought out the original village settlers, dredged the channel, and built forty-three cotton warehouses. With that, the cotton trade mushroomed.

One of the early cotton clerks was young John Chrystie, employed in a three-story warehouse at 59 Water Street. Chrystie's letters to his family in New York present an interesting picture of life in this active but isolated port:

> There is no excitement here of any kind except that of business & when there is none of that you can hardly imagine what a damned dull place it is. We sleep in our warehouse, we get up in the morning, go up to the hotel to breakfast, come down again, go up to dinner, come down again. . . . I hate the sight of a Cotton bale & yet the fates have ordained that some ten or fifteen thousand of them should be eternally under my nose—I almost fancy at times that I am a Cotton bale myself.

Chrystie did manage to get invited to some local parties, although he wondered if any of the local belles thought "such a poor bedevilled poverty stricken merchants clerk as I worth spreading any snares for." About his only pleasure was taking his flute to a back room, where he could "blow away like mad." Thus his seven years in Apalachicola were an ordeal. In 1842 he returned to New York City, where he became a broker, until he died only ten years later.

By the 1840s, Apalachicola's population topped a thousand, enough to have its own malaria and yellow-fever epidemics. Most doctors believed that a hot swampy atmosphere caused the illnesses. As a result, a local physician, John Gorrie, invented a compression machine that cooled the air in his patients' rooms, and by 1851 he had secured a U.S. patent for the design. But potential commercial backers pooh-poohed the air-conditioning idea as silly, and Gorrie died four years later without making any profit from his invention. Later generations, however, recognized Gorrie's genius, and the Smithsonian Institution put his original machine in its permanent collection. The state of Florida, certainly one to appreciate air-conditioning, chose a likeness of Gorrie as one of the two monuments it placed in Congress's Statuary Hall.

As for Apalachicola itself, the coming of the railroads to upriver towns in the 1880s cut off its cotton trade, which had been based on the far slower river transportation. Eventually the town turned to oysters, which could be harvested from boats in the shallow bay by merely using long rakes. But recently a life-threatening bacteria in some uncooked oysters has seriously crippled that industry, so now the town is trying to spur tourism. There are many specialty shops and art galleries, as well as quite a few historic sites, such

*A festive crowd enjoys the arrival of Apalachicola's first steam train in 1907.* —P. H. Yonge Library of Florida History, University of Florida

as the Gorrie Museum on Sixth Street, one block off US 98. Across the square from it is the Trinity Episcopal Church, dating to 1837, of which Gorrie was a founder.

Two of the original cotton warehouses still remain on Water Street, two blocks north of US 98. Once, the street's docks bustled with cotton barges from Georgia and sailing ships from overseas.

There are fifty more historic locales, one of the most pleasant being the old Gibson Inn on US 98, at the foot of the Gorrie Bridge. A map of the sites can be obtained from the Apalachicola Chamber of Commerce, at 84 Market Street, which is also US 98.

## Port St. Joe

Traveling west from Apalachicola, US 98 passes through aisles of tall pines, showing what the area looked like in prelumbering days. Sawmills took care of nearly all the primeval forest—and still today lumbering goes on, now largely out of sight. Port St. Joe's economy is based largely on products of the vast timberlands that surround it. The highway skirts the large plant of Box USA. The building

*Oyster boats nudge the docks along Apalachicola Bay.*

*Apalachicola's 1907 Gibson Inn still accommodates guests.*

formerly belonged to the St. Joe Container Company, which had long been a major landholder in the area. It also passes the extensive installations of Arizona Chemical, part of International Paper Corporation, which makes adhesives.

Port St. Joe has had a devastating past. The town, first called St. Joseph, began as a prosperous rival of Apalachicola in the 1830s, when its population soared to twelve thousand, making it by far the largest city in the state. In 1838 St. Joseph was selected as the meeting site for Florida's constitutional convention. Here, the delegates squabbled for more than a month trying to forge a document that would meet the approval of the many east Floridians, who wanted two states, divided by the Suwannee River, as well as the many citizens of Pensacola and its environs, who wished to become part of Alabama. The constitution, with a unified state, ultimately won the popular vote by a bare 119 margin in 1845.

The Constitution Convention State Museum re-creates the hall where the delegates met. Audio-animated mannequins portray such influential figures as William Duval, the first territorial governor, and David Levy Yulee, one of Florida's first U.S. senators.

Although St. Joseph's future seemed secure, in 1841 yellow fever struck. Probably never in American history has a town been so devastated by disease, for fully 75 percent of the men, women, and children died. Old St. Joseph was abandoned, and most of the homes were broken down and shipped to buyers in Apalachicola.

**US 98**

# Panama City—Pensacola

**103 miles**

## Panama City

Panama City, thirty-three miles west of Port St. Joe, is Big Time Florida. Each year, almost 3 million visitors come here and to Panama City Beach, with its relatively inexpensive motels and sprinkling of fine resorts.

During the Civil War, St. Andrews Bay (now crossed by the US 98 bridge) was a major source of salt for the Confederacy, with up to twenty-five hundred men actively gathering salt in the bay flats and transporting it up to Alabama. After the war, the region settled into a lethargy until 1905, when George West organized the Gulf Coast

Company to develop the site, which he named Panama City because it was on a direct line between Chicago and Panama. Midwesterners, attracted by the town's name, connoting warmth as well as the shortest route to Florida, began wintering in Panama City.

In the early days, Panama City was a quiet place, and the most popular activity was hunting turtles from sailboats. However, since the completion of the Gulf Coast Highway (US 98) in 1934, Panama City is not quiet any longer. Indeed, Panama City has actively recruited the fun-loving spring break crowd, who have helped make it one of the liveliest towns in the state.

## Seaside Village

West of Panama City is the village of Seaside, "the most celebrated small town in the world," as proclaims a local handout.

The hyperbole is probably not far from true. The village, which consisted of just two homes when it was begun in 1981, now contains over two hundred homes, painted in delightful pastels, plus nearly twenty shops and restaurants.

Seaside was planned so as to bring back the days when towns provided meaningful social environments, not merely sleeping quar-

*Homes at Seaside are built with a close neighborliness that has made the village a pacesetter in modern town planning.*
—Steven Brooke

ters. Thus the houses in Seaside have front porches, where family members congregate. Furthermore, Seaside residents are always strolling the narrow streets, which are actually designed to lead somewhere rather than end in private cul de sacs.

The Seaside idea has caught on. *Newsweek* called it "probably the most influential resort community since Versailles." And when Walt Disney officials were planning their own town of Celebration near Orlando, they inspected Seaside and borrowed many of its concepts. Other developers have done the same.

But Seaside has been built with more than just an eye for quaintness and human relationships. When Hurricane Opal pounded the panhandle in 1995, Seaside, with its solid construction and the protection of sheltering dunes (which the developer, Robert Davis, did not destroy in order to give home buyers a view of the gulf) lost no more than a few shingles.

## Grayton Beach, Destin, and Fort Walton Beach
*The Devastation of Hurricane Opal*

In early October 1995, Hurricane Opal hit the gulf coast between Panama City and Pensacola Beach, destroying nearly $2 billion of oceanfront property. Opal's fullest force slammed into Grayton Beach, immediately west of Seaside. The once-beautiful dunes that made this stretch of sand among the most desirable in Florida were virtually leveled. Twenty-one miles farther west, a fifteen-foot gulf surge crashed over US 98, ripping the highway apart for four miles between Destin and Fort Walton Beach.

The Hurricane Center was able to give only the briefest warning of the storm's approach to panhandle inhabitants, one hundred thousand of whom fled on the few highways leading north from the beaches. But the roads became jammed, so thousands had no choice except to return to their homes or to local emergency shelters where they rode out the storm. When it was over, the devastation was so great that two thousand national guardsmen were called in to keep looters from the doorless and windowless buildings.

## From Fort Walton to the Bay

Fort Walton was established during hostilities with the Seminoles and was named for George Walton, a high Florida official. Among history buffs, Fort Walton is well known for the ancient Indian mound dating to A.D. 1400. But pre-European settlements go much further back, for many different cultures have occupied this site, the first as early as 12,000 B.C. The mound is a National Historic Landmark, and the museum beside it, at 139 Miracle Strip Parkway (US 98), exhibits over four thousand prehistoric Native American artifacts.

At Navarre, a side trip on Florida 399, the road leads to Santa Rosa Island. The current road is new; the old one was hammered into rubble by Opal. Santa Rosa is part of the Gulf Islands National Seashore. There is a visitor center at historic Fort Pickens, on the western end of the island.

US 98 reaches Pensacola over a long bridge across Pensacola Bay. Parallel to the modern structure is the old bridge, which, although it is now used just for fishing, was epochal in its day because it first opened the gulf beaches to tourism. When this bridge contract was granted in the 1950s, it was the largest ever awarded by the state road department.

# Selected Bibliography

## General Florida Reference Books

Gannon, Michael V. *The Cross in the Sand.* Gainesville: University of Florida, 1965. Tells the history of Spanish Catholic efforts in Florida between 1513 and 1870.

———. *Florida: A Short History.* Gainesville: University Press of Florida, 1993. Excellent capsulated history of Florida. In paperback.

———, ed. *The New History of Florida.* Gainesville: University of Florida Press, 1996. The best one-volume history of Florida.

Head, Clarence, and Robert B. Marcus. *The Face of Florida.* Dubuque, Iowa: Kendall/Hunt, 1984, 1987. Gives a valuable geographic basis for further study of Florida.

Jahoda, Gloria. *Florida, a History.* New York: Norton, 1984. A very good short history of Florida. In paperback.

Morris, Allen. *Florida's Place Names.* Coral Gables: University of Miami Press, 1974. An enlightening name-history of almost all Florida towns.

Stockbridge, Frank P., and John H. Perry. *Florida in the Making.* New York: De Bowen, 1926. A most entertaining town-to-town account of Florida during a trip in 1925.

Tebeau, Charlton. *A History of Florida.* Coral Gables: University of Miami Press, 1980. This is the standard scholarly Florida history.

## Books on the Major Cities

### Jacksonville

Gilkes, Lillian. *Cora Crane: A Biography of Mrs. Stephen.* Bloomington: Indiana University Press, 1960. Relates the interesting career of the madam who became Stephen Crane's wife.

Stowe, Harriet Beecher. *Palmetto Leaves.* Facsimile reproduction of 1873 edition. Gainesville: University of Florida Press, 1968. Shows the softer side of this author in her winter home beside the St. Johns River.

Ward, James Robertson. *Old Hickory's Town.* Jacksonville: Florida Publishing, 1982. Excellent pictures and text.

Wood, Wayne W. *Jacksonville's Architectural Heritage.* Jacksonville: University of North Florida, 1989. Presents a different side of history. Good pictures.

### Miami

Fisher, Jane. *Fabulous Hoosier.* New York: McBride, 1947. A delightful account of life in Miami Beach from 1913 to 1939 by the wife of its dynamic founder.

Muir, Helen. *The Biltmore: Beacon for Miami.* Miami: Pickering, 1987. This thin volume gives a colorful history of a famous hotel.

Weigall, T. H. *Boom in Paradise.* New York: King, 1932. A highly entertaining account of Coral Gables and Miami at the crest of the 1925 real estate boom. Written by one of George Merrick's public relations staff.

### Orlando
Hollis, Richard, and Brian Sibley. *The Disney Studio Story.* New York: Crown, 1951. A well-written book with many illustrations.

Kendrick, Baynard H. *Orlando: A Century Plus.* Orlando: Sentinel Star, 1976. An excellent short history of Orlando.

Shofner, Jerrell H. *Orlando: The City Beautiful.* Tulsa: Continental Heritage Press, 1984. Many historical photos and a vivid text.

### Tallahassee
Long, Ellen Call. *Florida Breezes, or Florida, New and Old.* Gainesville: University of Florida Press, 1962. (Recent facsimile of the 1883 edition.) A picturesque account of Tallahassee in the nineteenth century by the daughter of an early Florida governor.

### Tampa and St. Petersburg
Fuller, Walter P. *St. Petersburg and Its People.* St. Petersburg, Great Outdoors: 1972. Largely a firsthand account by a prominent realtor of St. Pete's development.

Hernon, Peter, and Terry Ganey. *Under the Influence: The Unauthorized Story of the Anheuser-Busch Dynasty.* New York: Simon & Schuster, 1991. An excellent description of four tempestuous generations of the Busch family. Unfortunately there is very little about Busch Gardens in Tampa.

Jahoda, Gloria. *River of the Golden Ibis.* New York: Holt, 1973. A colorful history of Tampa, St. Pete, and other locales along the Hillsborough River.

Mormino, Gary R., and Anthony Pizzo. *Tampa: The Treasure City.* Tulsa: Continental, 1983. A coffee table–size photo book with good text.

Pacheco, Ferdie. *Ybor City Chronicles: A Memoir.* Gainesville: University Press of Florida, 1994. A skilled writer tells of growing up in Ybor City during the 1930s and 1940s.

## Books Relating to the Events Along the Highways

### Florida's Turnpike: Wildwood—Miami
Dodson, Pat. "Hamilton Disston's St. Cloud Sugar Plantation, 1887–1901," *Florida Historical Quarterly* (April 1971).

Edgerton, David R. *Memories of Mount Dora.* Mount Dora: Link, 1993. This is a good account of the town by one of its most prominent citizens.

Hughes, Melvin E. "William Howey and His Florida Dreams." *Florida Historical Quarterly* (January 1988). A good, short history of this colorful figure.

### I-4: Daytona—Orlando—Tampa
Bartram, William. *Travels of William Bartram.* New York: Dover, 1955. First published in 1791. Good descriptions of Blue Spring and other locales along the St. Johns River during the British era. A Florida classic.

Fry, Joseph A. *Henry Sanford, Diplomacy and Business in the 19th Century.* Reno: University of Nevada Press, 1982. The best biography of Sanford.

Gill, Brendan. *Many Masks: A Life of Frank Lloyd Wright.* New York: Putnam, 1987. As far as discussion of Wright and Florida Southern College, this is the best biography.

Hemenway, Robert E. *Zora Neale Hurston, A Literary Biography.* Chicago: University of Illinois Press, 1977. This is the standard biography.

Hurston, Zora Neale. *Dust Tracks on a Road: An Autobiography.* Chicago: University of Illinois Press, 1942, 1984. Describes growing up in Eatonville.

———. *I Love Myself When I am Laughing.* Edited by Mary Helen Washington. Old Westbury, New York: Feminist Press, 1979. A good collection with such selections as "How It Feels to Be Colored Me" and "My Most Humiliating Jim Crow Experience."

### I-10: Jacksonville—Pensacola
*(see also references under Tallahassee)*
Parks, Virginia. *Pensacola: Spaniards to Space-Age.* Pensacola: Pensacola Historical Society, 1986. A slim, well-done volume that adequately covers this interesting city's highlights.
———, ed. *Iron Horse in the Pinelands: Building West Florida's Railroad, 1881–1883.* Pensacola: Pensacola Historical Society, 1982. Although this book is only ninety pages, it is rich and entertaining.
Portier, Reverend Michael. "From Pensacola to St. Augustine in 1827." *Florida Historical Quarterly* (October 1947). A firsthand account of a hair-raising round-trip in the days before roads.
Rimini, Robert V. *The Life of Andrew Jackson.* New York: Penguin, 1990. A detailed account of a complicated and violent man. Space is give to his military activities in northern Florida.

### I-75: Georgia Line—Tampa—Miami
Bartram, William. *Travels of William Bartram.* New York: Dover, 1955. First published in 1791. Recounts this British botanist's 1773 trip from the St. Johns River to the Alachua (Paynes) Prairie.
Bigelow, Gordon E. *Frontier Eden: The Literary Career of Marjorie Kinnan Rawlings.* Gainesville: University of Florida Press, 1966. This is a definitive study of Marjorie Rawlings that covers both her personal life and the Florida setting of her writings.
Blacker, Irwin, and Harry M. Rosen. *The Golden Conquistadores.* Indianapolis: Bobbs-Merrill, 1960. Has thirty-four pages with quotations from de Soto's chroniclers.
Clark, Ronald W. *Edison: The Man Who Made the Future.* New York: G. P. Putnam's, 1977. One of many good Edison biographies.
Grismer, Karl H. *The Story of Fort Myers.* Fort Myers Beach: Island Press, 1982. A detailed study of Fort Myers history.
Jahoda, Gloria. *River of the Golden Ibis.* New York: Holt, 1973. Contains a vivid account of Major Dade's disastrous march from Tampa.
Mahon, John K. *History of the Second Seminole War: 1835–1842.* Gainesville: University of Florida Press, 1992. Good, detailed account of the hostilities. Also has a chapter on the First Seminole War.
Rawlings, Marjorie Kinnan. *The Yearling.* New York: Scribners, 1938, 1967. Rawlings's masterwork. An engrossing portrayal of Florida pioneer life around 1880.
———. *Cross Creek.* New York: Scribners, 1942. Reissued in paperback by Collier Books, 1987. An absorbing account of Rawlings's experiences in Florida during the 1930s.

### I-95: Georgia Line—Cape Canaveral—Miami
Chandler, David Leon. *Henry Flagler: The Astonishing Life and Times of the Visionary Robber Baron Who Founded Florida.* New York, Macmillan, 1986. Highly readable.
Collins, Michael. *Carrying the Fire.* New York: Ballantine, 1975. An exciting, firsthand story of the American space program by an astronaut.
Curl, Donald W. *Mizner's Florida.* Cambridge, Mass.: MIT Press, 1986. A detailed and well-written account of the flamboyant architect who put Palm Beach's fabulous Worth Avenue on the map.

Dickinson, Jonathan. *Jonathan Dickinson's Journal.* First published in 1699. Current edition published in Port Salerno, Florida, by Florida Classics Library, 1985. One of America's most exciting journals and a Florida classic.

Englebrecht, Curt E. *Neighbor John.* Ormond Beach: Ormond Beach Historical Trust, 1993. Excellent recollections of John D. Rockefeller's twilight years at Ormond Beach by his personal photographer.

McIver, Stuart. *Yesterday's Palm Beach.* Miami: Seaman,1976. Contains 140 pages of wonderful photos.

Shelton, William Roy. *Countdown: The Story of Cape Canaveral.* Boston: Little, Brown, 1960. A most readable narrative of early days at the cape by one who was there.

Tucker, Tom, and Jim Tiller. *Daytona: The Quest for Speed.* Daytona: News-Journal, 1994. A lively account written by two journalists affiliated with the *Daytona Beach News-Journal.* Contains many vintage photos.

Von Braun, Wernher, et al. *Space Travel: A History.* Cambridge: Harper & Row, 1966, 1985. An oversized book with many good pictures. Written, at least in part, by one of the key men in NASA's early space program.

Waterbury, Jean Parker, ed. *The Oldest City: St. Augustine, Saga of Survival.* St. Augustine: St. Augustine Historical Society, 1983. A detailed but highly readable account of one of Florida's most interesting cities.

### US 1: Miami—Key West

Hemingway, Ernest. *To Have and Have Not.* New York: Scribner's, 1937, 1962. The famous author's firsthand, though fictional, story of Key West in the early 1930s.

Hoffmeister, John Edward. *Land From the Sea: The Geologic Story of South Florida.* Coral Gables: University of Miami Press, 1974. This thin volume presents the geology of southern Florida in a popular, though well-researched, manner.

Lynn, Kenneth. *Hemingway.* New York: Simon & Schuster, 1987. This is a major study of the author's life with good details on his years at Key West.

Proby, Kathryn Hall. *Audubon in Florida: Selections from the Writings of John James Audubon.* Coral Gables: University of Miami Press, 1974. Brings to life the artist's travels through the Keys in 1832. There is also a good résumé of his life.

### US 41 (Tamiami Trail): Naples—Miami

Douglas, Marjory Stoneman. *The Everglades: River of Grass.* Miami: Banyan Books, 1978. This is the book that brought the Everglades and its peril to public attention. A Florida classic.

Kay, Russell. "Tamiami Trail Blazers: A Personal Memoir." *Florida Historical Quarterly* (January 1971). An exciting account of an epic motorcade across the roadless Everglades in 1923.

Tebeau, Charlton W. *Florida's Last Frontier: The History of Collier County.* Coral Gables: University of Miami Press, 1966. Author devotes a full chapter to the construction of the western portion of the Tamiami Trail.

### US 27: Clermont—Miami

Adams, William R. *Historic Lake Wales.* St. Augustine: Southern Heritage Press, 1992.

Bok, Edward. *The Americanization of Edward Bok: An Autobiography.* New York: Scribners, 1920, 1965. Tells the amazing story of this influential magazine editor. Unfortunately, the building of Bok Tower is omitted.

Ulmann, Alec. *The Sebring Story.* New York: Chilton, 1969. The inside story of this famous racetrack by one of its founders.

### US 98: Tallahassee—Pensacola (see also references under I-10)

Schuh, Niles. "Apalachicola in 1838–40: Letters From a Young Cotton Warehouse Clerk." *Florida Historical Quarterly* (January 1990). Back issues of the *Florida Historical Quarterly* are available at most Florida public libraries.

# Index

We encourage you to patronize your local bookstores. Most stores will order any title that they do not stock. You may also order directly from Mountain Press by mail, using the order form provided below, or by calling our toll-free number and using your Visa or MasterCard. We will gladly send you a complete catalog upon request.

## Roadside History titles of interest:

| | |
|---|---|
| _____Roadside History of Arizona (paper) | $18.00 |
| _____Roadside History of Arkansas (paper) | $18.00 |
| _____Roadside History of Arkansas (cloth) | $30.00 |
| _____Roadside History of California (paper) | $18.00 |
| _____Roadside History of California (cloth) | $30.00 |
| _____Roadside History of Idaho (paper) | $18.00 |
| _____Roadside History of Idaho (cloth) | $30.00 |
| _____Roadside History of Florida (paper) | $18.00 |
| _____Roadside History of Florida (cloth) | $30.00 |
| _____Roadside History of Nebraska (paper) | $18.00 |
| _____Roadside History of Nebraska (cloth) | $30.00 |
| _____Roadside History of New Mexico (paper) | $18.00 |
| _____Roadside History of Oregon (paper) | $18.00 |
| _____Roadside History of Texas (paper) | $18.00 |
| _____Roadside History of Texas (cloth) | $30.00 |
| _____Roadside History of Wyoming (paper) | $18.00 |
| _____Roadside History of Wyoming (cloth) | $30.00 |
| _____Roadside History of Yellowstone Park (paper) | $ 8.00 |

*Please include $3.00 per order to cover shipping and handling.*

Send the books marked above. I have enclosed $_____

Name_____

Address_____

City_____State_____Zip_____

☐ Payment enclosed (check or money order in U.S. funds)

Bill my: ☐ VISA  ☐ MasterCard  Expiration Date:_____

Card No._____

Signature _____

**Mountain Press Publishing Company**
P. O. Box 2399 • Missoula, MT 59806
Order Toll-Free 1-800-234-5308
mtnpress@montana.com
Have your Visa or MasterCard ready.